D0837333

FIND OUT WHAT REALLY HAPPENED
TO DEBBIE AND KATHY.
DISCOVER ALL THE EERIE AND DISTURBING
DETAILS ABOUT . . .

- The UFO landing that began Debbie's terrifying experiences and left her eyes so burned that she required emergency medical care . . .

- The camping trip that turned into a nightmare—complete with the photos that show why it was the vacation from hell . . .

- Kathy's bizarre sleepwalking that masked the memories she had buried out of fear . . .

- The black helicopters that have buzzed their houses—helicopters that the government says don't exist . . .

- The "man" spotted by a neighbor trying to enter their house, a figure that left no footprints in the snow . . .

- The pregnancy confirmed by Debbie's doctor that suddenly vanished after her terrifying dream that aliens took her unborn child . . .

- The daughter named Emily who is out there . . . with *them.*

ABDUCTED!
The Story of the Intruders Continues. . . .

QUANTITY SALES

INDIVIDUAL SALES

ABDUCTED!

The Story of the Intruders Continues

Debbie Jordan
and Kathy Mitchell

Introduction by Budd Hopkins

A DELL BOOK

Published by
Dell Publishing
a division of
Bantam Doubleday Dell Publishing Group, Inc.
1540 Broadway
New York, New York 10036

ISBN: 0-440-22116-1

Reprinted by arrangement with Carroll & Graf Publishers

Printed in the United States of America

Published simultaneously in Canada

October 1995

10 9 8 7 6 5 4 3 2 1

RAD

I would like to dedicate this book to the memory of my beloved husband, Karl Osburn Learner II. He chose to leave this world on May 16, 1994.

I loved my husband with all my heart and I know that without him, this book would not have been possible. I wish with all my heart that he could have lived to see it in print. It was as much his dream, as mine. He believed very deeply in the existence of extraterrestrial life and he believed in me more than anyone I ever knew. I feel blessed to have shared the last two years with him and I hope he knows how much he's taught me about people and life and love. He wanted so much to know the truth. I pray that now he does and that now he knows peace. I love you, Sweetie. Forever.

—DEBBIE JORDAN

PREFACE

WHEN WE SEARCH FOR THE TRUTH, MANY TIMES WE AVOID looking in the most obvious place: inside ourselves. This can be a frightening place to look for the answers because then we must take responsibility for *our* involvement in the story. The courage to "genuinely know the truth" is the kind of courage Debbie Jordan has.

The strange events that happened to Debbie and her family in 1983 caused a tear in the fabric of their lives. With no reputation to uphold, no money to gain, no academic tenure to protect, Debbie had *no choice but to try to find out not only what was going on, but also why*. Desperation and a few synchronicities led her to a careful and compassionate researcher, Budd Hopkins. Budd helped Debbie, as he has so many others, to rip the veil of confusion.

Debbie ignored the old adage, "Be careful what you wish for, you just might get it." She wished to know the truth, but after finding it she would never view this world or reality the same way again. She learned a secret only to find she could tell no one. She felt no one would believe and few would understand. She now feels she *must* tell, whether you believe or not.

When I first read of Debbie's experiences in *Intruders,* by Budd Hopkins, I empathized with her terror. Then I cheered for her courage as she overcame the fear. After meeting her, I was inspired by her sojourn inward to understand her part in these alien encounters. I share, as we all can, her compassion to help others understand what this is all about. Now, I am proud to be called her friend.

This book is about Debbie and her family's journey for their truths. Perhaps they are your truths as well. By reading this book you have shared, first hand, in the events and experiences that possibly millions of people are having—events that are changing the consciousness of this planet.

FOREST CRAWFORD
Certified hypnotherapist and
Illinois State Director, MUFON
(Mutual UFO Network)
September 2, 1993

INTRODUCTION
by
Budd Hopkins

THE MONTH OF SEPTEMBER 1983, WHEN I RECEIVED MY FIRST letter from Debbie Jordan, seems half a lifetime ago. So much has happened to Debbie and to me, as well as to the world's understanding of the UFO enigma as a result of that first communication. The changes have been so profound that it is almost impossible now to recall the state of our knowledge of the UFO abduction phenomenon prior to the "Kathie Davis" case, to use the fictional name I gave Debbie at the time.

The 1987 publication of *Intruders* brought before the public the results of the investigation that followed my receipt of Debbie's original letter and photographs. That complex three-year inquiry produced major new information about the patterns, scope and apparent aims of the UFO abduction phenomenon, data which has since been replicated in the research of independent investigators throughout the world. A brief review would include, first of all, the fact that the extensive physical evidence in this case effectively demolished the notion that UFO abductions are purely "mental" events with no outside witnesses. At the beginning of Debbie's June 1983 experience, she and her mother independently reported seeing strange lights on the Davis property. And where Debbie remembered seeing the landed UFO, the ground was affected in peculiar ways: the grass died, and, below, many cubic feet of moist, dark soil was changed into a grayish rocklike material that for years was unable to support vegetation. Extending outward from the roughly eight-foot circle of altered soil—the spot where the craft apparently rested—was a forty-nine-foot-long straight swath of similarly damaged earth. This evidence dramatically supports the idea that the object Debbie saw that night left behind clear-cut physical traces and was, therefore, neither a fantasy nor a dream.

To support that notion, when the craft apparently lifted off, Debbie's next-door neighbor saw a brilliant flash of light through the trees at the location of these ground traces. Seconds later, as some kind of craft passed noisily overhead, the neighbor's home suffered a complete power outage. Equally strange, all the lights spontaneously came back on, with no disturbance to either fuses or circuit breakers. This neighbor's testimony further eliminates any suspicion that the event can be regarded purely as an artifact of *Debbie's* mental processes.

In the days following her abduction, Debbie experienced a series of unpleasant physical aftereffects suggestive of low-level radiation poisoning. But it was not just Debbie who experienced such problems—the behavior of birds and animals around the affected soil was unusual, to say the least, and the lesions and severe hair loss her dog suffered led to its eventual death. Debbie tells the story of these physical sequelae at some length in the following pages, as she, her sister, and her family experienced them.

Even more important than the fact that this case demonstrates the physical reality of UFO abductions is the evidence pointing to a long-term alien reproductive experiment. Prior to 1983, a few investigators were aware of a sexual, or reproductive, component in some of the small number of abduction reports that had been investigated; I had run into such suggestions as early as 1976. Yet most abductees had been reluctant to volunteer information about this highly personal aspect of their experiences. And since investigators generally hesitated to bring up the subject, issues of reproduction and sexuality had remained for years in the margins of our knowledge of the abduction phenomenon. In a pioneering decision, Debbie Jordan was the first woman to fully reveal this most intimate aspect of her ordeal. Her uncommon courage has made it easier for hundreds of men and women since then to unburden themselves, thereby immeasurably aiding UFO research and facilitating the work of therapists and investigators.

What Debbie's account revealed is no more or less than the central reason for alien interaction with humans. Despite deep alien curiosity about human sexuality, about our basic maternal and paternal instincts, and about the way human beings form relationships with one another, it is our genetic makeup that appears to be the focus of alien attention.

The story of this watershed event has been told fully in *Intruders,* so there's no need to present it here. What has never been made public, however, is the background of Debbie's decision to allow this part of her story to be included in my book. The details of her disappearing pregnancy and the later presentation to her, inside a UFO, of what she took to be the hybrid result of that pregnancy comprise the most personal and poignant saga one can imagine. Nothing Debbie said during the many months of my investigation was as moving to me as her description of what it was like to have her baby forcibly taken from her, and, years later, to feel the sudden rush of maternal love for the strange but beautiful little girl the aliens presented to her . . . and then the profound anguish of separation as the child was once again taken from her.

One night, as the investigation was winding down and I began to discuss my ideas for a book about her case, Debbie seemed thoughtful and rather quiet. After a long pause, she said that there was one thing she did not want me to write about. She asked me not to include anything about the little girl, whom she had named Emily, and about whom her feelings were still too raw, too sadly troubling. Her love for this child and her sense of helplessness at having been separated from her were still too overwhelming to handle. She wanted none of this—the pregnancy which vanished and her short, precious meeting with Emily—to be included in a book that strangers would read and skeptics would deride, or even ridicule. It was a private tragedy she was not yet able to share.

Believing as I did that information about alien genetic experimentation was the single most important issue for our knowledge of the phenomenon, I asked her if she would agree to a tentative compromise. I promised to continue working on the book with this part of the story included, but added that after I'd finished the manuscript, she could read it and if she still wanted me to, I would delete the sections dealing with her missing pregnancy and her involvement with the little girl.

With this understanding, I continued writing, hoping she would change her mind. And then one night, as we drove together to an airport, Debbie was unusually silent. I don't remember her precise words once she began to speak, but they were something like this: "Budd, I've been thinking a lot about Emily and my pregnancy and that whole thing, and I've decided that you can put it in the book. I know this has happened to a lot of other women, and I sure know they must feel like I do. It's about the saddest and the strangest thing you can imagine. In one way I don't want this part of me and my life to be so public, but this is the way I've come to think about it: maybe I'll never do anything great in life, or have the chance to have an effect on things in any major way. Maybe this is the one really important contribution I'll ever be able to make . . . to let other people know what happened to me so they can understand what might be happening to them . . ."

As we drove along that night, Debbie spoke very softly, as if there were literally months of thought behind her words. I knew how moved she was, and how much her decision cost her. There were tears in my eyes, too.

In the years since then, Debbie has become a role model for hundreds of other abductees, frightened, confused men and women who have seen in her a strong, very human and vulnerable young woman who has survived and ultimately triumphed. If she can face these devastating problems and surmount them, so can they. The trajectory of her life follows an ideal line: From the low point of stasis and depression and denial, she lifted herself up and ahead to face her disturbing memories and fears. In 1983, she wrote her letters, throwing several away until she was able, finally, to mail one. And then, feeling a little safer, she began to explore her experiences. She met other abductees, formed new friendships, but faced new bouts of denial and depression, all interspersed with a steady sense of gain over the confusions she'd lived with for so long.

Understanding her feelings more clearly and moving away from the helplessness she'd known for so many years, she agreed to let her story be known for the good of untold numbers of other men and women. It took a while longer for Debbie to gather the courage to speak in public for the first time about her experiences. But that seemed to her a necessary next step in facing—and facing *down*—the tears that had nearly crippled her for so long.

I remember vividly that first public appearance, in 1988,

at one of John White's conferences in North Haven, Connecticut. Debbie had asked me to stand at the podium next to her for moral support, and when she stepped up to speak there was a period of silence. "I've never done this before," she told the audience, "and I'm really kind of scared. Just let me take a minute to get myself together, and then I'll be all right." I'm not sure if these were her exact words, but that was the sense of what she said. She lowered her eyes and was silent. We waited. The silence deepened. All the people in the auditorium were leaning forward, tense, inwardly wishing her well. The silence continued, and then she looked up, smiled, and said, "I'm okay now," and began her relaxed and wholly natural talk. At the end, there was a standing ovation. Everyone sensed that hers was an unmistakable voice, a voice of honesty and humility, a voice of simple wisdom. It is the voice one finds in the pages of her book. *Abduction—The Intruders Story Continues* is a work that represents the current stage in the lifting trajectory of Debbie's life. The confidence she has acquired over the years is fully revealed in the limpid directness of her forceful writing.

The appearance of her sister Kathy as coauthor is yet another demonstration of the strength and resilience that UFO abductees so frequently possess. In Kathy's case—as in Debbie's—it was not always so obvious. When I first met Kathy, she was both wary of my investigation and curious to find out the meaning of so many odd fears and memories that had inevitably colored her life. After some tentative interviews and regressive hypnosis, experiences she movingly describes in the pages of this book, Kathy decided against a more extended exploration. It was clear that she felt the privacy and well-being of her husband and children might be at some risk if she allowed an investigation. However, it also seemed to me that she was fearful of what might be discovered if she allowed the process to go forward.

In clear, eloquent prose Kathy lets us see into her mind, helping us to understand why she ended the investigation a decade ago, and why, now, she feels strong enough to tell the full story behind her decisions. In a certain sense Debbie and Kathy represent two diametrically opposed responses to the same stimulus: the first, the path of openness and risk, the second, the path of caution and privacy. And yet now, a decade later, the sisters who chose opposite paths find themselves in exactly the same place, sharing with the world their years of private anguish and their present sense of slowly building strength.

Over the years, I've learned many things from my investigations into the UFO abduction phenomenon. I know that some kind of nonhuman intelligence is interacting with us, but on its own terms, telling us only what it wishes to, and manipulating us with cold objectivity. I also know that some part of our government is aware of these intrusions and depredations but for its own reasons is deliberately denying this fact to the public at large. There is a sad and depressing parallel here: the government lies and the aliens lie. Each, apparently, has a hidden agenda; neither can be trusted.

But if the issues of government secrecy and alien intentions occupy the thoughts of many investigators, I find myself thinking far more often about the victims of both, about the pain they've suffered and the strengths they've shown. I think of Debbie and Kathy, two sisters from a modest midwestern family who suffered greatly but who finally triumphed—two marvelous representatives of the bravery and resilience of the human spirit. I am proud to have known them both.

—New York, 1994

AUTHOR'S NOTE

Debbie

I'M JUST AN AVERAGE PERSON. I TRY TO LIVE BY THE GOLDEN Rule as best I can. Often I find myself trudging through daily life, trying to make the best of a bad situation. And trying to get as much enjoyment out of life as I can. We all do that. Sometimes I do something wonderful, sometimes I make awful mistakes. Don't we all? Isn't that how we learn?

When I found myself in the extraordinary situations I write about in this book, I reacted just as you probably would. I had a hard time believing it. Any of it. I had serious doubts about my sanity and that of the people I soon found myself working with. "How on Earth could normal people believe this stuff is real?" It was easier for me to think I was just nuts.

Once I got to know the people I was to work with, I realized that these people weren't crazy. They were sane, intelligent, and if they were to testify in a court of law, I would accept their testimony as fact. And when I began to see the evidence that other people like me were presenting to them, I found that I could no longer rationalize all this stuff away. There was just no way other people could have remembered the things I remembered if they hadn't seen it for themselves.

In the beginning, I did not tell Budd Hopkins all the things I had remembered. It was too embarrassing and I was still trying to rationalize it all away. I would see the drawings other people did, knowing full well that I had not told anyone on the face of this Earth, those things that they were also remembering. I knew *something* was going on.

Budd used to show me things other people had done, or said, after I had told him my memories, perhaps thinking to himself that confirmation of my event would give me some peace of mind. I appreciated the thought but, actually, it made me sick to see that other people were remembering *my* stuff!

There went my neat little way of rationalizing!

I come from an average midwestern family. I'm lucky, I guess, because my family is close both geographically and in heart. We see each other almost every day. My parents are still married after forty-seven years; I haven't even lost a close loved one through death and I'm almost thirty-five years old! We weren't rich but we were by no means poor, having all the necessities, and most of the "extras" of life.

We came from a very stable background. We weren't kissy-huggy people, but if one of us was ever in trouble, we were all there, behind the person, giving all the support and love we had. There was no child abuse or sexual abuse of any kind in our family and I resent researchers who insinuate that all abduction experiences stem from this. They are wrong.

I was, I suppose, a bit of a "wild child." I listened to rock and roll, hated school, and rebelled whenever possible. I had problems with depression, anxiety, and low self-esteem as a teenager. No one could ever figure out why I was like this, when I came from such a good background. When I started to uncover the history of my family's involvement with UFOs and started working with Budd Hopkins and Dr. Aphrodite Clamar, I finally found relief. I got better. I have remained well since and it leads me to believe that they were obviously on the right track. It's my understanding that you can't relieve the symptoms unless you deal with the root problem. I think my recovery says a lot.

When I found myself standing on a stage in North Haven, Connecticut, back in 1988, I was terrified. I was about to bare my soul for the first time in front of a whole room full of strangers. When the applause died down and the room became silent, I found myself thinking, ''Well, either I'm going to open my mouth and talk, or I might as well just fall down now!'' My heart pounded. I didn't want to be there, and yet I had to tell the world. I was driven by a force stronger than me to be there that night—just as I am driven to write this book now. I decided that honesty would be the best policy, so I told the crowd I was terrified. That no matter what I was up there to talk to them about, I was very self-conscious and somewhat shy and this was going to be real hard for me. I think that was pretty obvious. I received a standing ovation for that bit of truth.

I'm following the same policy in writing this book. I don't expect a standing ovation. I don't even expect all of you will believe everything I write. I just pray that you will read with open minds and open hearts. Of course, I have no definite proof for most of what I will tell you in the following pages. But if you've already made up your mind that you're not going to believe it anyway, no proof would ever be good enough for you. I hope you'll be able to see the circumstantial evidence as I did and it will, at least, make you think twice about all this. Put yourself in my shoes for a moment. Imagine how you'd feel, what you'd say, if you had seen and experienced the things we have. If one idea I present here will make you think twice before you hurry to make a judgment call, cause you to remember something you needed to remember, or open your mind just a little bit more than when you first picked up this book, then I will have accomplished what I believe I am here to do.

This book is for all the people like us, who are searching for the truth. Even if it doesn't answer questions, perhaps, at least, it will help us to ask the right ones.

This book is also for my children, in the hopes that someday it will help them to understand their mother and their family a little better. I hope they know how much I love them.

I'd like to thank my family, my friends, and all the people who have chosen to dedicate their lives to finding the truth. I love you all.

Despite the limitations of the human language, as I read the spiritual things in the final chapters, the ideas resonate with such "rightness," that I know I have chosen the correct words. I hope that it will touch the core of your being, just as it has mine.

This is not an easy book to finish, because the story, like growing and learning, never ends. All I can do is keep my faith, an open mind, an open heart, and keep writing.

AUTHOR'S NOTE

Kathy

FOR THREE GENERATIONS MY FAMILY HAS BEEN INVOLVED IN many bizarre UFO, extraterrestrial, spiritual, psychic, and poltergeist experiences. I don't know how or if any of these experiences relate, but taken as a whole, they unite us as a family.

Our family is fairly ordinary at face value. We get together every weekend and holiday, play cards, and get loud. To an outsider we probably appear to be the Waltons gone berserk. We could be your neighbors, your coworkers, your friends, and you would never know the secrets we only share among ourselves and with a handful of close friends. You might even be related to us but not be aware of any strange happenings and encounters we have logged in our mental banks.

Debbie has been the only one to come forward and spill her guts, much to our shock and horror. Ten years ago, she decided to go public. She continued to use the name Kathie, which was given to her in the book *Intruders* in a meek attempt to protect her identity, but she still used her own face, much to our chagrin. The rest of us did consider rearranging that face for her—to protect her identity, of course. (Just kidding, folks.)

Now, after ten years of being in the shadows, I've decided to come out into the light.

I present myself to you now and will share some of my experiences. I offer no scientific data to back them up. I have no physical evidence, no souvenirs, no mathematical equations to prove my extraterrestrial experiences. I only have my word. Proving extraterrestrials exist doesn't seem as important to me as learning how to mentally deal with the aftermath of these experiences.

Bear with me now as I allow my soul to seep out of the crack in my armor.

My life on this earth began November 30, 1947, in the suburbs of Indianapolis. A strange giant of a man slaps my naked bottom, probably for waking him up, plops me on a scale, and proclaims six pounds, five ounces. I think to myself, four ounces, and thus begins my lifelong fixation with my weight.

For the next eleven years, I was an only child. That was really pretty good living. I always got my own way and never had to share with anyone. I always felt older than friends of the same age. When we played house, I was always picked to be the mother. I feel like I've been Mom all my life now, and it's getting a little stale.

In the early 1950s, I heard and read a lot about UFOs. It was a new phenomenon then and I used to hear my parents talk about sightings when they would read articles in the paper. All that talk never frightened me: it just seemed to be a fact of life. I can remember watching popular science fiction shows with great interest, but I always took them with a grain of salt.

Talking about UFOs didn't frighten me, but I remember being terrified of the dark, spiders, and being closed up in small spaces. Many nights I lay awake, needing to go to the bathroom, but so afraid to get out of bed that I would simply wet my pants. That caused me great anguish, but it seemed the lesser of two evils.

Even with my great fear of the dark, I have vivid memories of sitting in front of my bedroom window, alone at night, and simply staring into the sky. I don't recall ever seeing any UFOs back then, but I remember wishing "they" would make themselves known and take me away with them.

It seemed so very harmless to sit and wish "they" would come down and make themselves known, but when "they" do come into your life, the effects will forever alter your being in an array of unnerving situations. From that day on, you begin to realize that maybe your life is no longer your own. You are humbled in the knowledge that perhaps you are not as strong as you had always thought. You are scared of the fact that an unknown source, which the majority of the population doesn't even recognize as real, can manipulate you into whatever suits its needs or purposes. You subconsciously maintain that fear every waking and resting moment of your life, knowing that you could be confronted at any time, more than likely when you least expect it.

Sleep makes you feel especially vulnerable to "them." Consequently, sleep is distubing to you. Sleep somehow dissolves your defenses, even though you know you have no defense, and sleep opens your mind to all the subconscious realities you refuse to recognize while you're awake. Therefore, sleep becomes your enemy.

I have spent many years fighting sleep. Pacing the floors alone in the dark, fearing windows, shadows and noises. Fearing everything except what I was really afraid of. I paced not only while I was awake, but I paced while I was asleep, waking up in some of the most bizarre situations. I have awakened just before stepping out of the front door. I have awakened stark naked, sitting in the living room in front of the window eating an ice cream cone I fixed in my sleep. I have awakened in various parts of the house, always wondering what I have done in my sleep, where I have gone, if anyone has seen me, and if I am going crazy. I associated my fear of sleepwalking with my fear of sleep, and only after twenty years, when I finally came face to face with my greatest fear, when I learned to contend with the eerie, unbelievable phenomenon in my life, was I finally able to sleep with any regularity.

When the investigations began of my family and myself, I was very excited, but as the studies became more intense, as I was pressured to invite strangers into my mind, I began to feel extremely defensive. I protected my subconscious as one would protect a child. I began to feel anger at anyone trying to make me remember my innermost thoughts, my secrets, my experiences. I somehow felt or knew that those experiences were supposed to remain locked in my mind, not even to be revealed to myself. I would compare that feeling to that of a prisoner of war: captured, cornered, and interrogated. Someone forcing that prisoner to confess to that which she feels she can't. First defiant, then beaten into submission, then relieved upon the completion and feeling lucky to have survived.

The aftermath of a UFO experience is like being accused and sentenced for a crime you didn't commit. You are professing to that which you know is true, but no one believes you. It feels like it's you against the world. No one listens, no one believes, no one cares. If anyone does believe, he is labeled "guilty" too. It's a terrible out-of-control feeling that makes you feel sparated from the norm, an alien yourself, an outsider.

With the support of my family and friends, I believe I am

now ready to take the plunge into my mind. It has taken me many years to finally get over the feeling that I "can't tell."

I would like to thank them all for simply being there. I'll try not to embarrass my kids too much, but I hope that they will finally realize just what their mom is all about.

PROLOGUE
1965

IT WAS LATE AFTERNOON, GOING ON FIVE P.M. I HAD DRIVEN MY mother to a local bingo game. I hadn't had my driver's license very long—I was just sixteen—so I loved chauffeuring people around. I liked being behind the wheel of a car. Most kids do. It makes you feel like you're an adult and gives you such a feeling of power—you're in total control of two tons of engine and steel. Or at least you think you are.

I turned down the familiar two-lane road that would take me home. I was in no hurry. There was still plenty of daylight left. The evening was coming slow, as it does early in the fall. And I had no special plans, unless you'd call babysitting for your little brother and two sisters special. I stopped at familiar cross-streets—every traffic light, it seemed, turned red as I approached—and drove by familiar houses. The familiarity made me feel easy, comfortable with my life.

Then, suddenly, I wasn't.

I wasn't on the road. I was frantically turning the steering wheel every which way I could, but the car was totally out of my control. I thought for a moment I was headed for the empty parking lot behind a church, although I didn't know why. Then I thought I had stopped: But why? I needed to get home, needed to see to my little brother and two sisters, needed to get them some supper and put them to bed, and at eleven I had to pick up my mother. Urgently.

Everything seems to have stopped. I look up. I'm leaning over the steering wheel, looking up through the windshield, and directly over the car, about the height of two telephone poles away, it's hovering. It's not like anything I have ever seen before. An oblong craft, approximately seventy feet in length, it resembles two dinner plates on top of each other. Its surface smooth, like stainless steel, it stands out against the sudden blackness of the sky. Red and white and amber lights flash on its underside. It is unearthly; it is magnificent.

My view is completely unobstructed. Through the windshield my arms, still folded over the steering wheel, begin to feel a warmth like that of the summer sun. I reach for the glove compartment, where I always keep a small camera, as I'm thinking that I've got to get a picture of this or who will believe me. The camera is gone. Faintly, through the closed window, I hear a humming sound coming from the hovering craft. I roll down the car window so I can hear more clearly. The car radio is playing. Without taking my eyes off the craft, with my right hand I reach for the radio, to turn down the volume. The very instant I touch the volume-control button the craft starts very slowly to rise straight up.

I am not on the road. I am not in the empty church parking lot. I am not even on the ground. From the side window of the car, on the vacant pavement retreating below me, I see a bright circle of light marking the spot where I had thought the car had stopped.

And then the car has stopped.

* * *

I am somewhere else, inside the car, in a closed dark room.
A misty light pours from a doorway that leads to another
chamber. Though bright, it fails to illuminate the surroundings immediately outside my car, but it does silhouette three
figures. Their frames are humanlike but small. They stand
maybe four feet in height. (Actually, the figure in the center
appears to be somewhat taller than the other two.) Their
arms seem to be long and their heads large in proportion to
the rest of their bodies. Their heads are rounded at the
crown and narrow slightly at what would in humans be the
chin.

They do not speak. Still I know that I must get out of my
car. I know that I must enter the lighted room beyond. I
know that I don't want to—I am scared—but I know that I
am going to have to because I cannot resist their will and
they are going to make me go. To observe them is one
thing, but to have them move you, to intrude upon you, with
their minds . . . that is another story.

I am in another room. The room is all white. There is a
table. I am lying on a very smooth table in an all-white
room. A figure—this one very tall; a very tall and very thin
alien figure—is standing at the foot of the table. While no
feature suggests it and no particular characteristic points to
it, for some unaccountable reason or by something like intu-
ition I have the feeling that this alien being is female in
gender.

Its (her?) skin is dark and brownish, leathery in appearance. The body is rigid. The head is like nothing I have seen
on earth, like nothing except maybe the head of a praying
mantis if you'd enlarge it beyond the size of a human head.
Wide on top, it slopes at an angle downward and in to a
pointed chin. The head simply sits on the body—no neck is
visible—and moves with quick, jerky, insectlike move-

ments. The eyes, huge and luminous and liquid and black, are trained solely on me.

I am lying on a table in a white room. A rigid, stringy figure six feet tall is standing at the foot of the table, staring at me. Curiosity fills the gaze of its huge, black eyes the way wonder might widen the eyes of a small child exploring the objects in a room for the very first time. Its attention captured, it gazes down the length of the table at me. It cocks its neckless head at me; though common enough, the gesture strikes me as being strange and inhuman, chilling.

I am lying on a table, watching this curious creature curiously watching me. I am watching, I am waiting. I am not as curious. Maybe I'm afraid. But mostly I am only waiting, waiting to see where this mind will make mine go.

1

DEBBIE
1983

THIS WAS THE BEGINNING OF THE ODYSSEY THAT WOULD LATER become my life. The story was first reported by Budd Hopkins in his book, *Intruders: The Incredible Visitations at Copely Woods.*

As I looked at that huge, odd-shaped mark in my parents' backyard, a million thoughts raced through my mind. Somehow I knew what it meant, I knew how it had gotten there, and yet, I still couldn't believe my own eyes—my own thoughts. Images of big, black eyes, feelings of panic and confusion filled my conscious mind. When I heard my mother's nervous laugh and the words, "That's where our UFO landed," I slammed back to reality, shocked at what I heard coming from her mouth. Secretly my heart skipped a beat. Out loud, I asked, "What planet are you from?" To myself I said, What the hell is wrong with me?

My father was bitching about how his beautiful yard was now screwed up and wondering out loud if he had mowed the grass too short. That was typical of my father. He had this obsession with his lawn. Ever since we moved into this house he had pampered and protected his beloved grass as if it were one of his favorite children. I swear, sometimes I thought I heard him outside at night talking lovingly to the seed as if it would help it grow better. God help those responsible for this travesty.

Meanwhile, I was already beginning to remember how the yard got so messed up. And I sure didn't like what I was remembering. It was too much like the nightmares I'd been having lately. And that was just unthinkable.

It was the Fourth of July weekend, 1983. The whole family had come over to have a little celebration picnic and go swimming. Later we were going to set off some fireworks. This had become something of a family tradition since we had moved in. Our house was the only one big enough to hold the whole family. It also helped that we were in an area where the houses were spread far enough apart so as not to set the neighborhood on fire with our spectacular display of K-mart fireworks. This was also the first time anyone had been in the backyard since the night of June 30—the night I saw the light in the yard. The night I believe the mark was left in the backyard.

On that night, I had been getting ready to go to my girl-friend's house to do some sewing. I was divorced and living with my two sons at my parents' home. My girlfriend had a lucrative little costume-sewing business going, and I was her assistant. At that time in my life, this was my only source of income, meager as it was.

I was standing at the kitchen window, washing chicken grease off my hands. Something caught my eye, outside in the backyard. I noticed an odd-looking light emanating from the swimming pool pump house. Now, the light in and of itself might not have been so strange. But because I had been out there earlier in the day, loading the pool with chlorine, and distinctly remembered wrestling with the rusty slide lock on the pump-house door, I knew that door shouldn't even be open. Later I was to find out that the light bulb had been burned out in the pump-house light fixture for several years.

I called to my mother to look at this odd light. She came to the window with me and noted that it was indeed odd, although she didn't seem to be too impressed by what she had seen. It was a very bright white light that seemed to have a life of its own. It almost appeared to radiate through the open door, in bursts. I didn't think of it at the time, but later I realized that light from a yellow incandescent bulb would probably not look like this under any circumstances.

I had a strange feeling that I had better stay home, but I shook it off and left anyway. As I got in my car, I decided to drive back behind the house, on the turn-around, just to make sure that I didn't see any prowlers lurking about— human ones, that is. As I made my turn and approached the back of the house, I saw that the light was gone, and, to my surprise, the back door to the attached garage was now open. I don't know why I didn't stop right then, but I didn't. I drove over to my friend's house, approximately two minutes away on the street directly behind mine.

As soon as I got to her house, I called my mother. I told her what I had seen and asked her if she wanted me to come home. I was thinking about burglars, not aliens! Mom insisted that everything was all right. She said that she would lock the doors and keep the porch light on for me, and she told me not to worry. I hung up the phone thinking that all was well and started to tell my friend what I had seen. No sooner had I hung up, when the phone rang again. I grabbed it on instinct. It was my mother and she sounded very strange. She asked me to come home "right now." She sounded kind of scared and ominous. Not at all like my mother, someone who was never scared of anything. My friend's husband heard my concern as I talked to my mother, and he yelled from the bedroom, "Why don't you call the police? That's what they get paid for." My mother heard this and replied, "I don't want anyone here, except you."

What my mother had failed to tell me was, after I left to go to my friend's house, she had seen the light I had pointed out to her go out. And soon after, there appeared a soft, white light that surrounded the bird-feeder, directly in front of the kitchen window. The light seemed to be about the size of a basketball. She said that she tried to figure out where the light was coming from, and looked for a car or someone with a flashlight, in the back driveway. She soon realized there was no way a car or any other kind of light could have been making that ball of light surround the bird-feeder in that manner. There was no beam, and even if a car had been in the driveway, it couldn't have been at the angle it needed to be to make that ball of light and not show a beam. She told me that as she stood there, watching this light, it began to grow fainter and fainter, until it finally disappeared. It was then that she got the idea to call me home from my friend's house. The best part of this was that she didn't even remember this whole little episode until almost a week after the fact. One day, she said to me, "Oh, by the way, Debbie, I just remembered why I called you home the other night." I said to her, "Gee, thanks, Mom. If I had known that, I would have *never* come home again!"

I jumped in my car and raced home. The trip took all of two minutes. When I got there, I pulled up alongside the house and jumped out of my car, right at the back patio room door. Mom was standing there, waiting for me. I went in the patio room, grabbed my father's shotgun, which wasn't loaded, and started back through the kitchen to the back porch. Mom made a comment that the gun wasn't loaded, so I said to her, "Well, I'll just beat them to death, if I have to."

For me to have even gone out there that night was strange, totally out of character for me. I am the biggest chicken who ever drew a breath, and I normally would have just run the other way. Plus, I hate guns with a passion and always used to complain to my father for even having them in the house. For me to actually grab one with the intention of using it, in any way, was very much "not like me."

I proceeded to go from the back door of the kitchen to the pump house out by the pool. I don't remember seeing anything strange in the yard at that time. I forced open the rusty lock and stuck the gun in through the tiny opening I had made. I yelled out some pretty raunchy threats and then kicked the door open with my left foot. There was nothing in there I could see in the dim light of the moon. As I turned to look at the open pedestrian door of the attached garage, I realized that my dog, Penny, had been in there. Surely she was out, now that the door was open.

We were keeping her in the garage at night, as she was in heat and we didn't want to have to get rid of yet another litter of unwanted pups. She was the Irma la Douce of the neighborhood.

I decided to look for her in the back of our property. It was a little strange that she hadn't already found me. Usually, when I go outside and she's out, she's on me like stink on garbage. She thought I was her "mommy." Actually, I was the one who fed her.

I heard some whimpering coming from under Dad's old truck. It was parked in front of the workshop in the back lot. I looked under the truck and there was Penny. I called to her several times, but she absolutely would not come out from under the truck to see me. That was really strange. I grabbed her by the legs to pull her out, and she fought me like a mad dog. I finally gave up trying to get her to come out. And I was starting to have a real uneasy feeling about this whole thing. This was beginning to feel like another bad dream.

I decided to go back toward the house and check out the

attached garage. Someone could be hiding in there. I made the same kind of approach to the garage that I had made to the pump house. I spewed a few obscene remarks and flung open the door as I hit the light switch. Nothing, not a soul, could be seen. I walked around for a minute or so, looking behind boxes and old mattresses. All of a sudden I began to feel very hot. It felt as if the skin on my body was burning off. I felt real panic race over me and thought to myself, Damn, I gotta get outta here, *now!* As I turned to run out the door, I froze. The next conscious memory I had after that was of walking up the back steps and thinking about my kids. Were they all right? I saw my mother standing in the open screen door, and I remembered telling her, "It's cool." Then I remembered her saying, "Good, now I can go back to sleep."

After this episode, I no longer wanted to sew. For some unknown reason, I felt like I needed to get wet. I felt grubby and hot. I decided to have my girlfriend come back to my house to swim with me. I went back to her house to fetch her and within twenty minutes, we were on our way back to my house for a swim. No mention was ever made as to the amount of time I had been gone. Later, we all began to realize that I had been gone much longer than I had remembered and I believe that she may have felt guilty about not noticing it then. A trip that should have taken all of fifteen minutes, actually took over an hour.

When we got back to my house we headed for the pool immediately. As we walked across the yard, her daughter suddenly jumped and yelled "Ouch!" She said that as she walked over a spot in the yard. She apparently stepped on something that burned her foot. She said that it felt prickly and that her foot then started feeling a little numb. We were probably in the pool for about ten to fifteen minutes when suddenly we began to feel sick to our stomachs. Just before that I had noticed my eyes had begun to burn and my vision was "turning white." All the lights that I looked at had some kind of halos around them and it felt like I had glass in my eyes. Not unlike the effects that too much chlorine in pool water would have on your eyes, except that I hadn't gotten water in my eyes. And this was much more intense. We all felt creepy. My girlfriend even remarked that she felt like someone was watching us, so we finally gave up and ended our swimming for the night.

The next morning, I woke up with the ugliest looking eyes you have ever seen. They were swollen shut and running like a faucet. The pain was so bad that my mother took me to the emergency room of the local hospital. The doctors in the emergency room immediately sent me to the eye specialist next door to the hospital, and his girls worked me in within ten minutes.

As he examined my eyes, I could see the look of bewilderment and concern on his face. He asked me, more than once, if I had looked into the arc of a welder. By the third time he'd asked me this, I was getting pretty hateful. I felt like I'd been hit by a train and my eyes were killing me. I snapped back to him that I was not some kind of stupid person and I knew better than to ever do something like that. My eyes had apparently been burned, as far as he could tell. He prescribed several medications and gave me instructions on how to care for my eyes. It took several weeks for them to heal and I had to make a return trip for a follow-up exam. My eyes have never been right since. They are very light sensitive and weak. I have problems with night vision and sometimes my eyes water, ache, and burn for no reason at all.

That was the strange night that I kept thinking about as I looked at that mark in the yard. I found myself thinking about my sister, "Laura," and what she had seen in 1965 and how we razzed her half to death over it. I thought about the book that scared me so much that I had tried to read a month or so before. (The book was *Missing Time* by Budd Hopkins.)

I had made a habit of going to the library a lot over the last year. It was a cheap form of entertainment and we lived right across the street from one of the better libraries in the city. My children liked for me to take them there once or twice a week for story time. To pass the time, I would browse through the shelves for anything that looked interesting.

I had come across one particular book, whose bright orange cover and big, bold title lettering caught my eye. I had assumed the title, *Missing Time,* and the word *abduction* on the cover referred to some kind of crime mystery. (Well, in a way it did, I guess!)

I have a rather unusual way of reading books. I read the last page first and then look for any drawings or photos that might be included. Then I just scan through the rest of it, randomly, until I pick up on something that catches my eye.

I noticed in the back of the book there was a notation stating that if you felt you'd had an experience similar to what the author had written about, you could write him in care of the publisher and he would try to get back to you. I thought that was odd. Why would anyone who had been abducted want to tell this guy? Wouldn't they just call the police? I didn't realize what kind of abduction Budd was talking about. When I began to look through the pictures in the middle of the book, my skin began to crawl. My first instinct was to put the book back on the shelf, and that's exactly what I did. Throughout the afternoon I kept finding myself drawn back to that shelf. So, before I checked out for the day I went back, grabbed the book, and put it in the pile I had ready to go.

Later that evening, after I put my kids to bed for the night, I picked up the book again and began to look through the pictures. Something about those pictures was so hauntingly familiar. Every time I tried to look at the picture of the creatures with the big black eyes, I started to panic. I tried to read a few times but I'd have to stop. I realized that each time I tried to read, I'd start to hyperventilate and get dizzy. This went on for several days before I finally gave up and put the book down for good, I thought.

That book was about people who had been abducted by aliens in UFOs. Right! UFOs! I thought to myself, Why in the hell am I connecting this mark in our yard to UFOs? Why? Why did my mother say that? And why did that book scare me so much?

I began to have one of my nightmares right there in the yard. All I could see, superimposed on the mark, were two huge, black, almond-shaped eyes. It was so lifelike, so real. And it was as if they were trying to tell me something. I was trying to make myself remember and it was making me sick.

I wasn't feeling very well, physically, anyway, and I sure didn't need *this,* too. My stomach was queasy a lot and I'd had diarrhea something fierce. My head hurt and I hadn't been able to sleep or eat much. My whole body ached. I felt crazy. I felt like I was losing my mind.

I'd already been under enough stress as it was. I'd gotten divorced the year before, moved myself and my two little boys back to my parents' home, tried to figure out what I was going to do with my life, and I tried to make two families get along in the same house. All this had already begun to take its toll on all of us.

I had signed up for group therapy at the local hospital to try to learn how to cope with my anxiety and all the changes we had been through. I was hoping to gain enough self-confidence to be able to get a good job and raise my kids, alone. In retrospect, I feel sorry for those people who were in my group.

In 1983 I was wrestling with something a lot bigger than

just getting a divorce. Now I realize why I have always had a problem with anxiety and low self-esteem. I was exhibiting symptoms of post-traumatic-stress syndrome even back then.

One evening, while in my group meeting, around the night of June 30, 1983, we were listening to some poor fellow talking about how upset he was that his wife had left him. He didn't think he would be able to live without her. It really pissed me off! I remember thinking to myself, You wimp! You don't know what it's like to be scared. You have no idea! You think you can't make it without her? You're scared to be alone? Well, let me tell you something, buddy, you don't know what it's like to feel fear until you've felt the kind of fear I live with every day. Exhibiting incredible insensitivity, I jumped up and screamed just that, right in his face, and then ran out of the room like some kind of wild woman. I plopped myself down on the front porch of the house where we were holding our meetings and bawled my eyes out.

I felt like such a fool. I didn't mean to hurt that guy's feelings or diminish what he was going through. I just couldn't hold it in any longer. My counselor came out onto the porch and put his arm around me as I sat there, sobbing. I'll never forget the look on everyone's face as I ranted and raved. And I was so embarrassed. He said to me that he wanted to help me, but that I had to remember what it was that was bothering me so much, and that I had to tell him. I couldn't remember anything that I had the nerve to tell him, so I could tell him nothing. I asked him what it felt like to go crazy.

I'd like to make an important point. Once I began to work with Budd and all the other fine researchers and doctors, I began to learn how to cope with my feelings and I got better. That's more than I can say for anything I or anyone else has ever tried. I think that says a lot for what Budd is doing, how he does it, and what he discovers during an investigation. Whatever he did, it worked. And I'm a lot different now.

But back then, my kids were driving my parents crazy, and my parents and my life were driving me crazy. This mark in the yard was beginning to be like the straw that would break the camel's back. And I didn't even understand why. That just made it worse, because I hate not being able to understand something.

I have this "thing" about trying to make things fit into a rational place, so I decided that there had to be a reasonable explanation for what had happened in our yard. I just wasn't about to attribute it to what I thought were a few bad dreams and a few weird things that I assumed happened to everyone. I just couldn't.

I dug out the trusty old Yellow Pages and began calling anyone I could think of who might help explain it all away. I called the agricultural agent for the state of Indiana but was told that he was out of the office for a while.

I called several local universities and asked to speak to their agricultural departments. I explained to them that this mark (for lack of a better term) had appeared in our yard, just out of the blue. I told them that it was an eight-foot-diameter circle with a forty-eight-foot-long by two-foot-wide swath coming off the east edge of the circle. The swath extended south, from the circle, and ended in a perfectly rounded tip. The edges were very well defined and it had not changed shape since it appeared. The grass inside this mark was folded down on itself as if it had been crushed. And the soil had a particularly pungent, bitter odor. I also explained that the grass outside the mark appeared normal except for a small area directly to the west. This area was near the attached garage and looked as if it had been dusted with something that just scorched the tips of the grass, but it didn't burn it up or crush it, like in the mark itself. I also told them about a section of trees directly north of the circle that had been damaged. In a swath of trees about ten feet wide, the leaves had begun to turn yellow and wilt from the trunk to the top. Of course, I left out the weird nightmares, seeing the light in the pump house, and getting sick. I didn't tell them about how my girlfriend's daughter's foot had burned as she walked over the swath that night and how she began to get nauseated and feel her leg go numb up to her knee. I knew in my mind that this was all connected and somehow UFOs had something to do with it. But I realized that I would never be able to convince them of that. And besides, I wanted a real answer, not something cooked up to pacify a crazy woman!

The answers that I got from various agents from different schools were practically the same. They explained to me that it couldn't have been a mold spore or any kind of fungus because they generally just don't appear all at once and they will grow and change shape to some extent. Also, they all agreed that they had never heard of anything affecting the soil like ours was affected.

The dirt wouldn't even hold water. It just rolled off it like it would a rock and the soil was like that down to some twelve inches deep. They had no explanations whatsoever. Everyone could tell me what it wasn't, but no one would even offer a speculation as to what it could be. And no one was willing to ever come out and test it. I thought that was kind of strange.

I called the local power company, the local gas company, and even a few local lawn-care services. (I was, by this time, desperate for any kind of rational explanation!) I checked with the weather service to see if there had been any lightning anywhere in our area that night that might have hit the ground and made that spot. I also asked them if lightning could do that kind of a thing to a yard. I think they thought I was nuts.

I must have inherited my propensity for trying to make things "fit" from my dad. He, too, was running his own kind of investigation on the appearance of the mark. He discovered that the drainage tiles underneath the mark had been broken, smashed in many places. Shortly after the night of June 30, 1983, the transformer atop the utility pole next to the mark blew up. When the power and light company came out to repair the damage, they were mystified to see that all the wires running to the transformer had been melted together. The man my father spoke to could not explain how that could have happened, and he was as perplexed as my father, who has been an electrician for thirty-five years.

My dad is also an amateur radio operator, and he noticed that the antenna switch in the house had been destroyed, apparently by whatever had destroyed the wires outside.

Several days had passed and every time I looked at that mark in the yard I could feel myself getting more and more anxious. I had all but given up trying to find an explanation for it. My thoughts continued to drift back to the book that I had looked at a month or so before the mark appeared, before the night I'd had the strange encounter with the lights in the yard—that book, *Missing Time*.

Recalling that there had been an address in the back of the book, I decided to write to the author. I had begun to feel that maybe there was something going on in our family that he might be interested in. My nightmares had begun to seep into my waking state and I had begun to have what I called flashbacks. I could be involved in the most mundane task with my mind blank and suddenly start to see whole scenes whiz before my eyes as if I were watching them on a movie screen. And I was the unwilling star. Sometimes I would only see eyes. These huge, liquid black eyes, boring a hole through me. At other times I would see whole faces, gray faces with slits for mouths. I began to remember seeing bright, flashing lights and hands, funny hands moving across me. I could almost see, again, these faces as close to mine as they could get, "talking" to me in some strange manner. I could see balls of light moving all around me and dark shadows moving about my parents' yard. I had memories of being hit by "lightning," right in the chest. And thinking that I was dying. Try doing the dishes while you're being hit by lightning! I could actually feel the pain over and over. Each time I'd relive this, I'd really relive it, feeling, hearing—touching, the whole nine yards. I'm sure that anyone who had been watching me when this would happen, would have thought I was completely nuts. I began to feel like there was something right on the surface of my subconscious that I couldn't remember, but that if I didn't, I'd burst. It was like trying to remember the name of a song that's on the tip of your tongue, but you just can't get it. Every time you think you've got it, it's gone. And you can't stop thinking about it.

I went back to the library and got that book. I raced home with it, promptly found the address in the back and wrote it onto an envelope. Then I began to write a letter—a letter that would change my life forever. Had I known what I was starting when I wrote that letter, I'm not sure I would have. At that point in my life I was nowhere near ready to go through what I went through during the investigation. Although I must say that now I'm glad I did it.

I had no idea what I was expecting Budd Hopkins to do for me. I can't figure out if I wanted him to confirm my suspicions about the night in the yard and the mark that appeared there, or if I wanted him to tell me that it was all just a bad dream that would go away and that I wasn't crazy, after all. Perhaps I just wanted to know that I really wasn't as alone as I felt in all this. Whatever my reasons, I later began to realize that it must have been my destiny. Sitting in Budd's studio one day, looking through hundreds of letters that were just like mine, it struck me that my letter had been in this mess with all the rest. How in the world did mine happen to be the one of the few that he could actually get to and answer?

I was not experienced at writing letters of that type, just as I am not experienced at writing a book, so needless to say, several drafts were written and found their way into the trash can. I had figured out a way to write it without taking on total blame for all the craziness that I was trying to relate to this man. I focused a lot on my sister's experience in 1965 when she had been taking Mom to a bingo game and had seen a UFO on her way home. I couldn't actually say that I had seen one myself, because I couldn't remember all that happened to me that night. So I decided to tell him about her at the beginning, thinking that maybe he wouldn't throw the letter away if I could tell him about her actually seeing a UFO first. Then I'd spring the weirder stuff on him later in the letter. I was also thinking about how my sister was going to kill me if she ever found out that I had told a complete stranger about that night in 1965. She was real touchy about this particular event. We teased her a lot about it for years.

When I finally finished an acceptable and readable letter and had the fifteen photographs I had taken of the mark back from the drugstore, I asked Mom to mail the package. She later told me that she had no intention of mailing it, but when she went to the mailbox to send off some checks, she remembered that she had the letter in her purse and just dropped it in. She doesn't know why she did it after she had already decided that she wasn't going to. I guess now that I'm glad she did.

From the time the letter got mailed, to the time I actually heard from Budd, I continued to grow steadily worse. Physically, I found myself nauseated every day. I broke out in mysterious rashes and noticed that my hair was breaking off and falling out at the roots at an alarming rate. I dreaded washing my hair every morning because I couldn't believe how many times I would have to clear the drain of hair so the water could empty out. It was getting more difficult to make it look like anything and I was beginning to get to the point where I didn't even care if it did look okay. I had begun to sleep a lot during the day and stay up all night because I felt safer sleeping during the day, when other people were up. At night I would check on my kids several times, sometimes sitting by their bed for hours, watching them.

At this point I still didn't know what it was that I was so afraid of, but I knew that I could never let my guard down or "they" would be back for me and my kids. I noticed that I felt very uncomfortable whenever I got near a dark window, especially the upstairs bathroom window that overlooked the mark in the yard. I refused to swim in the pool after dark, and that was something I had loved to do before the night that light came. I had also begun to go out in the evenings when I just couldn't take it anymore. I guess I just needed to get away from that house and those unconscious memories that were eating me up inside. I didn't go out as much as I would have liked to since the kids were so little, but I went whenever possible. I had one girlfriend I would go out with. As it turned out, she was also one of the people that I had an encounter with back in 1977, before I married my first husband.

A lot of times I wished I could go out, but just didn't feel well enough to get dressed, let alone dressed up. Three times in one week I went the local emergency room thinking I was having a heart attack. Of course, I wasn't having a heart attack, but I was having massive anxiety attacks. It's pretty bad when the local hospital employees start to call you by your first name when you walk through the door. I started having irregular heartbeats that became so bad that one night I wound up in the cardiac intensive care unit. That condition was diagnosed as "nervous heart syndrome." I was put on a couple of different beta-blockers, and the condition is now under control. Basically, I was a mess.

I was never so surprised in my life as when my mother told me that "the guy who wrote that book" called. I had never expected to hear from him at all! At the very most, I expected some kind of form letter explaining that what I had written was interesting, but that he just didn't have time to look into it right now. But, a call! Wow!

Did I really want to talk to him? Would he think that I was just another nut? What in the hell would I say? Maybe I'd find out he was the one who was nuts, and then where would I turn?

Budd was very polite on the phone. I could tell by the way he talked to me that he was trying to get me to tell him more about myself and the night that prompted me to write him. I kept trying to change the subject back to my sister's experience in 1965. I think I must have answered more questions from him that night than I've ever been asked in my whole life! He was definitely very thorough.

Soon after I talked to Budd, I called my sister. I told her that I had heard from the guy who wrote the book and I confessed to her that I had told him about her sighting in 1965. I figured she would be mad at me, and boy, was she ever! But I knew that Budd would want to talk to her about it, so I told her to expect a call from him. It was too late to take back what I had written him. Now it was time for me to face the music with her. Oh well, I thought, she'll get over it. Typical sister response.

2

KATHY

The Beginning

As I looked down at the eight-foot circle burned in the yard, the tiny voice inside my head was speechless for the very first time. As my eyes followed the forty-eight-foot path leading away (or to) the circle, I just couldn't seem to grasp the reality of this situation. Little did anyone in the family know that the circle would be the beginning of an amazing journey into ourselves. That journey would alternately bring us together and tear us apart in our search for answers to our past and future.

Little did we know then that the circle would be our only proof in three generations of UFO and unusual poltergeist phenomena.

The circle appeared June 30, 1983, in my parents' backyard in suburban Indianapolis, a few days after a night of bizarre, half-remembered incidents. As I was not present in the house at that time, I only know details told to me by others who were there. I did write everything down shortly after that. This is what I wrote in 1985 when I was trying to write a history of our family:

My mother and sister were alone at the house one evening, and saw a light in the pump house, by the pool in the backyard. Mom was also witness to a circular, glowing light that lit up the bird-feeder in the yard in front of the kitchen window, then she called Debbie to come home. At that time, she could not determine the source of the light. She could determine that it was not a beam of light, and it was very soft and glowing in nature—not harsh or illuminating. It was simply a perfect glowing circle of light about the size of a basketball. No other part of the yard around the bird-feeder was illuminated, in any way. And she didn't even remember this event until a week or more later. Debbie arrived home to investigate the grounds. She took a gun with her. The gun was not loaded but would sufficiently impress anyone she might point it at. She investigated the surrounding yard and pool house, but found no one or nothing—or so she remembers. The fact that she went outside alone, thinking there was a prowler about, is totally unbelievable to me. You would have to know Debbie. She is, as I am, a total chicken at heart. If I was certain there was a prowler anywhere around, I would stay as far away as possible. Because she did voluntarily go outside alone, that proves to me that someone or something beckoned her against her will to leave the safety of her home and go out into the darkness of the night alone. It will be months later before we are able to uncover the rest of the story. Several days later, they noticed an eight-foot circle of dead grass in the backyard with a swath of dead grass coming from the circle in a perfectly straight path that was approximately two feet wide and forty-eight feet long. On the Fourth of July, when my oldest son questioned what happened in her yard, Mom jokingly replied that was where a small flying saucer landed.

Later, she questioned why she would make such a remark like that, since at the time, it certainly seemed like a strange thing to say. The dead circle and lengthy strip of dead grass in the yard continued unchanged after months of fertilizing, watering, and reseeding. Along with the yard markings came an unconscious uneasiness about the happenings of the night in question. The ground inside the circle and strip repelled not only water, but any new life, including weeds. The family dog refused to go anywhere near the spot and two years later, had lost all her hair. Her skin was cracked and bleeding. She was blinded, literally eaten up with cancer, and in such agony that, eventually, she had to be put to sleep. The dirt in the affected area was like ground-up cement.

The marking in the yard was to stay exactly the same, winter and summer, for the next five years.

I studied the circular marking numerous times in those five years but I refused to touch the dirt or even walk on it. It gave me a very uneasy feeling and I felt it might be fairly unhealthy, perhaps radioactive. I'm no rocket scientist but I know enough to at least keep myself from glowing in the dark. My father had been given a new Geiger counter by my uncle several years before. At one point he broke it out and tried it on the mark in the yard. He couldn't even get the thing to zero, let alone get a reading. He took it to his place of employment, to test it, and it worked fine. When he brought it home to try again, it still wouldn't zero, the needle buried to the maximum reading. He gave up, and I avoided the mark from then on.

Debbie had tried to read a book called *Missing Time* by Budd Hopkins, before the night that she and Mom had seen the light in the yard. The book was about UFO abductions, and gave the author's address, so that people who felt that they had witnessed strange UFO sightings or occurrences could write to him. The markings in the yard, a UFO encounter I had in 1965, the many chilling dreams, and all the various strange happenings that surrounded family members, had prompted Debbie to write a lengthy letter to Budd.

Much to everyone's surprise, he contacted her, and thus began the investigations that have turned up an array of startling facts. Dreams, feelings, and numerous eyewitness events began tying together three generations of family members.

I won't reiterate Budd's findings. He spent several years and a large amount of personal funds to investigate and scientifically prove the facts he disclosed in *Intruders*. But I will state his conclusions:

On the night in question, June 30, 1983, the glowing light my mother and sister saw was apparently from an unidentified flying object that, for some unknown reason, had chosen to land in their backyard.

Debbie was apparently abducted by beings from a craft that had landed in the center of what was to become a dead circle of grass. At the same time, my mother was put into some kind of trance during this abduction.

I'm sorry I wasn't there to see all that. Up until then, I had been the only family member to see an actual UFO, or at least, remember seeing one. I had told and retold my encounter only to the immediate family, many times over the last twenty years. (I'll tell you about it in a later chapter). My encounter left me with a feeling of being special or "chosen."

My family would probably be considered more open minded than your average midwestern family, and we had always thought that we, the human race, were not alone in this vast universe. We figured that was the only intelligent conclusion.

In 1965 I had actually seen a UFO close up and walked

away without a scratch—at least no scratches visible from the outside. Now, almost twenty years later, I was no longer alone, the only one to have been witness to a UFO, the only one to catch all the flak. Not one, but two family members would now share this burden with me. Goody. Their experience would be a tough one to follow.

The only evidence I had of my encounter was my word. My only witnesses flew off in the UFO. The only "souvenir" I brought back was locked in my mind. At least Debbie and Mom had the circle and "runway" to substantiate their amazing encounter.

That circle was to remind them daily that "something" did happen that night in 1983. Without that circle remaining there, defying explanation, the night in question could have been rationalized away as just another bad dream, the same way our family has rationalized many of the other "bad dreams" we have had.

When Debbie told me that someone named Budd Hopkins would be calling me from New York to talk about my 1965 sighting, the hair on my arms stood on end. I could not believe that she was not only opening up her life to some total stranger, but volunteered my life as well. Talking about all of this to the family for twenty years is one thing, but talking to a total stranger is something else. I had told only a handful of people about my experience.

It only took one person's ridicule to make me realize the subject of UFOs is not easily mingled into everyday conversation. At that time my worst heckler was my husband "Johnny."

Johnny came from the South and was raised in a very impoverished environment where the family's main interest was finding their next meal. UFOs were certainly the last thing on their minds. His motto had always been, "If I can't see it, it doesn't exist."

Consequently, when I told him of my sighting as a teenager, he just assumed it was a quirk in my nature. When the family would get into a serious discussion, he would just shake his head.

There was no reasoning with him. It was only his view or the wrong view. In his opinion, only an idiot would actually tell anyone.

Well, this should be just swell, telling him some big city slicker would be calling the house to talk about UFOs.

Before I even told Johnny that Budd would be calling, I began to feel the twinges of being caught in the middle. Yankees to the left, Confederates to the right. Each gently tugging at an arm. As time passed, the tugs would become stronger. I would become wedged in the middle, my heart wanting to do one thing, but my mind holding me back. I would remain in this psychological limbo for many years. I formed a protective shell around my mind and kept the cracks patched so nothing would leak out. I didn't have much to spare, as it was.

Preparing for the call, I began to mentally recount the events of my sighting, making sure I had each detail in its proper order. I had played the picture in my mind hundreds of times since 1965. I told the story, the parts I actually remembered, at family gatherings so often that it seemed to fall effortlessly out of my mouth like the Pledge of Allegiance. I had never actually questioned the missing parts or the unusual circumstances. I had never wondered why it was broad daylight when my "five-minute" sighting started and pitch black when it ended. I had never questioned any of the discrepancies, and neither had anyone else.

Now, after twenty years, a stranger was interested in my story and I had an uneasy feeling that he would question all the missing parts. All the parts that I didn't want to think about. All the parts would change that night from interesting parlor conversation into a nightmare. All I could do was sit back and wait for Budd's call.

3

DEBBIE
Meeting Budd Hopkins

MY HEART POUNDED AS I DIALED BUDD'S PHONE NUMBER. When he answered, I nearly hung up on him. Nervously, I introduced myself and explained that I had written to him, that he had called when I was out, and that I was returning his call. Then I hoped he would talk for the rest of the conversation! That phone call seemed to go on forever. I kept trying to place the focus on the photos, the mark in the yard, and my sister's encounter in 1965. He kept trying to get me to talk about me. I felt like a jerk.

That call turned out to be the first in a long line of calls that would take place over the next few months. In order to save money on phone bills, I began to write to Budd as well. He set me up with a "buddy," someone I could call and tell about what had happened and how I was feeling.

I really liked "Mary" (a pseudonym). We seemed to click right off. Mary had been instructed not to tell me too much about what she had gone through, so as not to "contaminate" my subconscious. Despite that, we never seemed to lack things to talk about.

As the weeks passed I began to recall things that had happened when I was a child, things that at the time seemed normal to me but in retrospect were, indeed, strange. I couldn't believe that I had forgotten these little incidents. I think it says something about the incidents, in that I remembered them while talking about the UFO subject.

I remembered how, when I was a child of four or five, I had been frightened by a dream I had in which I thought a giant pterodactyl flew over my house and was looking for me. I remembered a trip I had taken with my older sister when I was six or thereabouts and how I had gotten lost. While I was trying to find my way back to where I should have been, I ran into a strange house and met a little boy with big black eyes who tricked me into what I thought was a playroom. He performed experiments on me and hurt my leg by poking something into it. I remembered waking up one night and seeing someone big standing next to my brother's bed staring very intently at him, then closing my eyes quickly and feeling him do the same thing to me. His face right next to mine. I was petrified! I remember waking up in my bed one night when I was really young and seeing someone lying beside me, trying to suck the breath out of me through my mouth. Whatever or whoever it was, it wasn't much bigger than I was, but it had a funny-shaped body and large head. I couldn't believe I had forgotten all these strange memories! And somehow, they seemed to make much more sense now.

One night I was in my room upstairs watching TV. I heard something—a vague, beeping noise—in my head and then I heard my name being called by several voices, in unison. They were neither male nor female. It blurted through all my mundane thoughts, from out of nowhere. It was all too familiar and it scared the hell out of me. I bolted up from my bed and rushed into the bathroom. I sat in there for a moment and tried to regain my composure, telling myself that I had just imagined it. "Go back to bed and relax. You're imagining things," I told myself. As I was going back to my room, across the hall from the bathroom, a small ball of bright white light whizzed past my head. It had come from my son's closed bedroom door and went toward the stairway. It disappeared as it began to go down the stairs. I jumped, bolted to my mother and father's room, opened the door and told my mother, who was trying to sleep, that my chest was starting to hurt again. (I didn't want to tell her about the voices that I heard. I was still trying to deny that I had heard them because it just sounded too crazy.) I asked her if she had seen the ball of light and her comment was, "It must have been lightning. Go take an aspirin and go back to bed. You'll be okay."

I knew it wasn't lightning because there were no windows in the hallway, and besides, the weather had been nice all day. I decided that to keep waking them up would be useless, and inconsiderate, so I went downstairs to take an aspirin. While I was walking through the living room to go to the kitchen, I noticed a bright white light, right outside the living-room window, and I thought I could see a silhouette of a small man standing in the light. I grabbed the phone and proceeded to call my buddy, Mary. God bless her heart. It must have been one in the morning and she was as sweet as she could be. I was hysterical. She talked to me for a good forty-five minutes. Every once in a while she'd ask me, "How are you feeling? Can you still see the light? Do you hear anything? Do you have any Valium or some wine?"

I don't know how I made it through that night, but with Mary's help, I did. We talked until I couldn't talk any more. We talked about anything and everything under the sun. Anything to get my mind off what I was feeling. I don't know if anything happened after we hung up, but I slept through it, whatever it was, and that was okay with me.

Eventually Budd decided that I needed to go to New York where he lived, so that I could be hypnotized by a psychiatrist who he knew was willing to help me, free of charge. I prayed that she would tell me I was crazy. At least that could be treated. Budd was beginning to realize that my June 30th incident, and my sister seeing the UFO in 1965, were only the "tip of the iceberg." Fleeting, telltale signs of something much bigger and more incredible than anyone would have ever imagined. I was so desperate for some help that I agreed to go.

Of course, it was my responsibility to pay for my way there and I was nearly broke. I decided I would sell my washer and dryer to raise money for the bus ticket and food. My washer and dryer were the only things I had in this whole world worth more than two cents! (I must have a guardian angel of finances, because I had exactly thirty-four cents left in my pocket when the bus pulled into the station back home in Indianapolis. I cut that one close, didn't I?)

In October of 1983 I left for New York City. I was scared half to death. This was the first trip I had ever taken by myself and I was terrified of getting lost and stranded in a strange place. (That's something I still worry about today.) Hell, I almost had a panic attack in the car on the way to the bus station! I just didn't know if I really wanted to go through with this. I was afraid of what I'd find out and I was worried about how I would handle that. I was worried about leaving my kids. Without me there to watch over them, what would happen to them? What would happen to me if "they" found out what I was doing? What would happen to me and my family if anyone else found out about this? Would we be the laughing-stock of Indiana? Was this guy I was going to see okay or was he even crazier than me? He could have been some kind of psychomaniac for all I knew. I was taking some big risks in going to see this guy, but I had to believe that everything would be okay. I was so desperate that I was willing to risk it all, in the hope of finding a way to live with the situation—or to get rid of it—once and for all. I had to, for myself and for my kids.

New York was one hell of an experience all by itself. I had been born and raised in Indiana, but had never been any farther east than Ohio. So I was in culture shock from the moment I saw the huge skyline of New York City over the horizon. The bus trip itself took every bit of seventeen hours and after the first couple of hours I was ready to get off almost anywhere. For one brief moment, as the city began to look bigger and bigger, I seriously considered turning around and going home. I was overwhelmed, to say the least.

When I stepped off the bus, Budd was there to greet me. I recognized him right away from his picture in the back of his book. I was very relieved to see a familiar face in that mob, but I couldn't help thinking to myself, What the hell am I doing here? This is crazy. I must be crazy!

Newspaper under one arm, hands full of stiff coffee and muffins, Budd led me through the bus station and onto the subway that led back to his apartment. My first subway ride was a "trip" all on its own. I was so jumpy from the long bus ride and because of all the stuff on my mind, I nearly went through the roof of the subway car when the lights went out for the first time. Nobody told me this was normal. Budd must have been at least a little amused at my reaction. I think it also helped him to see just what kind of state I was in at that time.

Both he and his family were very kind to me the whole time I was with them. I don't know of any other researchers who give nearly as much of themselves and their time to their subjects as Budd gave to me during the investigation of our case. I feel very lucky to have found him.

As soon as I dropped my bags in my room, it was time to go to the doctor's office. Not a moment was wasted during the whole time I was in New York. After all, I only had one washer and dryer. Who knew when I would be able to do this again?

My very first hypnosis session was very nerve-wracking for me. I was exhausted from the long, bumpy bus trip and I was afraid of what might come out under hypnosis. Also, my sister had a nasty experience with hypnosis several years earlier while trying to lose some weight. I was afraid that I, too, would have a bad experience with it and I sure wasn't up to that right then. Especially not that far from home!

Not a whole lot came out in this first session, but it was enough to give me a taste of what hypnosis was all about. When we were through for the day, I felt more comfortable about it and, after a long nap, was ready for more.

As it turned out, much was accomplished during this trip and the many that followed. Consciously, I recalled the night in April of 1978 when I had seen two gray, big-eyed creatures in my bedroom standing next to my bed. I had told my husband about them the next morning and he asked me what I had eaten before bed that night. He didn't remember a thing, even though he lay in bed right next to me during the whole experience. And I never once had the presence of mind to wake him. I believe it was then that we realized I had only consciously remembered the end of a much longer scenario. To this day, I don't consciously remember most of it. Under hypnosis, I had recalled feeling a sharp pain in my head, right behind my nose. I remembered tasting blood in my mouth and feeling as if something was going up one of my nostrils. I felt very cold and I had to use the bathroom. I also saw those eyes again—those huge, black, shimmering eyes that I could never forget. The beings in my room that night, in April 1978, had those eyes.

I also got a chance to meet my "buddy," Mary, face to face. The first thing I did was apologize for the late-night phone calls. I was glad to see her smiling at me when we shook hands!

She invited me over to her apartment for dinner one night and I had some kind of breakthrough in my memory while I was cutting up salad veggies. I suddenly began to remember all kinds of little things that had been locked in my subconscious for many, many years. I got more and more anxious as I related to her all the things that I was recalling. She, in turn, was also getting pretty anxious herself. She was glad that I was remembering things that I evidently needed to remember, yet, at the same time, I got the feeling that my spontaneous recall was flipping her out a little bit. Still, she hung in there with me and I'll never forget her for that. I can never thank her enough. I think it was that night with Mary that actually convinced me that my family and I were actually having truly strange encounters with someone paranormal. It was fascinating to see how everything was beginning to fall into place, beginning to make some kind of sense. I had come from a family that always seemed to have strange things happening to them and I had assumed that everyone lived like this. Boy, was I in for a big surprise!

When Budd deposited me on the bus home, he left me with the comment, "Once we start to look into your case, the 'visits' will stop." I knew this was meant to make me feel better, but, honestly, I actually felt worse leaving than I did coming. I now felt as if I were a very bad girl, that I had told something I shouldn't have to someone I shouldn't have and that I was going to be in big trouble when I got home. I felt that "they" were going to come back after me and they were going to be mad! I wasn't even supposed to remember this stuff, let alone tell anyone about it, especially someone who would stop it from happening again. Later, Budd and I were to find that what he said to me that day was far from what really happened.

4

KATHY
Introduction to the Bizarre

MY HEART POUNDED AS THE PHONE RANG. MY SUBCONSCIOUS knew this would be "the call." I scanned my memory, putting each detail in order, to make this call as efficient as possible. Long distance has a way of cutting me right to the chase, even if I am not paying the toll.

It was Budd. He introduced himself, and he seemed genuinely interested in our family and in our encounters. He spoke calmly and cheerfully as he asked for details about me and any other family stories I could recall.

Even though he was very pleasant, I am extremely skeptical about trusting people with my innermost thoughts. I have always been standoffish, always cheerful enough to have plenty of friends, but never inviting them inside my soul. If anyone starts invading my inner space, I begin to back off and put up my barriers.

As I talked to Budd, these barriers were already in place.

He asked me about my history, and I began remembering all the sleepless nights over the years. I was always a chronic sleepwalker and found myself waking up in numerous embarrassing situations. Sometimes, sitting by the living-room window in the dark, alone. Other times, just restless pacing, feeling a void in a life too full. Searching for answers to any unspoken questions.

Some nights I never woke—just paced in my sleep, leaving a trail of clues where I had been, to be found the next morning. Half-eaten food and my clothing in various parts of the house were telltale signs of a restless night. One night I awoke, startled from sleep, to find myself in a rocking chair in the living room in front of the window. In my hand was an ice-cream cone I had made in my sleep. Feeling rather foolish, even though there was no one awake to see me, I returned to my room. The window glass of the kitchen door reflected my naked body. What a startling sight! My nightgown lay on the bathroom floor. Sometime in the night I had disrobed, made myself a snack, and found a comfortable chair by the window—all in my sleep.

That incident made me fear for my sanity. I wondered what other things I might have done in my sleep and hadn't awakened to realize. At least I didn't go outside in the middle of the front yard. I hoped I hadn't, anyway. Can you picture a naked woman sitting in the middle of the front yard, eating an ice-cream cone? My neighbors would die laughing. I wonder if that would be covered under my homeowner's insurance?

My sleepwalking was disturbing not only to me, but also to Johnny, who was beginning to feel the results. Many times I would wake him up for work, have his lunch packed, coffee ready, only to discover that it was midnight or 1 A.M. Since he didn't leave till six, it was ridiculously early. After this happened three times in one week, he made it a practice to never get out of bed until he checked the clock himself.

I remember waking up one morning and finding myself turned around in the bed. My feet were on my pillow and my head at the foot. Blades of grass and bits of dirt were scattered about on the sheet. I remember thinking that was odd, but I merely brushed it off, logged it into my mental bank, and went about my routine.

As I continued talking with Budd, he asked about a particularly bad reaction I had experienced with hypnosis several years earlier. My mind began reeling again. I am the type of person who can look right into a person's eyes, carry on a conversation, and never remember a word you said, because my mind is racing a trillion miles per hour on a hundred different topics. I have mental lists ranging from kids, Johnny, work, home repairs, bills, and other assorted subjects. I keep these lists constantly changing. As one item becomes more pressing, it goes to the top of the list, etc. . . . .

I scanned my memory and began to tell him of my trip to the hypnotist.

I had gone to a group hypnosis session to lose weight. After years of sleepwalking and eating day and night, my pleasingly plump figure had ballooned. A friend of mine had gone to a group hypnosis session to lose weight with marvelous results. My friend lost one hundred pounds and I figured since I didn't need to lose quite that much—only ninety-five pounds—I should do well. I made an appointment two weeks in advance and began counting the days to a slim, new body. What could be simpler, just be programmed not to eat, and—no pain, no strain—instant results. The day of my appointment arrived in a downpour that lasted for hours. The city drain could not handle the rush of water in such a short time, and the road in front of my house became flooded. Cars were stalling, and it looked totally impossible to get through. That was disappointing, but I was determined nothing would stop me from my session, so I ventured out, water seeping into my car through closed doors, and made my way to higher ground. With the determination of a postal carrier in a blizzard, I finally made it across town, to a new lease on life.

Thirty other people also arrived, money in hand, all wishing to achieve self-improvement of one kind or another. Each person had a personal interview with the doctor before the session actually began so he could determine the person's hangups or the bad habits he or she wanted to change. The majority of the group were there for weight loss. The rest wanted to quit smoking. One man smoked four packs of cigarettes a day. One woman had only five pounds to lose. I wanted to strangle her. I could lose five pounds in my eyelids and no one would notice.

After everyone had received their pep talk, we gathered in a circle, dimmed the lights, pulled the shades, and proceeded.

With bowed heads and closed eyes, we were told to relax and breathe deeply three times. The doctor had a deep voice, with a heavy German accent that was not only persuasive, but somewhat calming. The first instruction was to concentrate on our feet. We were told they were very heavy and it was impossible to move them. At that precise moment, each foot felt as if it weighed a hundred pounds. He directed our attention to move along, up our legs, feeling the same heaviness and immobility, until the entire body was totally relaxed and in his control. This process took approximately thirty minutes and I was beginning to feel restless. Somehow I had envisioned not being awake through this procedure. I thought I was simply going to go to sleep, and wake up with a whole new outlook. Since I was aware of everything going on around me, my greatest fear was being realized. This must not be working. How awful! All that waiting, getting my hopes built up, only to be torn down by a cut-rate quack. An even worse fear was that I had thrown away thirty dollars. Now my disappointment was quickly turning to anger. What a waste! I felt like a fool. My immediate impulse was to jump up and run out of the room. I was pretty sure I could move my legs and body, but I didn't try. I thought to myself that he didn't have any control over me, he just thought he did—and I could simply get up and go any time I wanted to. But I didn't. I didn't move a muscle. Maybe I won't try moving, I thought. After all, I had never been hypnotized before, if he told me I can't move I guess I should sit still. I didn't want to break myself or anything.

The room was dark and cool, and I could feel the air on my bare arms. I was aware of the circle of people around me. Were they all under the spell of this German miracle worker, this mind programmer, this man who had my thirty bucks? Was I the only person not under his control? I couldn't be sure, but I figured I would humor him and act the part. I really could move   if I wanted to.

As the doctor made his way around the circle of limp bodies, he talked individually to each person. He had made notes earlier about each person's personal hangups, and he specifically mentioned them as he passed before the group.

Why am I sitting here? I don't want to hear about other people's problems. This is all beginning to irritate me. He's going to mess around and make me mad and I'll move my foot. I'll show him he's not so smart. I'll lift my arms and expose him as a fraud. No, I couldn't do that, that wasn't my style. . . . I was chicken. So I endured the session right to the gruesome end, but with each suggestion the doctor made, I began to mock him in my head.

"You're not hungry now and won't be when you wake," suggested the doctor.

You jerk, I thought. I'm starving. I was, too. I had been in such a rush to get there, I didn't have time for dinner.

"You'll feel very attractive and feel good about yourself," the doctor added.

Are you blind, fool? I mocked in my head. I'm two hundred pounds of quivering wrinkles. My stretch marks have stretch marks.

"You will have boundless energy," continued the doctor.

Cripes, I'm beat! This running around to get here has me worn out, I thought silently.

"You will feel better, physically, than you ever have in your life," claimed a determined doctor.

Holy cow, if I have to keep my head down one more minute, I'll scream, I whined to myself. I was getting very tense. I could hardly contain myself any longer. I was aware of the people around me and I felt that I was probably the only person unfulfilled. I'm getting a headache. That stupid doctor gives me a headache, this whole place gives me a headache.

Finally, after a few more grueling minutes, the session was over. The overhead lights came on, blinding everyone. The group sat there squinting like moles coming out of their holes. Twenty-nine of the participants were euphoric, flitting around like kids in a candy store.

"I feel great," exclaimed the lady who wanted to move to Hershey, Pennsylvania.

"Wasn't that wonderful," exclaimed the chain smoker. One lone survivor of the group sat alone, wanting to cry, something she never does. Hungry, tired, ugly, she sat alone, her head pounding. That lost soul was me. What a bummer, I thought. Life stinks. I'm going home and eat everything in the house. I did that very thing.

The next few days were very hard for me. I found myself falling prey to depression. I ate all day long, anything and everything. My body was heavy with a fatigue I was unable to escape, no matter how much sleep I got at night. My speech became slurred, gradually at first and so severely by the fourth day it was almost comical. From the moment I lifted my head following the group session, I had a headache. That headache was to plague me almost daily for several years.

By the third day following the session, I was near panic.

It didn't take a genius to tie all the symptoms together with my visit to the hypnotist. On the fourth day, I decided to call the doctor and talk to him about my newly acquired problems.

The hypnotist wasn't a quack, as I had privately accused him of being. I had checked into the program carefully before I ever made the appointment. He was then and still is now a very well regarded physician who had decided to start this program to benefit weak-willed people who obviously cannot help themselves. He seemed to be genuinely interested in the people involved in the sessions, but the program was new, just a couple of months old, and I was in the sixth session. Obviously all the bugs weren't worked out.

When the doctor answered, I felt a mixture of calmness and fear come over me. He was very kind and expressed sympathy for my plight, but since the program was so new, he thought it was best to leave well enough alone. Fearing he might cause more damage to an already wounded subconscious, he convinced me the symptoms would subside in time. That was easy for him to say. He wasn't the one talking in circles, with a mouthful of food. He wasn't the one sitting around all day, thinking life was a cesspool. Nevertheless, he had to know more than I did, so I hung up the phone, truly believing I could conquer this minor handicap. I was wrong. Twenty-four hours later, I was rushed to the emergency room with symptoms of a stroke, split vision, severe head pain, disorientation, and severe vertigo. After numerous tests at the hospital, the doctor sent me home with a diagnosis of a migraine headache, a shot, prescriptions for pain medication and antidepressants. Now I really felt like I had turned into a mental cripple. All I ever wanted to do was lose some weight.

Taking my various medications for only two weeks, I decided I was tougher than that. I may have been fat, but I was certainly no weakling. I finally pulled myself together, trashed the pills, put mind over body, and was back to my old self in no time. I had several more migraine headaches but with practice I was able to apply the techniques of self-hypnosis to find relief. It's ironic that the cause of my problems also turned out to be the cure.

I was finally together again, with mind and body, and a few years later I went on a diet, without the aid of any outside crutches, and lost fifty pounds.

The reason for my unusual symptoms following the hypnosis session seemed quite clear to me. I thought I caused them myself. As the doctor spoke, I twisted everything around in my head, not realizing then that I was programming myself subconsciously to the opposite of everything he commanded, thus nearly rendering myself out of control.

However, people who have spent many years studying UFO cases, with possible abductions, will argue that somewhere in my past, I have been rendered helpless by some type of mind control, and have been forced to do things that possibly have severely frightened or hurt me. As a result, if someone tried to control my mind, or to force me to remember something that I wasn't supposed to remember, my subconscious would immediately rebel. I'm not sure just which opinion I will go with—my fault or my defense.

As Budd and I continued our conversation, he asked about my sighting in 1965. He listened quietly as I recalled my encounter, word for word, as I had done for nearly twenty years. My conscious memories of that night are as follows:

On a crisp fall evening, at approximately 4:30 P.M., I was driving my mother to a local bingo game. I hadn't had my driver's license very long, and I just loved chauffeuring people around. There is something about being behind the wheel of a car that makes a kid feel like an adult. It's a feeling of power, when you can maneuver a piece of machinery at your will, to be in total control, or at least to think you are.

Returning from my completed mission, feeling good about myself, I made my way down the two-lane road back home. I was stopped at almost every light, but I was not on any time schedule, unlike the adults who became impatient at the lights, or who raced to cross the intersection on the yellow light. How foolish they seemed to me. Why are all adults always in such a hurry? Kids never worry about time because they don't think they will ever run out of it.

It was early fall and there was plenty of daylight left, but there was no rush to get home. I was babysitting my brother and two sisters tonight, so I had made no social plans. It wasn't too bad watching the little ones. They went to bed early, then the rest of the night was mine until eleven, when I had to return to pick up my mother. I was thinking how uncomplicated my life was, and it was a nice feeling.

Nearing my home, I passed all the familiar houses and buildings that made me feel comfortable with my life.

Suddenly my car had come to a stop, but I was no longer on the road. I was behind a church, off the main road. I think I remember turning into the church parking lot, but why? What an odd thing for me to do. I had no intention of turning there. I needed to get home. The church was empty and there were no cars in the lot. I was leaning over the steering wheel, looking up through the windshield. Almost directly over my car, at approximately the height of two telephone poles, hovered an oblong craft resembling two dinner plates on top of each other. This was what I had been waiting for all my life. Where was this craft as I watched through my telescope night after night as a child? Why did it appear then, so unexpectedly catching me off guard, so totally unprepared? So alone. No one would believe this.

It was a magnificent sight to behold. The surface appeared smooth, like some kind of stainless steel. I quickly estimated its length to be approximately seventy feet. This was definitely no water tower light, definitely no airplane, definitely like nothing I had ever seen before. It was very beautiful, in an unearthly, appealing sort of way, contrasted against the blackness of the sky. There were red, white, and amber lights flashing on its underside. Nothing obstructed my view. It was there and it was real, but what was it? I felt a warmth, like summer sun, coming through the windshield on my arms, which were leaned over the steering wheel. I determined quickly in my mind, that I should take a picture of it. As a rule, I always carried a small camera in the glove compartment of the car, everywhere I went, but not this time. The camera was not there. Faintly, through the closed window, I could hear a humming sound coming from the motionless craft. I rolled down the window and could hear more clearly. The radio was playing and I reached over to turn it down, never taking my eyes off the ship. The instant I touched the volume control, I saw the craft very slowly start to move straight up. Then in a blink of an eye, it was gone, leaving an empty void in the autumn night.

It somehow doesn't seem fair that a person should wait for years hoping to witness such an event only to have but a fleeting moment. To be alone, with no one else to verify your facts, not even to get one picture as your positive proof —there is, somehow, no justice in that.

Leaning back in my seat, I just sat for a few minutes. Who would ever believe me? My car was sitting next to a row of houses, probably not thirty feet from me. Inside the first house, I saw a light on in the kitchen, but no one was looking out. The yards were empty, the lot was vacant, not one solitary person anywhere to verify what I had just witnessed.

I pulled my car out of the lot, back onto the main road. I don't remember whether the engine was running or if I had to restart it. I continued my interrupted journey back home.

It was several blocks before I saw headlights of another car, far too late for anyone inside to see what I had just seen. Too bad for them, I thought to myself.

As I finished my story, our call was drawing to a close. Budd suggested the possibility of hypnosis to help me remember any missing details of the night. He stated he would be calling back and would like to talk to Johnny. Fat chance! I thought to myself. That would probably be when donkeys fly.

As we hung up, I noticed the hair on my arms standing straight up between the goose bumps.

5

DEBBIE
The Journey Begins

AS THE BUS PULLED OUT OF THE STATION THAT NIGHT, I CRIED
like a baby. I felt about as dark and dreary as the rain I was
watching pour down the side of my dirty bus window. At
least in New York I had felt safe. (Imagine that!) I figured,
in that big city, with so many people around, "they" would
never find me and I'd be safe. Now, I was headed back to
"the boonies," where I'd be a sitting duck.

I found out that Budd wasn't a psychomaniac like I had
worried about before I left home, but I hadn't decided if I
believed all that I had remembered while I was there. It all
sounded too crazy to me, and yet, at the same time, it all
made sense. I was more confused now than before I left
home.

The first stop was somewhere in Pennsylvania. As the bus
pulled into the station, I thought to myself, I'll be damned if
I'm going to share my seat with one more smelly, toothless
Neanderthal! I pretended I was asleep and I flopped my big
old self over that seat. Let's see someone try to move this! I
was in no mood to be nice to anyone and I didn't want to
have to talk to anyone, either. I was all talked out.

Everyone who was to get off at this stop, got off, and

within minutes, I could hear—and feel—new passengers boarding. I lay as still as I could and even tried to muster a few fake snores for effect. Suddenly I felt very strange. This prickly sense of anticipation washed over me and I got the distinct feeling someone was boarding the bus that I needed to see. I peeked up over the back of the seat in front of me and what I saw nearly took my breath away. There stood the most beautiful man I have ever seen. And he was looking directly at me as he walked up the steps of the bus! It was as if he knew I was there before he even got on the bus.

He was about six-feet-four, medium build, yet slim. He had shoulder-length, wavy, medium blond hair, steel-blue eyes, and the most perfectly structured face I have ever seen. The way he smiled at me really knocked me out. I thought to myself, "Well, by God, if I have to share my seat with anyone on this bus, baby, I sure hope it's you!" Then I realized that I was staring at him, so I immediately ducked back down behind the seat. Once again, I felt like such a jerk.

Within a minute or so, I felt someone looking at me, you know what I mean? I looked up and there he stood, right over me, with that big, ornery grin of his! My heart just stopped. I immediately scooted myself over on the seat, hoping that he would sit beside me. But instead, some soldier back from overseas jumped in from nowhere and sat down next to me.

With a mouthful of food, half of which he spit all over me as he talked, he said hello and began to tell me all about his latest tour of duty. I looked at the stranger and thought to myself, Oh great! I was thoroughly disgusted now. Then I noticed that the stranger had sat down with my seat-mate's buddy. I could hear him talking to the buddy, and I couldn't believe what I was hearing. He said to the buddy, "I see that you are very tired after your long trip. There is an empty seat right over there. If you like, I will trade seats with your buddy and you can take that empty seat. That way, you and your buddy can get some sleep. I don't mind sitting with the young lady.''

Everyone agreed to the swap, and shortly I found myself sitting next to *him*! He promptly turned to me and said, ''Hi! I felt sorry for those guys. I knew they were tired. But I really wanted to sit with you. That's why I got them to trade seats.'' There went that smile, again! I couldn't take much more. With that, he asked me what I had been doing on my trip and where I had been. I didn't want to tell him about UFO stuff, so I just told him that I had been in New York visiting friends and doing a little snooping around. He promptly threw his head back and laughingly said, ''Oh, the extraterrestrials will love that!'' I dropped my jaw. (I'm sure that was attractive!) I looked over at him and said, ''Excuse me! I never said anything about extraterrestrials. Why did you say that?'' He just looked at me with that smile and said, ''Never mind.''

This was only the beginning. I was about to leave on the wildest trip of my life. And ''Lars'' would be the most unusual person I will ever meet.

Unfortunately, I have to use a pseudonym for the strange, wonderful man I met on my journey home. I can't find him to get his permission to use his name. Perhaps he will read this, and I can only hope that he will try to contact me through the publisher. I have a few questions for him and would very much like to talk to him again!

As the bus pulled out of the station, Lars began to ask me all kinds of questions. He wanted to know what I did back home, if I was married and if I had any children. I managed to get in a few questions myself, before I completely slipped under his ''spell.'' I found out that he was thirty-three years old, that he liked to ride motorcycles on ice, and that he worked for a friend who owned a motorcycle courier business in Cincinnati. He told me that he loved children and that he thought it really must be neat to have a little piece of you live on after you're gone, in a child. He said that he had been somewhere on the East Coast, visiting a friend whose child had been involved in an accident and had sustained some brain damage. He claimed he knew of a clinic there that had been doing research on the brain and had developed a way to make the brain regenerate new cells in people who had developed brain damage. He spoke so technically that I thought that he must have been some kind of doctor. I noticed that his voice was very soft and smooth and he seemed to be speaking with some kind of a sing-song accent. It was very slight. So slight, in fact, that I first thought that he was faking it for my benefit. I asked him where he was from and he told me that he was from Sweden. Actually, he said he was from ''near Sweden.'' That didn't make much sense. It didn't sound like a Swedish accent to me, but what did I know? I found out later that he was, indeed, from somewhere other than the U.S., because he read to me out of a paper that was written in some kind of foreign language. It was very sweet, the way he put his arm around me and laid the paper over our laps and read to me, having me repeat each word as he had spoken it in his language and then telling me what it meant in English. It reminded me of a father, reading the funny pages to his little girl. That's what I felt like, his little girl, his charge.

Throughout the entire trip, he was extremely protective of me. I don't think five minutes would go by before he would be asking me if I was okay or if I needed anything. In retrospect, I wonder how he knew I was in such need at that time? I don't believe what I was feeling inside showed that much on the outside. Especially to a stranger. I'm just too good at hiding my feelings for that to be true. How did he know I was at a turning point in my life and was probably more vulnerable than at any other time in my whole life? Did he realize that he was acting as my guardian angel or was it out of his control as well? Whatever the case may be, I will never forget his kindness, nor will I ever be able to thank him properly.

I noticed, after a while, that he never seemed to show any signs of a beard growth, despite the fact that we were together for more than seventeen hours. I also noticed that every time he touched me, however lightly, on the arm, or face, his touch was exceptionally warm and I could feel that warmth flow through my whole body, relaxing and calming me. I didn't realize at the time how unusual any of this was.

Sometime in the middle of the night, the bus made an unscheduled stop. It appeared that Lars and I were the only ones awake on the whole bus. Wherever it was, it was pitch-black night and we couldn't see anything outside the bus, except what little was lit by the running lights on its sides. I saw the driver get off the bus and start to walk into the darkness of the night. I wondered where he was going. If he had needed to use the restroom, there was one at the back of the bus, so why would he go outside to do that? Then I wondered if he was going to check on something on the bus itself. Why would he walk out into the night and not walk around the bus? It just didn't make sense to me. I told Lars this and he told me not to worry about it. I bet we sat there for at least five minutes.

After the bus driver returned, we continued for a little while more. Then we stopped at an odd-looking truckstop/restaurant. By this time, I was the only one awake on the bus. Even Lars had fallen asleep with his head on my shoulder. I had to crawl over him in order to get out of the bus. He was dead to the world. The bus driver followed me into the truckstop.

I was hungry, so I went to where they were serving food. I noticed that the only people in the whole bus station were me, the driver, who had gotten himself a cup of coffee, and an old man and two girls. The old man and the two girls were working in the stop. And everyone was staring at me! I noticed they all had the same large, dark eyes that the bus driver had and their staring gave me the creeps. I shook it off as just being tired and worn out, both physically and mentally.

I purchased a sandwich and some orange juice. I thought if I ate something, I'd feel better and things wouldn't creep me out so much. When I sat down to eat, I noticed that they were staring at me even more intently than ever. Boy, this was going to be a hard one to shake!

As I ate, I realized that the sandwich tasted just like the orange juice and they both tasted like cardboard. But I was hungry, so I ate it. I looked up from time to time to see the bus driver and the old man and the two girls leaning against the wall, looking at me, still! They all had a funny kind of half-grin on their faces. Oh, well, so they're weird. After all, what kind of life could someone have if they're working in a truckstop at two in the morning? (Nothing personal, mind you.)

I finished up and then realized that I needed to go to the bathroom. I found my way back to the bathroom and thought it kind of strange that it was a "one-holer," since this was supposed to be a busstop/truckstop restaurant. I also thought to myself how unusual this building looked for a truckstop. It was kind of neat, all round and full of panoramic windows.

When I went to wash my hands, I looked into the mirror. For a brief moment, I thought I could see, not my own reflection, as I had expected to see, but the image of a tiny blond girl whom I didn't recognize. She was wearing a cobalt blue, turtleneck top. Whoa! What was in that crappy food, anyway? I rubbed my eyes and looked again. Thank God that time I saw the ugly mug I always see when I look in the mirror. It was time to get back on the bus, *now*!

As I passed by the old man, the girls, and the bus driver,

they all nodded at me. Adios, weird people! Get a life! I thought to myself. One lone passenger had stumbled off the bus while I was in the restroom. He passed me as I made my way back to the bus. He looked at me as if I were nuts, and he was semi-comatose. He rubbed his eyes and shook his head, then turned around and boarded the bus right behind me.

Off we went again. By this time Lars had awakened and was wondering where I had been. He had a funny grin on his face and he asked me where I had been and if I had enjoyed my snack. We continued our conversation.

Out of the blue, he blurted out that he wished he could dance with me right then. That was a strange thing to say, and yet it meant something to me. At home, whenever I felt stressed out or just wanted to "let go," I would turn my stereo up real loud and dance my heart out. Music means a lot to me and when I dance, I "become" the music. It moves through me and moves me. It's not a pretty sight but I really enjoy doing this. That's why I do it when I'm alone in the house. Often I would get this unnerving feeling that someone was watching me but they didn't mind how I looked, they just wanted to dance with me, and did. That they enjoyed my spirit's freedom when I did this. It may sound silly, but now, I found myself thinking, You must be the one who dances with me. I was definitely not myself on this bus trip! As I thought of this, Lars just looked at me and smiled.

At one point, he reached over to me, took my face in his hands and pulled my hair back over my ears. He said that this was the way women wore their hair where he came from and that I would look beautiful with my hair like this. Then, he asked me if he could kiss me. I said, "Okay." This was not like me, at all. I don't just kiss anybody, especially some stranger on a bus, for crying out loud! The kiss was the softest, most gentle kiss I have ever had and when he finished, he looked at me as if he had never kissed anyone in his whole life, and he acted like he loved it. Believe me, I don't kiss any different from anyone else and I'm sure I'm not that good! From the way he reacted you'd have thought I was Venus, the goddess of love, or something!

From that point on, I think I was in some kind of trance or something, because I just don't kiss strangers. Hell, I don't even look at them, most of the time.

On the trip to New York, I didn't sleep at all and I sat there with my purse wrapped halfway around my head to guard against strangers. The way I was behaving now was not at all like me, in any way.

We finally reached Columbus, Ohio, around dawn. Lars was to get off the bus and catch another one to Cincinnati after about an hour. I had a one-hour layover before my bus would leave for Indianapolis. We decided to go to the Burger King in the station and get something to eat for breakfast. When we started to order, Lars turned to me and asked me what the difference was between bacon and sausage. Then he asked me what he should eat. I told him what the difference was between those two foods and told him that they were both good by me. He proceeded to order just about one of everything on the menu. When he saw how small the orange-juice containers were he complained, loudly, and then ordered four of them. The girls waiting on us looked at him as if he were some green-haired alien. I was kind of embarrassed by how weird he acted but one smile from him and I forgot all about that. I got my food and we sat down. As I sat there looking at him, I was thinking to myself, I don't want to leave this guy! I don't know if I can live without him. Hell, I'll never see him again, he doesn't even know my address or phone number. Just as I thought this to myself, he looked up at me with a startled expression on his face. Then it immediately turned back to his fabulous smile and he blurted out, through a mouthful of food, "Don't worry, we'll see each other again. Give me your address and phone number." Then he said to me that there was a place near my home he wanted to take me to someday. It was a long, silver trailer and he would take me there to eat and dance. He couldn't promise when he could come back. It could be months or years, but he'd be back to see me someday, promise. I believed him then and still do. I wouldn't be surprised if someday I get a knock on my front door, and it's him.

I said to him, "But, what if I move or something?" And he said, "Don't worry, I'll find you."

After we ate, we still had plenty of time before our buses were to leave so we decided to walk around the bus station. We passed a group of people sitting on the benches, who were dressed like old-fashioned Amish people. They absolutely stared a hole through us as we walked by. I'd bet we were a sight, him so tall, and me so short, but the look we got from them was even stranger than just them noticing our different heights. They actually looked totally dumbfounded. I was talking to Lars when I noticed them. It was almost as if I were talking to myself and they thought I was some kind of nut. I never did figure that one out.

I decided that I should use the bathroom before I left, so I told him that I was going to the restroom. He said, "Okay," and as I walked through the restroom door, he began to follow me in! I quickly pointed out to him that he shouldn't go in there, showing him the little international symbol for woman on the door. I explained to him that the person with the skirt was female and then I pointed out the little man on the other door. I told him he should use the one with the little man on it, as he was a man. As I washed my hands, I shook my head and thought out loud, "Jeez, I thought international symbols were supposed to be just that. Recognizable to any nationality." Whatever.

When I pushed open the outer door of the restroom, I almost knocked him down! He had stood at that restroom door the whole time I was in there, making sure I was going to be okay, or perhaps to make sure that I would come back out again! No wonder no one came in while I was in there. He probably scared everybody off! As we continued our walk, he began to complain, "I have a funny feeling, right here." He was pointing to his stomach. I said to him that his stomach was probably upset from all the crap that he had eaten in the Burger King. I asked him if he felt nauseated. He asked me what that meant. I said, "You know, like you're going to puke, throw up?" He still didn't get it. Then I said, "That means that all the stuff that you have put into your stomach, through your mouth, begins to come back up the tube and back out your mouth." (What a moron! I thought. Don't they barf in Sweden?) He said, "Yes, that must be what I'm feeling." I told him that I had some Pepto Bismol tablets in my purse and that he was welcome to a few, if he needed them. Of course, he didn't know what they were and became very interested in them. I had to explain to him how they coated the stomach, in order to relieve the uncomfortable feeling he was experiencing. I handed him a couple of tablets. He insisted on seeing the box and then proceeded to read each ingredient out loud, with great fascination in his eyes and voice. I was amazed. Then, instead of chewing up a couple, he popped them in his pocket. When I told him that they were not going to do him any good in his pocket, he got a confused look on his face. Then he said something about taking them later. There was a hint of embarrassment in his voice.

As we reached the end of the station, I noticed a row of newspaper boxes by the exit doors. He ran toward them and commented several times about how colorful our newspapers were. Then he asked me to buy him one. I did, and he seemed to take great delight in looking through it.

All too quickly, it was time for me to get on my bus. When I heard the announcement that my bus would be boarding, my heart sank. I felt like breaking out in tears. Lars walked me to the door and as I turned to board, he said to me, "When you get on the bus, look at the paper you bought for me and put your radio headphones on and listen to the music. You'll be okay now, and remember, I'll never forget you and I'll see you again someday. This, I promise you from my heart."

I did just what he had told me to do and I also cried my heart out as I did it. I couldn't believe that he was gone. I felt like I was going to die without him! What had he done to me? Why did I feel this way? If he had asked me to follow him to Cincinnati, I would have. Forget about my kids and my boyfriend. He was *it*. Boy, I really wasn't myself at all!

When I turned on my radio, a song started, as if it were meant just for me. The name of the song was "This Much Is True" by Spandau Ballet. I opened up the paper he had given me to a two-page ad about missing children. I looked at all those little precious faces covering my lap. Then I remembered my own two kids. I couldn't wait to get home. Those pictures were like a slap in the face, back to reality.

When I arrived, my boyfriend and my kids were there waiting for me at the station. It was so good to see them again! I almost ate them up. But in the back of my mind, I was thinking about Lars. Later, after we got home, I told James about Lars. I told him everything. I didn't realize at the time how it hurt his feelings to see his girlfriend so worked up over some strange guy. He also pointed out to me how strange this guy was. I hadn't realized how odd Lars really was acting. But it didn't change how I felt about him. James persuaded me to call Budd and tell him about my bus trip home.

I called Budd and he was absolutely fascinated by my tale

of the trip. He was even more interested in how I had reacted to it and how I was still reacting. I burst into tears
every time I thought of Lars and I think I cried through our
entire conversation. My heart ached for him, longed to be
with him again. Just to be near him, to hear his soft, sing-
song voice again, would have been enough. I felt like I was
really going crazy.

I used a little self-hypnosis to help me remember where
Lars had told me he worked in Cincinnati and it worked, I
remembered! Budd took this bit of information and actually
found Lars. He was a real person, not some alien or angel.
Thank God!

Budd had a lengthy conversation with Lars's childhood
friend and found out that all he had told me was true. He
also found out a few more interesting little bits of information on Lars. Apparently Lars was a rather eccentric man,
who was very interested in anything that had to do with the
occult or paranormal phenomena, including UFOs. We also
found out that he had been captivated by me and had talked
about me constantly since he had returned home. His friend
told Budd that Lars had a habit of taking off, sometimes for
long periods of time, like years, and no one would know
where he was or if he was even alive. Eventually he would
return, as if he had never been gone, with no mention of
where he had been all that time.

Budd gave me his friend's phone number and as my heart
pounded, I dialed it. I asked for Lars and in a few moments,
I could hear that smooth, sweet voice again. We had a nice
talk and I told him I missed him. He reassured me that we
would definitely meet again someday and that he had
thought about me often since our trip also. I got his address
and told him that I wanted to send him something, a small
token of my appreciation for his company during my trip
home. I sent him a bronzed coin with two hands clasped in
friendship on it and a little thank-you note. He called me

once more, to tell me that he had received the gift, that he loved it, and would keep it with him always. And every time he looked at it, he would think of me. That was the last time I ever spoke to Lars.

6

KATHY
Mind Games

As Debbie sat in the bus terminal in New York, I sat at home, wondering if I had made the right decision to exclude myself and my family from Budd's investigation. Was I choosing to stay in the shadows because it was easier or because it was more secure to keep the lid on this Pandora's box?

Many of the family had talked with Budd over the phone, and he had invited Debbie and me to visit him in New York to meet him and his family. He talked of a doctor he wanted us to meet, who would try hypnosis to uncover the details our conscious minds couldn't or wouldn't remember.

Just the word *hypnosis* made my teeth sweat. The pain of the migraine headaches was still all too clear.

Johnny was totally against it, as he also remembered my headaches.

My four kids had already begun laughing at the whole situation.

The Yankees and the Confederates were tugging a little harder now, as I struggled for answers to all the questions my conscious mind was asking.

The Confederates were victorious, and I decided against

going with Debbie to New York. Financially I wasn't that stable. At that time, I felt I couldn't take a week off from work. I also thought that my house would be in shambles when I returned if I left my family for a whole week. You have to realize that, after all, Budd was a total stranger to us, from a city that seemed very scary to a country bumpkin like myself.

We were living in a very small town where everyone knows everyone else's business. I could just see my kids taking an alien drawing to school for show-and-tell. Their assignments would be titled "The Summer My Mother Went Crazy." They all laughed among themselves, but outside our home, it wouldn't be a laughing matter.

Then there was Johnny, laughing the loudest. His friends were a bunch of regular guys who certainly could not understand any of this. Their wives were my friends, and it was so odd that all the women truly believed in UFOs and aliens, and one of my best friends even had a story of her own.

We all spent a lot of time together on weekends, and if the subject of UFOs came up at all, the men would just roar, Johnny included. It would really be hard for him to admit that he might possibly be a believer and keep his friends from tormenting the daylights out of him.

Yet a few more bricks in my barricade, raising it even higher.

Budd came from New York to meet us shortly after Debbie returned. I found him very personable, and he certainly had a lot of interesting stories about other people who had experienced UFO encounters.

Out of curiosity, I agreed to a session of light hypnosis. I was very nervous and my stomach wouldn't stop rumbling. As I felt myself begin to relax, I did wonder, however, why a person should have to go to such lengths to remember a part of her life. Why are most UFO abductions blocked out of the subject's memory? Is it a method of self-preservation that a person unconsciously refuses to remember such trauma, or are the memories blocked at the will of a stronger force? A force that commands you not to remember. A force that demands that you do whatever they wish. A force that continues to dominate, even years later, decades later, or maybe forever.

I was more relaxed now, thinking of ocean waves, gentle motion. Breathing in and out, slowly, methodically. Each breath seemed to strip the years, one at a time, from my life. I went back to a time when my life was carefree. Back to the days of a youth that seemed endless. Back to the days of being a self-assured teenager.

In my mind, I could see myself approaching the spot of my encounter. I was behind the wheel of my grandfather's car, which he had left to our family upon his death. I knew the car was turning into the vacant parking lot, but I could not determine whether I turned voluntarily or involuntarily. My next recollection is of looking up and seeing the UFO hovering over my car. I'm moving too fast; my mind tells me the same programmed version of the story that I have related for twenty years. I am asked to back up, to think clearly, to question my movements that night. I am told that I am safe, no harm will come to me. I am only remembering what has already happened. Memories can't hurt me.

I am quiet for several moments. I don't want to remember.

What am I doing here? How could I have let myself be cornered into remembering something I don't want to?

Pictures flash through my mind. My thoughts are racing back to that night.

Is it too late to get up and run out of the room? I continue my silence, like a forgotten vow or forgotten order.

Memory flashes quicken my breath. I can tell already this is not going to be any fun.

After several minutes, pictures of forgotten secrets unfold in a painful melodrama. I now see myself still in my car, but I am aware that my car is no longer on the ground. I see myself, as a stranger from the past, looking out the side windows of my car down to the pavement below. On the vacant pavement is a bright circle of light, targeting the spot where my car had previously been. I am aware of the coolness of my skin as I continue my journey into the past.

My next thought is of still being inside my car, but my car is contained in a closed area, some type of room. I am unable to distinguish the vague surroundings. It appears dark, but I am not sure if it's really dark or my mind won't let me see clearly. There is light coming from a doorway that leads to another room. The misty light is bright, but it does not light up the room my car is in.

Looking back, that light reminds me of my window as a child, a doorway to another world, where I would wake up and find myself sitting alone.

Silhouetted in the light from the doorway, I can see the figures of three humanlike beings. I cannot make out any features of their faces. The figures stand as shadows, perhaps a subconscious attempt or order, to protect me from a more frightening vision. Perhaps I did see their faces twenty years ago, but now refuse to remember. They are small-framed, standing approximately four feet in height. Their arms appear long in proportion to their body, and their heads are large and rounded, narrowing slightly at what would be the chin. The center figure appears to be somewhat taller than the other two. Perhaps he was just closer to me.

I do not remember any of the three beings speaking to me, but I knew I would have to get out of my car. I also knew I would have to go into the lighted room. For what purpose I did not know or remember, but I knew I would have to go. I didn't want to. I was scared. I knew they were going to make me go, and I couldn't stop them. I wanted to wake up now. The session lasted quite a while with a lot of long, silent breaks, as I refused to tell what my mind was recalling. Why couldn't I tell? Why wouldn't I tell? Why am I telling now?

One phase of my encounter has puzzled me more than the obvious time loss and actual sighting. If there are extra-terrestrial beings who have the power to pull my car off the road at their will, take total control of my mind and body, why did they allow me an unobstructed view of their craft for a few fleeting moments, for a memory I would retain forever? Did they just take my car and myself, do what they wished and deposit me back on to the road, void of any memory of their being at all, so that I had no story to tell, no memories to uncover, nothing to keep continually searching for? Do they want their "victims" to partially remember, to quest for answers, to educate the population at their own mental expense? Are they calculating the response? Are they counting the numbers? Are they laughing at our primitive explanations? Are they sorry if we are troubled? Are we progressing as rapidly as they feel we should? Are they seeing us as they were, long ago?

I can feel that they mean us no harm. With their advanced technology, we would pose no challenge with our defense.

Why do they keep watching us, and we them? Why can't they make themselves known to all? What are they waiting for?

A few pieces of my puzzle had slipped into place. I had remembered, finally. Now I knew a few more parts of what actually happened that night, as an innocent sixteen-year-old, and what little I did remember was now more than I wanted to remember. Except for my sleepwalking episodes, my life had been relatively normal for twenty years. I had not consciously realized that my personal being had been violated by someone, or something, not of this planet. My mind had been raped by intruders.

It was one thing to watch them from a distance, hovering about, just letting you see enough to keep you interested, but to have them rough you up, and move you with their minds, is another story.

The puzzle was still incomplete. I knew I had to go into the lighted room, but what happened in there? What did they do to me? What did they tell me? Why won't they let me remember? Will I remember all, when the time is right? Have they revealed secrets of their existence to me or just studied me, as one would watch a caged animal? Was there a purpose for my capture or was I just a game—a pastime for them, a trauma for me?

Over the next few months, flashes of forgotten memories began, like lost puzzle pieces, to connect my encounter, ever so slowly.

I can remember one major part of my story now, one part that tells me I did not turn into the parking lot. I can remember frantically trying to turn the steering wheel of my out-of-control car, while I was still on the main road. I know now that I did not drive to the rear of the church. I had only assumed that, since that's where I ended up. I did not turn in and drive back there. My car was taken right off the deserted main road—to where, I don't yet know. I still see the circle of light on the pavement, and I know that is where I was coming from, when I was midair, in my car.

That could explain why I am deathly afraid of heights, I don't like to drive fast, and I don't like to drive at night, especially alone.

Many months later, I remembered another part of the night.

I am lying on a very smooth table in another all-white

room. I can't remember anything in the room except the table I am lying on. At the foot of the table stands a very tall, alien figure. I have the feeling this being is a female, although nothing would point toward either sex. The skin of this being seems to be dark, brownish, leathery in appearance, reminding me of a six-foot-tall, lifelike stick of beef jerky. The body is rigid in appearance, very tall and thin. The head is nothing like I have ever seen on this earth, large at the top, and angling toward a pointed chin. The head seemed to be connected to the body in a very simple manner, with no visible neck, and moved with quick, jerky insectlike movements, exactly like a praying mantis. If I could enlarge a praying mantis head, and put it on a body covered with beef jerky skin, that is exactly what this being would look like. It stood at the end of the table I was on, and it watched me with huge, liquid, black eyes, in a curious manner, something like the way a small child might stare at an object he is seeing for the first time. As it gazed at me, it would cock its head in a strange, inhuman manner, as if it were more curious about me than I was about it. I lay on the table, watching this being with the same curiosity with which it watched me.

That's all I care to remember about my encounter as a teenager. Perhaps someday I will take the plunge into my mind to find out more details, but it may take another twenty years for me to gather up the courage.

At this point in my life, I feel I must have more incentive than just knowing for myself. So far, I can live without knowing. It has taken a lot of years to come to a comfortable realization with myself. I have spent countless sleepless nights. I have paced miles, in my sleep, and have tried to run away from myself.

After twenty years, I can relate my experiences with a little humor. I can now tell the story of my car being lifted off the road and sit back and say with a smirk, "Don't pay the ransom, I've escaped." But if I have to remember all the frightening details, all the pain and anguish, it won't be funny anymore.

7

DEBBIE
The Poltergeist Connection

MY FAMILY HAS EXPERIENCED ALMOST CONTINUALLY FOR AS long as I can remember something that other people classify as poltergeist activity. Weird things have happened to us in all the places we've lived, but when we moved into the house that my parents still live in now, it really increased. I don't think that it's so much the house, because, no matter where any of us live—me in my current new house, my sister in hers—it seems to follow us. There is just something about my parents' house that is exceptionally conducive to the phenomena. Maybe that's why my father was almost obsessed with living in it. My mother hated it from the word go. (She likes it now.)

One of my earliest memories of weirdness in that house dates from 1980, when I had gone over there to do some laundry. Both of my children were very small—Rob about fifteen months and Tommy only a couple months old. Dad was working the first shift and Mom was also at work in the local department store.

I was alone in the house. I made a habit of locking myself in this house when I was there alone. If you could see the location of the house, you'd understand why. It was in the woods and appeared to be way out in the country, yet we were actually pretty close to a couple of local "dives" and a variety of other unsavory areas.

I had "camped out" in the basement rec room with the toddler in the playpen and the baby in the "punkin seat." As I sat there, watching my soap opera and folding towels, I heard the kitchen door upstairs open, followed by very heavy footsteps going across the kitchen floor. Then I heard several lighter sets of footsteps follow behind. I froze. A few minutes later, I heard the stereo in the upstairs living room turn on and off five times in a row. I freaked out! I kept thinking about my two babies and was afraid we were in danger from these intruders in Mom's house. I was thinking burglars, not aliens!

I just sat there, listening intently, waiting for it to stop. After a few more minutes, it got quiet.

Then the baby started to fuss and I knew he was hungry. "Oh great! Couldn't you wait till Grandma gets home?" I started to panic. Images from television programs of Jewish mothers trying to hide their children from the German Nazis to the point of suffocating them to death, ripped through my mind. That's how scared I got. Would it come to that?

It was feeding time. I couldn't just let him lie there in my arms and cry. It was either suffocate him or make an attempt to go upstairs to get a bottle. The rational choice was to feed the poor kid.

I crawled up the stairs on my hands and knees. As I reached the slightly open door, I peeked around the edge of it and saw nothing. Taking a chance, I made a mad dash for the refrigerator. As I swung open the door, all the lids on everything in the refrigerator tumbled to the floor at my feet, including the baby bottle cap. I grabbed it and the open bottle, slammed the door behind me and I bolted back down the stairs to the basement. The baby would just have to drink his milk cold this time.

As I sat there, trying to feed Tommy the cold bottle, I began to hear footsteps going up and down the upper stairs that lead to the bedrooms. I decided to call my mother at work. I wanted to tell her what was going on and ask her what I should do. When I did, she told me to call my older sister to see what she would do.

When I called Laura, she said that she thought that she had heard someone pick up the extension upstairs and listen to us talk. Telling me that was not helping my panicked state of mind. I was beginning to feel like I was in a really bad B movie and I couldn't get out! She told me to hang up immediately and call the police. So I did.

After I talked to the dispatcher, I bundled up the babies and made my way out the basement door. By the time I got to the front of the house, the police were there. I took them back in through the door I had come from because the rest of the house was still locked up. (I saw the chain lock was still on the kitchen door and it hadn't been opened although I had heard it open.) There must have been half a dozen cars and the people who got out of the cars had their rifles out and ready. They searched the grounds and the house thoroughly and even looked in the attic. When nothing was found, they asked when someone would be coming home. I told them that my father would be home by three thirty and that I thought I would be okay until then. They said they would come back before then and check on us and they did just that. Twice.

I was surprised and relieved when I saw the police drive by to check on me and the boys. After the police came, nothing else happened that day. But that night, as my mother retold the story to my sister over the phone, she noticed that the interior light of the oven was on. This was strange, as she had never used the light in the oven and no one would have had any reason to turn it on. It was confirmation for her that I was telling the truth, that something strange had indeed happened in the house earlier that day.

Many strange, ghostlike things happened in that house from then on. I would see things moving, out of the corner of my eyes. Often, if I would look fast enough, I could actually see a shadow move around a corner, leaving a sort of distortion in the air of its wake. Once, when my mother was in the basement, doing laundry, she noticed that one of the copper pipes that was lying across another had been twisted into a neat little pretzel knot. While down in the basement, necking with a boyfriend, my little sister and her friend witnessed a coat hanger that had been twisted around the door knobs of an old metal clothes cabinet, untwist itself, and then the doors burst open, as if someone had kicked it open from the inside out. This put a damper on the necking session, to say the least. She never could get that guy back in the basement again!

Objects had a way of disappearing, then reappearing several days later in the strangest places. We were beginning to think that all this was some sort of test, as if someone wanted to see how supposedly rational people might react to irrational situations.

I had begun to date James by this time. He had given me a very nice "promise" ring to confirm our relationship. It meant the world to me.

One morning I woke up to find the ring James had given me was gone. I tore my room apart, trying to find it. I was devastated. I looked for that ring for three days and cried myself to sleep at night. During the time I never told him that I had lost it.

On the third day, I was running the sweeper in the boys' room, when I was overcome by the feeling that I should look under Tommy's bed for that ring I'd lost. I stopped the sweeper and looked under the bed. No ring. I resumed sweeping, when again I was hit with the feeling that the ring was under the bed. I looked again. This time something was telling me that I was looking but not seeing. To look closer, I moved the bed out from the wall. Running my hands over the carpeting, I suddenly got the idea to pull it up. I ran downstairs to get proper tools for the task and when I had found what I needed, I began to rip the carpeting away from the baseboards. Then, up came the padding under the carpet.

By this time, my mother had heard all the racket I was making and was watching me. She was not too pleased with what she was seeing. Nevertheless, I didn't give up. I felt that ring was there, even if I couldn't see it.

After a few minutes, I had the whole carpet, pad and all, up from the wooden floor and pulled almost to the middle of the bedroom floor. (This was a big bedroom with two twin beds and plenty of room left.)

There, on the wooden floor, about three feet from the baseboard, directly where the middle of Tommy's bed would be, was my beloved ring.

My mother stood there in shock as I jumped for joy at finding my ring. It wasn't until later that night that I began to question how I could have ever known that ring was there. My mom was so flabbergasted at what I had done that she stopped complaining about what I had done to her carpet, and called my sister to tell her what I had just done. Of course, I did fix what I had torn up, but let me tell you, it's a lot harder to put carpeting back than it is to rip it up!

Once Mom and I and the kids were watching television in the living room. It was a clear night, about 8 P.M. All of a sudden, we heard a loud popping sound. At that very instant, I looked up and saw that Mom and both the boys had covered their faces. I saw an incredibly bright green ball of light, about the size of a ping-pong ball, in the middle of the living room, approximately three feet from my mother's head, and about three feet off the ground. It filled the whole room, the whole house, with an eerie green light. The light bulb in the lamp blew out and shattered and the television kicked off with a thump. I jumped off the chair and ran to the kitchen window to see if there was a possibility that it could have been some kind of ball lightning. But all I could see were stars. The boys were crying and Mom was mystified. It was several days before the boys would go upstairs by themselves and they wet their beds at night, too, for a few days. I was just stunned and had the willies for a few days. Later that night, Mom asked Daddy if a light bulb going out could cause such a thing to happen. After all, he was an electrician, he'd know something like that. He just looked at her like she was dense and said, ''Not hardly.'' One more thing to record in my journal.

Around the same time my mother and I had witnessed a huge, boomerang-shaped craft pass right over our house and appear to light up, just for us.

My parents were awakened by the sound of someone beating on their front door at about 3 A.M. It turned out to be the police. There were several of them. My mother let them in and they explained that they had received a phone call, that they had traced to our phone number, and that it sounded like a woman who was in a great deal of distress. He told my parents that this woman sounded like she was trying to ask for help and was wailing and crying so badly that they had trouble understanding her. Mom came up to my room and woke me. She asked me if I had called the police. I couldn't believe what she was telling me. I had been in bed, sound asleep, for all I knew, all night. As she told me what was going on, I could see she realized that and knew that I hadn't called them any more than she had. I threw on some clothes and went downstairs with her. The police were looking all over our house and at one point had taken my father out to his workshop to check the door and the phone out there, thinking that someone could have broken in and used that phone to call for help. While they were out there, some of the other policemen began intently questioning Mom and me. They said things like, "He's outside now. You will be safe if you tell us what's going on. He can't hear you now. You can tell us." My mother really got kind of angry at this insinuation and told the cop, "Look, there is really nothing going on here. We were all fast asleep when you came here, and my husband is *not* doing anything to any of us, like what you are insinuating. Your computer must be on the fritz." Well, with that, the policeman called back to his dispatcher and had him ring up the number their computer had locked onto. A few seconds later, the phone rang. He picked it up and said thanks to the guy on the other end and hung up. Then he came back to the table and leaned down. Speaking really low, he said, "The call came from that phone right over there. Are you ladies sure everything is okay here?"

After some heavy convincing on my mother's part, the cops from hell finally left and the three of us sat around the kitchen table with coffee and cigarettes, trying to figure out what the hell just happened here. I started thinking to myself, My God, did I call the police in my sleep and not remember doing it? Did something funny happen here tonight and I can't remember it? What an awful feeling it is to not trust yourself anymore. I guess we'll never know whether I made that call. Was this somehow connected to the phone calls I received when I was pregnant with my youngest son? I looked in the papers the next day, trying to see if they had found a woman lying dead by some phone booth, somewhere, but never heard anything more about that night. My parents speculated that either our "ghost" had made the call or the police computers were really screwed up.

We did have a funny police story shortly after this happened. We were all in bed, sound asleep, when we were suddenly awakened by what we thought were the screams of a frightened woman. Jeez, she sounded so close to our house she could have been on top of it. And she was. Our screaming woman turned out to be the neighbor's pet peacock, trapped on our roof. Boy, did we feel like a bunch of dummies after calling this one in! I bet the guys downtown still talk about our family.

Shortly before the kids and I moved out, we had a run-in with about five hundred bees who decided to visit my children's bedroom one day. My oldest boy screamed for my mother to come up and see his room. He was using that "there really is something wrong" tone of scream, so we both raced up to see what was going on. I just could not believe my eyes when I looked into that room. There must have been at least five hundred bees, scattered all about the room. They were hanging from the curtains, clinging to the walls, all over the floor and both twin beds. They seemed very lethargic, almost in a stupor. I had never seen so many bees in one place in my whole life. It was very creepy, like some kind of Alfred Hitchcock movie.

The first order of business was to get rid of the bees. We bombed the room with bug killer and after they were dead, we began vacuuming and sweeping them off things. Then my father began looking for how they had gotten into the room in the first place. We didn't want a repeat of this one! He never could find where they had come in. There was no attic door they could have used. The windows had been painted shut long ago. There was just no way for them to have gotten in that room. If it sounds like the Amityville Horror, that's sure what it looked like!

Even after I moved out of my parents' house and into my own apartment, weird stuff seemed to follow me and my boys.

We are hit on the forehead by drops of water from out of nowhere. I jokingly refer to this as our "baptisms." We have had many encounters with small white balls of light that appear in our house and whiz past us, only to disappear before our very eyes. Many people who have been to one of our houses have seen the little white lights. They are about the size of a marble and you can almost feel static electricity as they pass by.

The metal railings on the balconies of my building rattled so hard one night that my neighbors came screaming down to my apartment, thinking that we were having an earthquake.

My neighbor Brigitte did not know who I was or what kind of experiences I was having at that time in my life. One day she told me about seeing six very small men in her bedroom, as she lay trying to sleep. This had happened long before she knew me well or knew who I was. She said they had pointed hoods on and stood all around the foot of her bed, looking at her. I told her she should have told them, "Debbie's downstairs, you've got the wrong apartment!" She laughed then, but at the time, she was far from amused. Before she had heard all the stories I had to tell her, she had once made the comment to me that, "Nothing strange ever happened here until you moved in."

One night, after my boyfriend James (soon to be my second husband) moved in, he was awakened by the sound of glass breaking in the kitchen and what sounded like plastic two-liter bottles falling in the bathtub of our apartment. He got up to investigate the matter but found nothing. This kind of thing has continued right up until now.

The first time I ever spent the night at the home of my current husband, K.O., as I was in the bathroom, I looked up to see the toilet paper roll unwinding itself onto the floor. I reached up to stop it and when I let go, it started again. I stopped it twice more before I left the room, pinching the cardboard tube to prevent it from moving, and by the time it was done, it had unrolled nearly a whole roll of paper. I asked my husband if this happened all the time, because he had lived there all his life and his grandparents before him. He was shocked and couldn't believe what I was telling him. I thought it was rather cool until I realized I was going to be the one to have to roll it back up.

Once as I stood in my hallway, talking to James, I saw a fuzzy creature the size of a large rat scurry down the wall from the ceiling. I know that I wasn't the only one to see it because my cat jumped at it and began to dig at the floor where I had seen it *go through*. It went right through the floor and disappeared. I just shook my head. What was I supposed to do?

I have never felt threatened or frightened by any of this strange stuff. Just curious and sometimes amazed.

After having spent an evening in my neighbor's apartment and then going back to my own to go to bed, I got a phone call from her demanding I tell her what was wrong. As she was getting ready for bed, she claimed she heard my voice, coming through her bedroom window, calling her name, and I sounded like I was in need of assistance. I had no idea what she was talking about, but reassured her that I was okay. In the back of my mind I thought, Here we go again.

James was awakened one morning by a man standing at the foot of our bed, looking out the window and back at the bed. He was very tall, with stooped shoulders and long flailing arms. James's description of this guy reminded me very much of a man I had seen in the apartment before James had moved in, who had threatened to rape and murder me, but not before I got what I "deserved," whatever that meant. I will detail this experience in chapter 11. The man James had seen sounded just like him.

We have also been awakened in the middle of the night by the most putrid odors I have ever smelled, wafting through the house. The smells are so strong that they wake us all up out of deep sleep. We get up and try to find the source of the odors, only to have them dissipate as quickly as they appear. The only way I can describe the smell is to say it smells like something has died and is rotting. Imagine a combination of burning matches and rotten eggs. This is the kind of smell that you can actually taste!

Our appliances turn on and off by themselves, our answering machine recorded itself calling other peoples' phone numbers. It's rather unnerving to check your answering machine messages and hear a phone dialing, then ringing. No one has ever answered the calls, but I'm curious about who my machine could be calling. I worry that one day someone will answer and it will be in another country. I can't afford the phone bill and I don't think the phone company will believe me when I tell them my answering machine did it!

Once, when my husband was working second shift, I had taken the boys to my mom's for the evening. When we came home I was surprised to see the television on. I am very good about making sure everything is turned off when I leave the house. As I walked over to the TV to turn it off, I noticed there were thumbtacks spread all over the oval rug on the living-room floor. It looked as if someone had taken the time to turn each one point up and space them equally far apart. I removed the booby-trap tacks and then went, once again, to turn off the set. It was then that I noticed the VCR was also on and there was a tape shoved into it the wrong way. Obviously it wouldn't work like this and I hoped it hadn't screwed up my VCR. When I pulled the tape out, I was shocked to see it was a tape of the movie *Close Encounters of the Third Kind*! I got cold chills.

I don't know what all this poltergeist activity means, but I believe with all my heart that it is somehow connected to the UFO activity. It seemed to me that just before something UFO-ish happened, something paranormal would happen, and they both seemed to come in cycles.

It happens, even today. As I began to type the first chapter of this book, my computer took on a personality all its own. After I had completed typing the *t* in the word *light,* and was adding an exclamation point to the end of the word, my computer started beeping and began typing exclamation points all over the screen. After this had gone on for a good three minutes, it stopped, backed up, and erased every one of the extra characters it had created. When it reached the point where it had started doing this, it stopped, and I could then go on. I tried everything I knew to stop this while it was happening, even trying to turn the thing off. It would not turn off! So I just sat there, arms crossed, watching, until it finished its little fun time. I noticed that as soon as I said out loud, "Knock this shit off, will ya!" it did stop. That was kind of strange.

When K.O., my present husband, was copying some text from one diskette to another, the text (my book!) suddenly disappeared, and what appeared on the new diskette were programs having nothing to do with my book. We don't know how they were transferred to that diskette. K.O. was an electrical engineer for twenty-five years for GM and he used computers for all that time, writing programs for GM's electronic equipment and products. I know that he knew what he was doing when this happened and that a mistake on his part did not cause this to happen. I guessed it was my "friends," as my father calls them, having a little fun with K.O.

No one has ever been injured during these paranormal incidents and we have learned just to live with them. It sure makes life interesting at times, and I bet I would be disappointed if it stopped now. As K.O. says, life with me is sure never boring!

8

KATHY
Paranormal Influences

WHEN BUDD FIRST CAME INTO OUR LIVES HE WAS CERTAIN THAT as investigations of our family progressed the sightings and unusual phenomena would stop. That had been the case in other studies he had done, but it wasn't the case for us. As months turned into years our family continued to experience many unusual events.

We had already been accustomed to the bizarre for a decade prior to the 1983 backyard experience. My parents purchased their house in 1973 and from day one we knew that it was really strange. I am so open-minded I would scare you. I was a believer in the ''New Age'' long before it was fashionable, back when it was merely called ''weird,'' but even I considered this house too bizarre for me.

So many unexplained things were happening in that house that I began jotting them down just for my own use. As far back as 1973, Debbie, Mom, and I actually witnessed an ashtray splitting in half with no one within ten feet of it. Lights would turn themselves on in the presence of witnesses. Light bulbs have exploded, spraying glass onto walls fifteen feet away. In one instance, a bulb covered by a glass shade exploded and while the glass simply should have dropped to the floor, it appeared to project horizontally, completely across the room, bouncing off the opposite wall and barely missing my mother, who was walking past at the time.

Doors have been seen opening and closing totally on their own, with no one anywhere near them on either side.

Light switches equipped with dimmers have been witnessed turning all the way down, then all the way up to the full brightness, then down again. If the family would happen to be talking about any of the extraterrestrial events they have experienced or about any of the unusual occurrences in the house, the lights would flicker, dim, or brighten as if an unseen force wished to be included in the conversation. All these incidents could be attributed to faulty wiring, but that cause is doubtful because my father is an electrician and completely rewired the house at the time the family assumed occupancy.

Various family members have had their name called as if by several voices in perfect unison, but no one would be there or claim responsibility. I have had that happen to me only once, and it was in my own home. I was alone at the time. The first time I heard it, I thought I was simply hearing things and sloughed it off as a result of an overactive imagination, but when it happened again within a minute, and I heard it clearly, I began to get spooked. Hearing your name called in a chorus of voices sounds harmless enough, but it is very unnerving, especially if you are alone. A few hundred years ago, I would have been burned at the stake for claiming to hear voices, now I will just be laughed at.

Several family members and I have had drops of water land on us that seemed to come from nowhere. They usually land on the face or arms. They are smaller than an ordinary drop of water, but they are actually water, or at least a liquid of some kind that looks like water. We have never had any of the drops analyzed. It's a very strange feeling to be smacked by drops of water when above you is a flat, dry ceiling, and around you are flat dry walls.

In my home and in my family's home, different members have felt something or someone touching them from somewhere behind—touching their arm or the back of their neck. Upon turning around, there is no one there. That will make the hair stand up on your arms, for sure!

The middle upstairs bedroom in my parents' home seems to have the strongest eerie feelings. When our youngest sister occupied that room during her youth, she swore that on several occasions she heard music coming from nowhere. She claims to have heard voices, laughing people, singing and dancing as if they were having a big party in the living room. This happened several times and each time, upon investigation, there would be nothing disturbed downstairs and no one would be there.

There is always a chill in that particular room, which would not be too unusual in itself, but there is also always the feeling that you are never quite alone in there.

Poltergeist activity and unusual phenomena are not limited to that eerie bedroom, but have occurred in every other room in the house. On several occasions our youngest sister witnessed a ghostly female apparition standing at the top of the stairs, never walking, moving, or speaking, simply standing there appearing relatively harmless and semitransparent, dressed in a long flowing gown from the Colonial era.

On other occasions, she has seen male figures dressed in tight-fitting black outfits pass to the side of her and yet upon turning around, she will see no one there.

Footsteps can be heard in almost every room of the house, especially up and down the staircase. That can be a little rattling if you are alone.

Since I have never been comfortable in that house, I would never doubt any odd occurrence happening there. I have never quite been able to place why the house made my skin crawl, but my sixth sense never seems to be wrong. Just a feeling that you are never totally alone, and I make sure I am never by myself there.

My family would jokingly talk about their family spirits, poltergeists, ghosts, or psychokinetic energy, whatever the case may be. They seemed to feel no fear of these spirits. They felt the spirits would not harm anyone; they just wanted people to know they were there. Not me, though. I decided right from the beginning they didn't like me, and I had no intention of provoking them in any way.

One unnerving experience for Mom happened after they were sufficiently settled in their new surroundings. She had been doing laundry and went upstairs to lie down on her bed to rest for a few minutes, taking clean laundry up with her. She had an armful of clothes on hangers that needed to be hung in their respective closets, but decided to just hang them all on the doorknob to separate later. When she couldn't go to sleep, she decided to get up and finish her housework. She was taken quite by surprise upon seeing all the clothes were now off the hangers and strewn about the floor. She was alone in the house at the time.

Poltergeist spirits? Who knows, maybe she just needed to add more fabric softener.

Another strange event centered around the pool table in the basement. The washer and dryer were also located in the basement about fifteen feet from the pool table, and it is necessary to pass the pool table each trip to and from the laundry room. On one trip, Mom casually glanced toward the table and noticed the balls were placed in the triangular set-up rack. She continued toward the dryer to fold the dry clothes and reload the washer. On her return trip past the pool table, less than five minutes later, she noticed the pool balls scattered about the top of the table. She was alone in the house at the time doing laundry and certainly had not stopped to play pool. The pool table is made of slate and of such an extreme weight that simply walking past would not jar the floor to enable any movement of the balls. The floor is concrete anyway, so that would be out of the question. Maybe it was time she started sending her laundry out to be done.

Our father has also been involved in several uncanny events that he has been unable to explain logically. He was alone one evening at the kitchen table reading when, out of the corner of his eye, he thought he saw someone walking behind him. As he continued to read, he also began to have the eerie feeling that he was not alone, that someone or something else was in the room. After looking up and around several times, he dismissed the notion. Several minutes passed as he continued to read. He was reading a novel not at all about UFOs, extraterrestrials, or science fiction, so it would not be the case that he simply got wrapped up in a subject he happened to be reading about.

Several more minutes passed as he continued to read. Suddenly the whimsical music of singsong chimes began to fill the room. He looked up and found the source of the music coming from a decoration on the dining-room table. The decoration was a blown-glass vase filled with an arrangement of silk flowers. Inside the base was a wind-up music box. After winding the music box, the entire vase revolved as music played, making a nice little table decoration if you like continually winding stuff up. He had purchased the decoration as a Christmas present for Mom and the thing had sat untouched since she had received it two years before.

He has also heard footsteps from other parts of the house when he was alone and on a few occasions heard the sound of breaking glass, but never finds any prowlers or broken glass.

I was not exempt from the bizarre during some of my

visits. One evening, very appropriately the night before Halloween, I had gone to visit Mom, who was babysitting for my two nephews. We were sitting at the kitchen table in front of a large window next to the back door, drinking coffee and hashing over life in general. As both of us were usually busy with our respective families, it was nice to visit with each other alone, if you don't count two little boys who never leave you in peace.

As we sat there, we saw the metal railing on the back porch begin to sway back and forth with such force that it was making the glass in the back door vibrate. Thinking to myself that I should leave for home since there must be a severe storm heading our way, I looked at the trees, expecting to see them dancing around in tune with the railing, which had since stopped. To my amazement, there was no wind. Everything looked quite peaceful. Mom and I were slightly puzzled, but we assumed that an animal must have bumped the railing and caused the commotion. Returning to our coffee and more conversation, approximately fifteen to twenty minutes passed quite serenely. Rising to the occasion, there was a small bunch of Indian corn tied together with a ribbon hanging on the outside of the wooden front door, protected from the elements by a closed storm door. Without warning the corn began to swing back and forth, crackling and bumping against both doors, diverting us once again from our coffee. Now, we looked at each other and decided there must be a storm coming. Neither of us wanted to leave the comfort of our chair, so again I looked out the window behind me. A second time, I determined there was no wind, breeze, or gusts of any kind to be seen. Jokingly I blamed the disturbances on their spirit friends. Since I lived twenty-five miles away, and I thought there must be a storm brewing, even though my eyes had not been able to confirm that fact, I decided to have one last cup of coffee and be on my way.

Recapping our conversation, I again confirmed that their poltergeist boarders didn't like me, when suddenly my chair legs were bumped, diverting my attention now to the floor under my chair. Looking down, I was expecting to see my youngest nephew crawling under my chair. There was no one there. I informed Mom that the place must be getting to me and I was certainly glad that I wasn't planning to visit on Halloween night since there was no telling what might happen. At that point, the legs of my chair were struck with such force that the chair moved two or three inches across the carpeted floor. Now, being of sound mind and ample body, that was quite a force. Rising immediately from my chair, I informed my mother that I could take a hint and I was out of there. The front yard has several fifty-foot trees, and before I reached my car, I was almost expecting to be knocked down by a giant tree limb. If I hadn't believed in the spirit world before, I was more than a believer now. In my mind I had visions of two or three ghostly figures huddled together, laughing themselves silly watching me run for the hills.

You win, I thought to myself. Trick or treat—and the trick was definitely on me.

9

DEBBIE
Government Involvement?

I HAVE HEARD MANY OPINIONS ABOUT WHETHER THE government is involved in the UFO enigma, be it in the form of a coverup of some kind, or something even more frightening, like being cohorts with aliens. I really don't have an opinion at this time. All I can do is report to you, the reader, things that I remember and let you be the judge.

Shortly after we began communicating with Budd, in regard to the mark in the yard and all the other weird stuff that my family had experienced, strange things began to happen.

One Sunday afternoon, I got a call from Joyce Lloyd, our neighbor to the north. She and I had become sort of friendly. She had been a witness to the night of June 30, 1983. Budd had discovered this during his investigation. She and I had begun to talk regularly after that. We became very close and even though many hundreds of miles separate us today, we are still quite close.

When she called, she expressed concern about the fact that she had seen a strange man in our backyard the day before. She had described him to be about middle-aged, dressed in a business suit and tie, carrying a large briefcase and driving a dark-colored sedan. She said that when he reached the mark in our backyard, he set his case down, opened it, and did something to the yard in that area. She could not see all that he did as his back was to her part of the time.

When he was done, he quickly packed up his stuff and left. We had been away from home at the time the man appeared. Too bad. It was good for him, though—Dad would have drilled him. I'm sure it was planned that way.

My family liked to sit at the kitchen table and watch the wildlife in our backyard. Several times while my mother and I were sitting at the table, someone in an older-model car would pull up, jump out of the car, and proceed to take several pictures of the back of our house and the mark in the yard. The ones I personally saw didn't look like government people to me. As a matter of fact, they looked downright scroungy. You have to remember, though, at this point in the investigation, no one knew who we were or where we lived. The book hadn't been written yet and Budd had not made this case public. How did these guys even know where to go to see something?

My father and I have both witnessed, on several different occasions, large black vans pull up alongside the road in front of my parents' house, and we have both seen several men get out and climb the telephone poles in front of the house. They were not from the phone company. We are sure of that because we asked the phone company. We don't know what this means. My father approached them once and was told to mind his own business. Then they abruptly left the scene. Apparently they thought they had been obscured by the row of trees that borders Mom and Dad's property. They thought wrong. Nothing slips past the Old Man.

The day after I moved into my house, I began to have problems with my phone. I'd pick it up and the line would be dead. The next minute the phone would ring and when we would answer it, there would be no one on the other end. The next day, I received approximately thirty phone calls. Every one of those were what I called "dead" calls, no one on the other end.

We had to go to the convenience store across the street to call the phone company about our problems. That was fun, trotting across a four-lane highway every time we had to use the phone. As soon as I told the operator my name and address, she suggested that I talk to the security department and ask that my line have a trap put on it. I thought this was kind of strange. I had said nothing about being concerned that my line was "tapped," but she mentioned that possibility. I told her not to bother, I just wanted my phone service working and please send someone out soon. I thought to myself, "Jeez, the phone lady sounded more paranoid than me! That's weird!"

Later that day, some guy in a phone company truck pulled into my driveway. He sat there for about an hour and then got out of the truck, swaggered up to my door, and proceeded to tell me that he knew what was wrong with my phone lines. I thought to myself, How can you know anything? You've sat in your truck the whole time you've been here, you goober! He said that I had a "swinging short" in the line that connects my house to the main line on the street. "Okay," I said, "fix it."

That night at about 10 P.M. I picked up the phone, on a whim, hoping that I would finally hear a dial tone. It had been three days since we moved in, and I missed that phone! Instead of hearing a dial tone, I heard a man's voice say, "Hello, are you there?" I said, "Who the hell is this, and what's wrong with my phone?" The guy said he was the phone company and if I would hang up, my line would be fixed shortly. "Fine!" I said. Finally my phone would be fixed.

It was another two days before the phone would work. No

one could ever figure out who the man on my line was that one night. He sure didn't fix my phone, though.

Until the June 30, 1983, incident, not one of us had ever seen a black helicopter. After that moment, we were to see them nearly every day for almost five years. They would fly over our house, below a thousand feet, well below, three or four times a day. Whenever any of us was in our cars and going somewhere, here would come one, and it would follow us wherever we went. Whenever we got ready to leave where we had been, here they would come again, to follow us back home. Sometimes they would come in formation, five of them. And sometimes they would be so close to us that if the windows weren't tinted dark, we could tell you the pilot's hair color. One got so close to my sister's car one time that he almost ran her off a country road she was driving on. She said that if he had been any closer, she could have opened her car window, reached out, and grabbed the wheel of this thing. He was that close to her car.

These helicopters are jet black, not Army green. There are no markings on them anywhere. They've been close enough to us that if there had been any markings, we would have seen them. Often, they fly well below a thousand feet. Sometimes lower than five hundred.

One evening, a black helicopter flew circles around my house for over an hour. The pilot, whoever he was, made more than forty-five passes above my house. Each time he made his approach, he would turn on this high-speed strobe light and aim it toward my windows. As soon as he made the pass, he would shut it off until the next approach. He was so close to our house that the noise cracked my bedroom window. My neighbors were calling, asking me what was going on, because they thought that it was a police helicopter and they were concerned that something was wrong at our house.

My children were playing in the field next to our house with several neighbor kids when I had heard a black helicopter coming around, so I went outside to get them in. They met me halfway around the house, screaming at the top of their lungs! Then they all proceeded to tell me the same story, all at once, my two kids and three other neighboring children.

They told me a helicopter had flown so close to them that it had stirred up dirt in the field, (They were covered with it, so I believed that part, for sure.) Then they claimed that a door opened on it and a man leaned out with some kind of camera on his shoulder. They thought he was taking pictures of them. They said he picked up some kind of instrument and began to talk to them. He asked if they wanted to go for a ride. This is when they came screaming home. These kids were genuinely frightened and it took me several minutes to calm them down. My oldest boy and the oldest neighbor boy both said that the man was wearing a dark green jumpsuit of some kind and he had blond, really blond hair. Boy, was I mad! Messing with me is one thing, but messing with my kids is something else. But what could I do? Who could I call and complain to? I called Indianapolis International Airport and told them about it and asked who was doing it. They said to call Fort Harrison because they had never heard of black helicopters, and, as far as they were concerned, they didn't exist.

I turned the tables on them one time and began to follow one that was following me. I followed him to Fort Harrison, but I was afraid to get any closer, so when he began to land, I left.

One even landed on the front lawn of the high school where I had worked. I was coming back from taking my oldest to a doctor's appointment. As we were going down the street my school was on, Robby yelled at me, "*Mom, there's a helicopter like the one that talked to us that day!*"

I nearly skidded off the road. Sure enough, there it was, on the ground, surrounded by Army guys, who looked as if they were guarding it. Later that afternoon I heard on the TV news that something had gone down in the woods next to Fort Harrison and that there was a search on for it. People had reported hearing voices calling for help in the woods, but nothing could be seen. They showed Army men, in full combat gear, with guns, marching through the woods, searching for the object. Some people reported seeing a fireball coming down from the sky and when they were told that it was probably a helicopter, I heard them saying, "No way, I know what a helicopter looks like and this wasn't a helicopter." I wondered if they hadn't put the black helicopter down at the school as a cover, in order to claim that's what these people had seen. They never did report what they found, except to say that there was never any sign of wreckage and that they didn't know where the calls for help had come from. I heard someone say that it sounded as if you were standing right next to them, yet could see nothing. Weird, eh? This all happened within five miles of my house.

I don't know who's flying these helicopters or what they want, but I wish they would buzz off. They have frightened my children, my animals, and my neighbors. I don't know if they are government-sponsored or something else, but I wish they'd go away.

Something interesting happened to me on my way home from Canada, where I went to help promote *Intruders* when it was published.

I had been there taping a segment for the *Dini Petty Show,* Canada's answer to our Oprah Winfrey. I appeared on the show with Budd Hopkins to talk about my family's case. I was quite nervous about my television appearances. No matter what the subject matter, I would be a self-conscious, nervous wreck! Nevertheless, I felt obligated to

Budd and Random House and I felt safe knowing that I was not going to be seen in my own country.

The show went well and Ms. Petty was a very nice, understanding, and open-minded person. Still, I was ready to go home. That kind of stuff really wore me out.

Getting into Canada had not been a problem. The lady at Customs was very nice and when she asked me what business I had in Canada, I told her about being on the television show. She just smiled, rolled her eyes, and let me pass with no problems. Getting back into my own country was a very different story!

As I approached the Customs counter, I noticed that the man behind the window seemed to be staring at me. I told myself that it was just my imagination and that I was probably a little jumpy from the trip and from all the UFO talk on the television show.

Before I left for Canada, I inquired as to whether I would need a passport or a birth certificate to pass from country to country. I was told that it would not be necessary when traveling to Canada, so I didn't have either of these things when the man at the Customs window asked for them. I showed him my Social Security card and my Indiana driver's license, but he told me that these things were not considered identification for passing from Canada to the United States. I nearly had a cow! Here I was, in a foreign country, with less than fifty cents to my name, about to miss my plane home and this guy wants to give me a hard time! What was I ever going to do? Why me? Why did he seem to want to make an example out of me? Had he seen me on the television show and thought he'd have a good time with me? Was there some other reason why my own country didn't want me to come back? I got semiparanoid very quickly.

He pulled me aside from the rest of the people in line and began to ask me the most ridiculous questions I'd ever heard. It was just like the stuff I'd seen on TV when some-one is detained by Customs for something and they ask all these stupid questions like Who is the president of the United States? You think they don't really ask those kinds of things but they actually did. It was like some kind of nightmare, some kind of cruel joke! I was in total shock.

Finally, this jerk of a Customs agent said to me, "You claim to be from Indiana, this one should be easy. Who is the vice president of the United States?"

I said, "I don't care who won the World Series, I didn't watch the Super Bowl and don't care who won. I'm neither Democratic nor Republican and I don't vote, in protest of the shitty way they run the government. As a matter of fact, I think they should let us vote for the guy we want *least* to be president and the guy with the least votes wins. I'm about to miss my plane, I don't have any money left, and I'm just about to lose my cool here. Dan Quayle is the vice president of the United States and I think he looks just like Alfred E. Newman on the back of the *Mad* magazines. Will you please let me go now?"

My terrified ranting and raving must have caused him great delight because he backed up from me, began to laugh out loud, and proclaimed that if I knew who Alfred E. Newman was, surely I must be an American. Then he told me to move along. He released me just in time to make my flight home.

No one would believe me when I told them what hap-pened at the airport in Canada. But I'm here to tell you it did happen and it wasn't one bit funny. At the time, I didn't protest as loudly as I should have. I was frightened and ignorant of the rules, but believe me, if it ever happens again, everyone will know about it. It was the most humili-ating, unjustified thing that ever has happened to me and I was very disappointed that my own country would do such a thing to one of its taxpaying citizens.

* * *

Just last year, I was sitting in my living room, watching my soap opera on TV. It was a nice, quiet day, all the work was done, and the kids would be home from school soon. I was enjoying one last hour of peace and quiet. There was a knock on my screen door. I was surprised to see a very nice looking man standing at my door. I don't know why, but I invited him in. I noticed that he was driving a brand-new car, very nice. He sat down and told me that Budd had given him my address. My little red flag went up. Budd usually doesn't do this without telling me first. Oh well, I thought to myself, let's just see what he wants. He began to ask me about the feeling I had before I went to sleep, sometimes, before something happens. That paralyzed feeling. Only he stated it wrong. That happened to me right before I wake up, not before I go to sleep. I corrected him, and I got the feeling that he already knew that. Perhaps this was a test. That was all he wanted to know about. He thanked me for my time and for letting him into my home. He said if he had any more questions, he'd be back. Then he left. That was weird, I thought. Of all the things that have been written about me, you'd think he'd have more questions than that, having gone to all the trouble to find me.

I received a phone call from a man who claimed to be a journalist from Washington, D.C. He claimed that they—whoever "they" were—were interested in the phone calls I had received when I was pregnant with my second son. They thought they had found out where the calls were coming from—somewhere in outer space! He said something about going to a "protected area" there in Washington, D.C., for some kind of meeting. He also claimed to have gotten my phone number from Budd, but that Budd had given him the wrong one, yet he found me anyway.

My neighbor Brigitte called me and said that this man

had somehow gotten the phone number of an old neighbor of mine, Rhonda, and that he had grilled Rhonda for my phone number. Rhonda's phone number was listed, but Brigitte's was not listed with an address. Why did he call these two old neighbors of mine, in order to get my number, and how did he figure out they were my neighbors? What was so important that he had to get hold of me, anyway? I never did figure out what the hell he was trying to tell me and I never heard from him again. Good. Probably a nut, rather than a government man.

The last thing I want to mention here, in regard to possible government involvement, is a memory I have of something that happened one night in 1986. I can't say for a fact that this really happened. It may be some kind of screen memory. I have never been able to find the man I was with that night to ask him. He disappeared after he took me home the next day. It's an interesting story, though, so take it for what it's worth.

A man I'll call Dave was coming to pick me up and take me to his cabin in the woods, for a romantic weekend—just the two of us. I had been introduced to him a few months before, by my best girlfriend. She worked with him at a large factory in Indianapolis.

From the moment we met, he couldn't keep his hands off me. He was crazier about me than I was about him. But I was giving him the benefit of the doubt, as I thought that I just wasn't used to getting that much attention from a man and that this might be good for me if I could just get used to it. He seemed to like my kids a lot and he was financially secure, so I thought, What the hell, I'm not getting any younger or prettier or skinnier.

When he invited me for this romantic weekend, I had mixed feelings, but thought maybe that was just what I needed to get used to his attentions. I had been seeing him for several months and I certainly trusted him enough to know that I would be safe.

When we arrived at his cabin, I remembered getting out of his car and thinking that I saw someone dart behind a bush next to the drive. I remember saying to him, "Hey, Dave, I think someone is snooping around your cabin!" I looked over the top of his car at him getting out, and the look on his face changed to pure terror. The next thing I remembered was seeing something go over my face, turning everything black, and feeling a sting on my right arm.

I remember coming to and still not being able to see, but feeling as if I were moving and hearing the sound of an engine. Then I blacked out again. Next, I remembered coming to for a moment and feeling as if I were descending in an elevator. Then I blacked out again. In my next memory, I could now see in front of me. I was being stood up and forced to walk down a long white hall. I noticed that there was white tile everywhere and a chromelike bar running along the wall, halfway up. The windows we passed had little wires running crisscross through the glass. I was surrounded by six men—humans—in orange jump suits and orange ball caps. They were all about the same height and build, much taller than my five-feet-four. Ahead of us were two men in white coats. They were older men with deep voices and very thick southern accents. I was no longer in my clothes but had on some kind of hospital gown and paper booties on my feet. I didn't want to be there, yet, somehow, I could not resist them. I was in a daze.

They took me to a room with glass walls. In order to get into the room, one of the two men in white coats had to put a little card into a slot at the right side of the door and speak something. The doors swung open and outward to create a huge entrance.

They put me on a table and proceeded to take samples of me—blood and skin and mucus—from every opening of my body. They also gave me several shots of something. I just sat there and let them do everything. I couldn't fight. While I was sitting there letting them do this to me, I noticed that the room I was in was actually a smaller part of a much bigger room. This huge room was divided into smaller rooms with glass walls. Huge sliding doors connected the rooms together. I could see other tables just like the one I was on in these other rooms. Fortunately I didn't see anyone else like me in there.

The older man with a white coat on—I called him the doctor—got up real close to my face and said to me, in a deep southern drawl, "Honey, you've got a bug in your ear and I'm gonna take it out for you right now. It won't hurt and you'll feel a lot better after I finish." Then he stuck this long, shiny metal instrument in my ear. It did hurt. When he pulled it out, he showed me what he had gotten out of my ear.

When I first looked at the little ball, it looked like a mosquito, all crusty, with its legs and wings out. Then, as he told me to look at that bug, it began to look like a BB, all bloody and crusty. The legs and wings went away. Then he said something else to me that I can't remember. With that, he looked at me, smiling, and said, "Well, I don't know why I'm even bothering to tell you this. You're not going to remember any of this anyway." I looked up at him and said, in the dopy state I was in, "Oh yes, I will. I'll never forget you, not as long as I live." He just laughed at me and then I blacked out again.

Next thing I remembered, I was in Dave's cabin, waking up on his sofa sleeper. I looked up and saw Dave's emergency monitor flashing in the corner of his room. Dave's an EMT, so he keeps it on all the time. I went back to sleep.

The next morning, Dave took me home. I was supposed to have stayed the whole weekend, but Dave changed his mind and decided to take me home right then. He hardly

spoke two words to me the whole way home, and after he
dropped me off that day I never heard from him again. On
the trip home, I felt awful, physically and emotionally. I
kept thinking that something had happened the night before,
but I just couldn't remember what it was.

When I got home, I lay on the couch and tried to get
some rest. I felt as if I had been up all night drinking and
had a terrible hangover. I don't drink. As I lay there, drifting in and out, I began to remember the story I just told you.
The longer I lay there, the more I remembered. It was not
like normal dreams, where the more you are awake, the less
you remember, so that by the time the day is over, you've
forgotten you even had that dream. By the end of the day I
had remembered it all and I was really upset by it. Who was
I going to tell? Who would believe it? I tried to call Dave
but never could reach him. I eventually told Budd about
this, but he didn't know what to make of it, so it went in the
peripheral file to be explored later. I never forgot it, though.

Several years later, my friend ran into Dave at the plant
she worked in. He asked if I was okay. That was all he said
about me. She told me that he had sold his cabin, grown a
beard, transferred jobs, and gotten married. She said he
seemed nervous and concerned when he asked about me.

A couple of years after this, I gave a talk to a MUFON
group about the experiences I have had and about how I
have changed because of them. During my lecture, I noticed
two men sitting in the front row. Both had on dark suits and
ties. One guy was wearing sunglasses in the meeting hall!

As I began to tell about some of the memories I had
coming back, about things that someone had told me, technical stuff, one of the men jumped up and said, "Where did
you get this information?" I told him that I got it the same
way I got everything else. I remembered someone telling
me this stuff. Then he asked me if the mark in my yard had
ever had a funny smell about it. I told him yes, absolutely.

That seemed to be the right answer for him because they both got up and left.

I really began to feel strange after that little interaction and was glad when my talk was finally over. I really wanted to get out of there. I asked the people who were putting on the presentation who those two guys in the front were. They told me that they didn't know who they were, but that they showed up from time to time, whenever they had a controversial speaker.

As I made my way back to my hotel room afterward, I suddenly began to realize why these men had bothered me so much. The one who had questioned me looked and sounded just like the doctor I had remembered taking the "bug" out of my ear years earlier. If it wasn't him, he's definitely got a twin. The man was in his fifties, about five-feet-eight or -nine, weighed about two hundred pounds. He had a really red-looking face, a big, bulbous nose, and snowwhite hair. He had the deepest voice I have ever heard and he had a very prominent southern drawl. He also had really blue, squinty eyes.

I'm just telling you what I remember. I'm not saying I know what it all means. Maybe someone reading this can shed some light on it for me.

10

KATHY
Who's Watching Who

AS WE HAD MORE AND MORE CONTACT WITH BUDD, JOHNNY continued to stay just far enough out of the picture to enable him to laugh at me in private. Although he didn't seem to be laughing quite as much as usual, it still irked me that he was so narrow-minded. Little did he know that soon he wouldn't be laughing anymore.

We had a small, very primitive cabin in the woods eighty miles from our home that was the perfect getaway from all the pressures of our daily lives. Some of our friends also had cabins close to ours and every weekend the guys would retreat to them to get back to nature, slow down, and relax.

Some of the wives and I accompanied our men to the woods at many times, but we soon found it too much like work. It was a novelty in the beginning, but we tired quickly, never having had the fantasy of turning back the pages of time to a more romantic era.

But the thrill of the wilderness and living off the land— hot dogs and bologna actually—only grew stronger for Johnny and his friends.

With the arrival of the weekend, I had plans to visit my parents' house. Budd was coming for the weekend and everyone was very excited. As usual, Johnny managed to avoid Budd and the entire subject of UFOs as much as possible. He didn't want to be any part of the matter, and he was determined to keep his distance.

I tried to convince him to stay home this particular weekend and go to my parents' with me, thinking that if I could just get him a little interested in the subject, he might understand how I could get so caught up in it. I thought it was especially rude of him to leave when we had a visitor coming, but he would not hear of staying. No way, Jose! He loved taunting me like poking a stick at a snake, yet he always knew when to stop before I would lash out with fangs of my own.

On his way to the door, with his ride waiting in the driveway, he made one last mocking remark to finalize his exit, "Now don't let them get you, Gert!" He always affectionately referred to me as "Gert" for some unknown reason. Well, that was the last straw! I stood at the door as he was leaving and popped back with, "I hope they suck you up and take you off somewhere. Maybe then you'll believe me, or at least I won't have to listen to you anymore!" Boy, I sure told him. That was probably the most ignorant remark I have ever retaliated with, but it was all I could think of at such short notice.

That weekend turned Johnny's life totally around. The king of the nonbelievers saw, at last, something he could not explain away. He had spent the night at our friend's cabin and upon rising in the early-morning hours to the call of Mother Nature, Johnny stepped outside onto the porch of the isolated cabin. Since there was no indoor plumbing, the restroom was anywhere you wanted it to be. Across the lake, about three hundred feet, he saw hovering over the trees an object he could not make out clearly. At first he thought it was a helicopter. It stayed stationary at treetop level for quite some time. Coming from beneath the hovering object was a very large beam of light shining down into the trees. Johnny could see two small, humanlike figures standing at the edge of the woods. They appeared to be around four or four and a half feet tall, with large heads, and of light grayish-white color. He thought at first they were the two buddies with him for the weekend who had gotten up early to start squirrel hunting. That was unlikely since it was still dark and only about 3 A.M. He remembers watching them for a while, he's not sure exactly how long, alone in the night. He then remembers going back to bed. He has no recollection of any timespan or any lost time. He has no recollection of any contact with these two beings. He also refuses any investigation into the matter, so we may never know the rest of the story. His next memory is of waking up and hearing his friends in the kitchen talking and drinking coffee. He asked them if they had been out earlier hunting, but they denied it. He never mentioned his experience to them that morning.

After returning home it was several days before he told me about his experience. I guess he finally knew what my family and I had been going through. I listened cautiously to every detail of that weekend, thinking to myself, This guy is putting me on. He thinks he is going to set me up for a joke or something, but I'm wise to him. For some reason I never questioned anyone else's experiences, but coming from Johnny it was so very unnatural, so out of place. He had dealt me such ridicule that I found it hard to believe him. If he was telling the truth it certainly was a just dessert.

As the weeks turned into months, I noticed a change in him. He no longer laughed at me. He still refused to be included in any investigation or hypnosis of that night but, after a while, I began to feel that he had been telling me the truth.

Was it merely a coincidence that I had wished him to be

involved and suddenly he was? Can it be possible to will another person to see what they have not been able to see in the past? I believe in almost everything, but that pushed me to my limits. It is surely impossible to will someone to be "sucked up" and have it happen. Well, whatever the case may be, I will certainly be more careful in the future about what I wish for. My next wish will definitely be for money! (On second thought, maybe the lesson of King Midas is reason to be even more careful.)

That one night of unexplainable circumstances, breaking past the skepticism of the nonbelievers, was not an isolated incident for Johnny. In the months ahead he was to experience more mysterious events, one that would be so frightening for him it would stop him from going to his beloved wilderness for almost a full year.

Driving to work one morning in December 1983, at approximately five thirty, and listening to his favorite country music tape, Johnny leaned back, feeling good with his life. He had traveled the same country road for the past two years and always enjoyed the scenery. Farmland reminded him of his Arkansas homeland. It also reminded him of his youth, when times were hard but happy. His family was painfully poor, living off the land, picking cotton to buy shoes for school. But being the youngest of seven children, his days were spent at his favorite pastimes, fishing and hunting.

Times are still somewhat hard now for Johnny. Finally being able to buy the house in the country he had always wanted, he found out how expensive it is to live in a rural community. I had been working for a few years and the extra income helped make ends meet. We had no money saved for emergencies, but we got by.

Johnny could relax in the fact that while so many people were out of work at that time, he and I had good steady jobs. One day in the future after the four kids were raised,

God willing, he and I would be able to build quite a nest egg for retirement, or at least we'd be able to eat steak once a week. As I said, he was feeling good about himself.

Casually glancing into his rearview mirror, Johnny was shocked to see the outlined shadow figure of a man wearing a cowboy hat sitting in the backseat of his truck. He slammed on his brakes, not knowing or caring if another car was behind him. He threw open the door and jumped out, half expecting to be stabbed, shot, or who knows what. Turning to face his assailant, Johnny's heart was pounding. The backseat was empty. He knew what he saw, but where was it? Wondering if he had gone mad, he quickly surveyed the surrounding land. Again he saw no one. The farm ground provided no hiding places for any fugitive and yet the backseat was empty.

Now visibly shaken, he returned to his truck. At least he hadn't caused an accident or been run down by another car. How could he ever explain that to the insurance company? "Well, this invisible guy was in my backseat, and I thought he was going to attack me or something. . . ."

Later that night, as he recounted every detail to me, Johnny was still nervous about the incident. Things like that make a person wonder if he is losing touch with reality, wonder if he has both oars in the water or if he is just going in circles and doesn't realize it. Whatever the case, Johnny sold the truck the next day and traded for one with no backseat. This time at least there would be no place for the shadowed cowboy to sit.

That incident no doubt shook Johnny's "I-gotta-see-it-to-believe-it" stability. He was positive he had actually seen a person in his backseat, but that in the blink of an eye there had been no evidence of any such person. I wonder if he somehow felt that my strange happenings were beginning to rub off on him. Did he feel that he had lived with me so long that he was beginning to think like me? He had laughed at me for so many years, it seemed only fitting that it was my turn to have a laugh. Paybacks can be a bummer, but being the swell kind of person that I am, I listened to his story and eventually accepted it as fact.

After a few days the strange early morning incident was laid to rest, filed away with the other "believe-it-or-not" occurrences rarely to be recalled. Even now when we talk about our many curious adventures, we religiously exclude Johnny. He remains adamant about keeping his life to himself and does not like it when I bring the matter up. He can dish it out but can't take it.

A short time later Johnny's mind was put to another test, leaving him even more confused.

Johnny and Mike, our third child, were on their way to work. It was summer vacation and Mike helped his dad carry material on the job and clean up tools to make himself a little spending money. Working with his dad was good experience for him and he learned very quickly that no one in this life just gives you money, not even your dad.

About 6 A.M., at almost the identical place Johnny saw his "shadowed cowboy," Johnny looked toward the sky and called Mike's attention to what Johnny was certain was a flying saucer. He pulled onto the side of the road and stopped the truck to get a better view. According to Johnny, as he watched the flying object, Mike seemed to be quite confused. Try as he might, looking in all directions, Mike claimed to see nothing.

Johnny related that he watched this flying craft for several seconds, trying without success to point it out for Mike. Still, Mike saw nothing.

According to Johnny, he spotted a strange flying object, pulled off the road, watched for a short while, pulled back onto the road, and continued on to work.

When we questioned Mike about the incident he denied

anything but going straight to work and coming straight home. He says he does not remember his dad pulling off the road or saying anything about a flying saucer. He swears the morning was totally uneventful, period. Even now when I question him about the incident, trying to get all the details correct, he is very confused and acts like I am trying to put words in his mouth. He acts like we are all a little strange. That is a typical reaction I have met with many times in the past.

So now I had to decide for myself who saw or did not see what. I had my husband coming in from work, very excited about a strange sighting he had witnessed that morning, and I had a son who stood there shrugging his shoulders, not wanting to call his dad a liar, but not claiming to see what he obviously thinks he hasn't.

So was there actually a flying craft that Johnny saw that morning that was not meant for Mike to see? Is it possible that in any UFO sighting so many people are allowed to view it and so many do not see?

I am reminded of my original sighting in the church parking lot surrounded by rows of houses on the remaining three sides of the church. Is it possible that even if there had been numerous other people outside at the exact time that none would have seen what I had? That would no doubt make it very easy to call a person crazy or a liar, or both. If ten people are together and one sees something odd or unusual and nine don't, who is right? Could it be that we are only seeing things in our mind, that what we claim to see is not really there at all? Perhaps the nonbelievers really do see UFOs but are so positive they don't exist that they refuse to let their mind grasp the perception. Maybe it's not meant for all to see. It's all too complicated for me. I can only go with the things I have seen and I can only tell what has been told to me as the truth.

Time passed, and that early morning incident was also

filed away in Johnny's mental bank. It was replaced by the daily woes that torment everyone: home repairs, bills, and trying to survive. Johnny continued his weekend retreats, drawn to the wilderness now more than ever. He was drawn like a lamb to the slaughter, leaving the day-to-day worries behind, entering the virginal land as one would enter baptismal waters, cleansing the sins of materialism from a troubled soul.

By now two of Johnny's friends had built cabins and equal time was spent at each. One weekend that same summer Johnny and Mike, accompanied by a friend, were settled in for a weekend of squirrel hunting and guitar playing.

By 9 P.M. when none of the other friends had arrived, Johnny decided to drive over to the other cabin about three miles away to see if anyone was there yet. Leaving his friend and Mike, intending to be gone only a short time, he made his way through the black wilderness night. Night in a forest is always blacker than you can imagine. Some nights you can't see your hand in front of your face. Not having the convenience of street lights, the moon and headlights are your only source of illumination.

Johnny never arrived at the second cabin.

As luck would have it, he had a flat tire there in the middle of nowhere. What really infuriated him was the fact that it was his second flat in a week. The same tire had been patched earlier that week. His newly acquired truck might not have a backseat, but it did have dry rotted tires. Johnny had intended to replace all four tires, but when you are just making ends meet, it's hard to squeeze in any extras until they become a dire necessity. He knew instantly he didn't have a spare tire. He'd had one, but found out earlier that week that it didn't fit the truck. So he proceeded to look for a jack, just so he could take the flat tire off.

In keeping with Murphy's Law, there was no jack. He did

find a lug wrench, so his next problem was to figure out how to get the tire off without a jack. That would be a good trick if he could work it. He managed to maneuver the truck over a ditch, trying several times, till he had the three good tires on solid ground and the flat tire rotating freely over the ditch. Now if he could just hold the tire still and loosen the lug nuts, he could roll the tire to his friend's cabin.

The poor guy never figured out why he would go to such trouble. Why not simply walk to the cabin, find help, drive back with them and then remove the tire? Perhaps in the frustration of the evening he wasn't thinking clearly. Perhaps the wilderness that he loved when he was with friends scared him when he was alone. Perhaps he felt that being armed with a flat tire was better than being armed with nothing at all. Perhaps he thought that if someone or something accosted him he could always smack it in the face with the tire, then run. Whatever the case, it didn't matter anyway because he wasn't able to get the tire off the truck.

There he stood in the dark, alone, frustrated, and thoroughly disgusted.

Then as if on cue from the edge of the woods, Johnny saw two small figures walking toward him. He described them as "small little fellows" being about four feet tall. They were whitish-gray in color, with overly large heads for their size. They had large, dark, liquidlike eyes. He claimed later they spoke to him but not with their mouth, which he described as only a slit. He said they told him mentally that they would help him and not to worry.

Not to worry—that would be easier said than done.

That's all he remembers of the "small little fellows." Try as he might, the only recollection he has is of rolling the tire down the road. Somehow, someone managed to remove the tire from the disabled truck. A man Johnny described as a hippie drove past and stopped to see if he needed help. The man drove him to the next large town until they found a service station that was open. Johnny later said he thought the guy was high on drugs or something. He claimed he drove like a maniac, scaring him half to death. It's odd to me that he did not associate his fear with the "small little fellows," but a drugged-out hippie can cause him much mental trauma.

They found a station that was open, had the tire repaired, returned to the crippled vehicle, and replaced the tire. Whether this hippie person was drugged out or not, it was certainly noble of him to go to such extreme effort for a total stranger. Johnny had never seen this man before nor has he seen him since.

Johnny returned to the cabin where our son and his friend were and was surprised to find out that it was now 8 A.M. His friend was very worried about him and had started to walk to the other cabin thinking he must have had an accident along the deserted roads and lay unnoticed all night. It was not at all like him to be so inconsiderate as to leave the pair alone all night with no transportation or telephone. He explained his lateness by simply stating he had a flat tire and the extreme length of time it took to have it repaired.

Johnny never got out of the truck, or never mentioned a word of his strange helpers. He just told his friend and son to get in the truck because they were going home.

I am certain that Johnny would never have told me but, upon their arrival home, his companions immediately told me how he had been gone all night, leaving them alone.

Well, this old gal is nobody's fool. That whole story sounded mighty fishy to me. I was mad because he had left our son all night, even though he was not alone. I figured he had not wanted to be bothered by having a kid around, so he went over to the other friend's cabin to drink and act like a fool all night and simply fell asleep. When Johnny swore he never made it to the other cabin, I began to be puzzled. When my son was insistent that his dad had not been drinking when he left them at the cabin—maybe two beers, which is not much for him—I knew then something was strange. Maybe our son was just siding with the guy who takes him hunting and fishing against the woman who makes him clean up his room.

Johnny has never been a loner. Coming from a family of nine, he was born in a crowd and liked it that way. It was not like him at all to have spent an entire night alone and I fully intended to get to the bottom of his story. I would deal with him and our Benedict Arnold son later.

When I questioned Johnny further about the previous night, all he would say was that he was never going back. Now something was really amiss.

The following Monday we visited with the friends who own the second cabin Johnny never made it to that night. They live in the same small town and frequently visit us, and we visit them. In Johnny's presence I made a point to bring up the weekend's events. Our friends and their son had been at their cabin that particular weekend and all three confirmed that Johnny had not made it over on that particular night.

That took me by surprise. So much for plan A, now I would have to move on to plan B. I wasn't sure just what plan B was yet but if it took the rest of my natural life I would find out what happened on the night in question.

It didn't take the rest of my life, but it did take several days before I got any more information out of Johnny about that unusual night.

Johnny is a true social drinker. Beer will sit in the refrigerator for days, weeks, or months, only until company comes over. I am not considered company—so when Johnny started drinking one night, several nights after his weekend incident, my first thought was that he must have a guilty conscience.

He sat for several hours at the kitchen table talking about

his life and what he wanted to do with it—and getting kind of sloshed. He lectured the kids about getting good grades and to try to learn more than he had in school. He said he wanted more for them than he had done for himself. He talked about getting out of debt, building a patio, fixing the cars up, buying new furniture, raising a garden, world peace, and anything else he could think of. He rambled on and on with words of wisdom, sounding like a ninety-year-old man who feels his days are numbered, wanting to pass on all the knowledge he has gained in a lifetime.

After a couple of hours the kids began drifting off one at a time until it was just him and me sitting at the table. Lucky me, I thought, I could endure his endless rambling because I simply tuned him out and gathered my own thoughts.

When he realized we were alone in the kitchen he leaned over and his voice got so soft I could barely make out what he was trying to say. He began recalling the events of his missing night. I was taken totally off guard as he began describing to me everything he could remember. Excuse me? What happened to world peace and report cards? Let's start at the beginning, I said to him gingerly. Is this a joke? I thought as I watched his face carefully, looking for any hint of a smile or sign that he was making the story up. Johnny never could lie well. His voice gets high pitched, he talks very fast, coughs a lot, and cannot look you in the eye. I watched for the telltale signs but never saw any. He was deadly serious as he recalled each detail he could remember.

I sat as patiently as could be expected, not quite sure just what to think. I could tell the experience definitely upset him.

What's the deal here? I wondered. Does this guy think I'm stupid or something? I continued to listen, quizzing him on several occasions.

I questioned him on what they said to him. All he could remember was that they said they would help him.

I bombarded him with every question I could think of, being careful to remember each so I could repeat them at a later date when he was totally sober. I decided it was impossible to argue with a drunk man and win, so I would continue the interrogation at a later date. I intended to be sly in my questioning, a little here, a little there, and sooner or later I would trip him up. Try as I might—and believe me, I tried—I never could. His answers were always the same, weeks later, months later, even to this very day.

After he had revealed the night in question to me the first time, he would talk openly with me about it, but never in front of the kids.

Johnny has refused to undergo hypnosis to uncover the rest of the story. Whatever happened in the dark of the wilderness night will probably stay locked in his subconscious for a long time. Even if he was not abducted or examined in any way, the fact remains that he saw two humanlike figures not of this Earth. He bears no physical scars from the night in question.

Johnny and our son, the other hunter, do bear the deep oval scar on their shins that has been linked to UFO abductions. Both scars are old and long since healed. Neither received the scars on the night in question, but from some time in each person's childhood from an unknown or unremembered source of injury. Being a very careful mother, I have searched my mind trying to remember when my son could have possibly received such a scar, but so far have been unable to recall any such accident or injury. Debbie and our mother also bear an identical scar. Two girlfriends of mine also bear the same kind of scar. No one, except Debbie, remembers how they came to receive such a deep oval scar. Debbie's were connected to her UFO experiences.

Whatever happened to Johnny that night turned him from

a total nonbeliever in aliens or UFOs to a man who now listens to stories of sightings or possible abductions and no longer laughs. He no longer scoffs and no longer travels without a spare tire.

11

DEBBIE
Transitions

On April 24, 1984, my mother and I witnessed the most unusual UFO sighting I have ever had.

I was giving myself a manicure that evening when I found that I had run out of nail polish remover. For some reason I decided I had to go out and get some more, even though it was getting rather late and I could have waited until the next day. I hopped in my car and ran down to the corner all-night convenience store. On the way home, as I came down our street, heading south, I saw what looked like the landing lights of a very large jetliner. I watched these lights for a moment. When I reached the railroad tracks that were approximately a quarter mile north of our driveway I stopped to get a better look at these exceptionally bright landing lights.

As I sat there at the railroad tracks, I saw the two bright lights slowly move together to become one intense light! I couldn't believe my eyes! Airplanes don't do that! I floored the accelerator and raced home. I ran in the front door yelling like a crazy woman for Mom to come out and see this thing. It was headed right for our house! Calmly she came out, had a look, and said, "Debbie, that's just an airplane.'' I knew it was no ordinary airplane and told her to wait a minute and she'd see what I was talking about. We stood on the front porch for three or four minutes. We could see the craft coming toward us through the trees. The bright light looked eerie as it shone through the half-bare branches above our heads. As it reached the clearing right above our house, it became obvious that this was no normal aircraft.

It was moving extremely slow—at about the speed of a dirigible—and its wingspan was huge. It covered the whole clearing in the trees above us. It looked to be about twice the length of our house, a bedrock tri-level. I don't know any plane that can fly that slow at that altitude—approximately two hundred feet—and not fall out of the sky!

We noticed a slight humming sound as it got closer to us, yet, when it was right overhead, the sound didn't get any louder.

It was shaped like a boomerang. Up in the front, where the two wings met, there seemed to be a round, dark area. Inside this dark area was a pulsing red light. I could also see a dark area behind the wings that looked rectangular, with a long pointed thing coming off the back—vaguely reminding me of a stingray.

As we stood there looking at the craft, it suddenly lit up! At this point, it was directly above us and the whole underside came alive with a nearly audible *whomp*. I could see many, many small white balls of light, dotted all over the bottom of this thing, and several long strip lights—like fluorescent tubes—bordering the edge of the two wings. It was striking, to say the least. The rectangular rear remained dark; only the wings lit up. My mother exclaimed how beautiful it was and stood there on the porch with her mouth open in awe. She commented that it seemed to have lit up ''just for us.''

I, on the other hand, was not so easily enthralled. All I can remember thinking to myself was, Oh shit, here we go again! I was not mesmerized as my mother apparently was. I was terrified. I remember grabbing hold of the screen door and standing there, one foot on the porch and one in the house. As the craft passed over the house I ran inside through the kitchen and out the back door. I wanted to keep my eye on this thing. I wanted to know where it was all the time. I wasn't about to let it sneak up on me. (Incidentally, I was so out of my mind with fear that I ran right past a loaded camera that was sitting on the desk right by the front door.)

I watched it pass over the house and then, when it was about half a mile away, I saw it turn on its axis, spinning its wings around to face the opposite direction, and travel back to the southwest. I couldn't believe what I had seen. No airplane can do that! I watched it until it was out of sight.

Mom and I immediately began to draw what we had seen. When Dad got home from work later that evening, we both nearly knocked him down telling him about it. He suggested we call someone to report this thing. I had received some literature from Budd about MUFON and CUFOS—two of the best known and most reputable UFO research groups in the country—so I got one of the journals out and called the UFO hotline number in the *CUFOS Journal*. Dr. J. Allen Hynek answered the phone. I was rather surprised at this. It was about 11 P.M. before we called. Rather late, I thought, for Dr. Hynek to be awake. Our sighting had been around 9:30 P.M.

We talked for about an hour and agreed to send him our drawings. He talked to each of us independently. He told my mother that he was beginning to believe that only certain people were meant to witness these events.

We noticed there were no reports about sightings of any kind on the radio or television that night or any night after that. This surprised us because the craft was huge and we couldn't believe that no one else had seen it! I look at this event as just one more confirmation that I really didn't need.

By February of 1986, I was nearly ready to move out of my parents' home and begin life on my own with my two boys. I was dating the man who would soon be my second husband, James. I had completed beauty school with excellent grades, and was working at my first job in the field. Life seemed to be settling down for me. Unusual things were still happening, but I guess I was slowly being conditioned. They didn't seem to frighten me quite as much.

One night that year, I was in my room watching television when my oldest son ran in acting very frightened and upset. He claimed that there was a "red spider" on his wall and that it scared him. He wanted to get in bed with me so he would feel safe. I had gotten used to this by now so I had him lie down on my bed, covered him up, and sat across the foot of my bed, continuing to watch TV. I figured he'd had a bad dream so I didn't bother to look for the red spider. Now, I wish I had because I believe he may have seen some kind of red light on his wall, somehow connected to the phenomenon, that scared him.

As I sat there looking at TV, I happened to glance at the open doorway of my room. I was absolutely stunned to see a blue light appear at the far edge of the doorway. As I continued to look, I saw—with both eyes wide open—and wide awake, the luminous blue outline of a gray alien-type figure strolling past my bedroom door. I sat there with my mouth wide open in total shock. He walked past my door and into what I will describe as an invisible doorway that began just before he got out of my field of vision. By this time, he looked blue and somewhat transparent. As he walked by my doorway he momentarily turned his head toward me, as if to balance himself while he walked. I got the distinct impression that he either was not aware that I could see him, or just didn't care if I did.

As he passed through this invisible doorway, wherever his outline touched or passed through it, it created tiny sparks that reminded me of Fourth of July sparklers. As soon as he passed all the way through, he was gone. And so were the sparks.

I sat there for a moment, trying to comprehend what I had just witnessed. Looking at my son lying there—fast asleep—I thanked God he hadn't seen what I had. How could I ever explain that one away? I also felt guilty because I hadn't gotten up to check on the red spider story. I was now sure it was connected to what I had just witnessed. This thing appeared to come from the direction of the boys' room. I was terrified and angry at the thought of this creature hurting and scaring my children.

I don't know how long I sat there on the edge of my bed trying to regain my composure. I recall hearing a slight humming sound coming from outside my bedroom window but I wasn't about to look out to see if I could see where the sound was coming from.

When I could finally get off the bed, I jumped off and ran to my parents' room. I insisted they get up and I begged Mom to loan me the money to rent a hotel room. She knew I was serious, so she got up. She made a pot of coffee and we sat there at the kitchen table for nearly forty-five minutes as I told her the details of what I had just seen.

No amount of coffee and cigarettes could calm me down. I finally went back to bed, first gathering up my other child and putting him in the bed with my other son so I could watch and protect them. I didn't sleep very well that night.

All during this time, I had been writing down things I had begun to remember on my own—without hypnosis. I had begun to create collages and pencil drawings of images I remembered seeing on the ships and something that looked like writing of some unknown origin. I thought these things might be of some importance to someone someday, and if I didn't write them down, I could not rest. It seemed to bother me until I wrote it down. Doing this was very therapeutic for me and after a couple of years I had collected quite a stack of material.

I gave a lot of this material to Budd, but there was just so much information that he decided to hold back on it so as not to confuse his readers. I have always felt the fact that I was remembering this information was important even though the material itself might not mean anything. I think Budd did too, although he was already becoming overwhelmed by the magnitude of our case and didn't know quite what to do with it all. I truly felt sorry for him!

During this time, I had also begun to collect seeds from the various plant life around my home. It became an obsession for me and I distinctly remember getting anxious for the time when the buckeyes would begin to fall from the trees. I needed to add them to my collection.

After a few months of this, my room started to look like a horticulturist's dream. I had seeds from just about every type of plant life known to the Midwest. I was proudest of my cattails, which turned out to be the hardest specimen to collect. What a pain in the rear it was to pull over to the side of roads and climb through muddy, swampy ravines to retrieve my prize. I'm sure I looked like a total nut! My reasoning for this was: I wanted to have a little piece of this world as it was then, so if it all changed one day, I would have something to show my children what my world—the nature of it—was like. I feel a very close attachment to nature to this day, although the compulsion to collect specimens of it has stopped.

Actually, it happened quite abruptly one morning. I woke up to see that just about everything I had collected was now gone from my room—overnight. Even my prized cattails were gone. I panicked and immediately accused my younger sister of taking them. She had been lusting after my cattails for a flower arrangement she was making. She was surprised when I asked her to please return my stuff and denied having taken them. I never saw any of my collection again and after that day, the desire—the drive—to collect them, stopped forever.

The same thing had happened to me a few years before that, only I seemed to be collecting men. Now, let me explain this.

Shortly after I moved in with my parents—after my first divorce—I began going out to the clubs with a girlfriend. As I said in a previous chapter, I had begun going out as much as I could to get away from that house and all the memories that were in it. Well, while I was going out, something else was also happening.

I am not what anyone would call a raving beauty, nor am I even particularly physically attractive in any way. The kids at school used to call me "five by five" because I was so short and fat. Yet, for a brief period of time, back when I first started going out, something happened that enabled me to attract any man whom I, for whatever reason I had decided, needed to be with that night. I could walk into a club, see the man I wanted, and by the end of the night, he was mine. It didn't matter whether he was rich or poor, extremely attractive or average, somehow I knew he was the one I should be with that night, and I would be.

I am not proud of what happened back then, but I have learned since then that I am not alone in this behavior. After I told Budd about it, he began to get reports from other women of the same types of incidents. Or, at least, he began telling me of other reports.

I recall meeting a man one night whom I eventually slept with. This is rather personal but I believe that it is important information and someone needs to tell about it because, apparently, it happens often. It's obvious as to why very few people talk about it.

While in the act of making love, we both noticed that something was wrong. Neither one of us could finish what we had set out to do and neither one of us could stop! We found ourselves looking at the other and asking what the hell was going on. We were both in a cold sweat and feeling rather sick to our stomachs. We also felt as if someone were in the room with us, watching us at work. Eventually we were kind of pushed apart. We both got up, got dressed, and commented, ''I'm outta here!'' Needless to say, we never saw each other again after that. This happened several more times before finally—just like the obsession with seeds—I woke up one morning and knew that it was over. But not before I had sampled about twenty different men.

As I said before, I am not proud of this—it makes no sense to me—and it is rather embarrassing to write about this part of my life in a book. But I know this has happened to thousands of men and women like me who have experienced the things that I experienced, and I think it means something. If more women would speak up about this, perhaps someone could get some answers to our questions.

After I moved out of my parents' house and into an apartment of my own, I figured that all this craziness would stop. It didn't!

One night, after my first husband had picked up the children for the weekend, I decided to take advantage of the quiet time by mopping my apartment floors. While I was mopping the floor near the patio door I heard a faint beeping sound. It sounded like someone's watch alarm. I stopped what I was doing to listen and see if I could figure out where it was coming from. I was not able to figure it out so I continued to mop. After I finished, I was worn out! I lay down on my cot, hoping sleep would come quickly. At the time I was sleeping on an old army cot that a girlfriend had loaned me. I had been sleeping on the floor and the cot looked pretty good!

As I lay there, trying to relax, I noticed, through the open bedroom door, some movement in the living room. I could see my rocking chair moving and the leaves on one of my large potted plants were rustling. At first I thought it must have been one of the kids, but quickly I remembered that they were with their father. I became nervous, so I got up and closed and locked my bedroom door. It seemed to be quiet for a while after that, so I began to drift asleep. Then I heard voices speaking in some foreign language. I also heard a rather loud banging noise coming from the living room. I sat up in bed to see a scary, ugly man burst through my bedroom door and lunge at me. He was very tall and skinny. He had very short hair, very pointed, yellowed teeth, and evil-looking yellow eyes. His arms were long and spindly and he was waving them wildly. He held a long, triangular stick that he kept poking at me. He was cursing and screaming that he was going to kill me, but not before I got what was coming to me, whatever that meant. I got the impression that he meant to rape and beat me first before he would finally let me die. He kept poking at me with that stick until he had poked me right into the corner of my room. There I sat, curled up in a little ball on the edge of my cot, practically smashed into the corner of the two walls, while this guy that I called the ''rubber-band man'' threatened to kill me. It was like a nightmare, but it seemed *too* real! Suddenly it dawned on me. I was going to die. This guy really was going to kill me. Then I panicked and began to pass out.

From out of nowhere came the beeping sounds I had heard earlier in the evening while I had been mopping. As soon as he heard the sounds, he freaked out. He began writhing in pain and turned to bolt from my room. I jumped off the cot and began following him. I saw him run through the sliding glass door and I mean *through* it! I opened it up and went out onto the patio to see where he had gone.

The next memory after that was being on what looked to me to be some kind of huge bus. I was sitting in front of a whole lot of big, long windows. I could see two strange-looking ships outside and I could see my apartment building down below.

These ships looked like a bug called a "walking stick." They looked sort of like an airplane with several sets of real skinny wings that were bent down, halfway out from the body. Then clouds of some kind—mist perhaps—started to surround the two ships. Soon I could not even see them anymore. Then a few minutes later—as the mist dissipated —they were gone. I heard a voice, coming from out of nowhere, telling me that this had been a test. "Do not be afraid, you are safe." That's the last thing I remembered about this whole event. I don't know what it all really meant, but I wanted to share this memory with you.

On May 15, 1987, I married my boyfriend James. He had been through so much with me I figured he really must love me, so I shouldn't let this one get away! He knew what kind of person I was and he had seen enough to know that I wasn't as crazy as I might sound to someone who hadn't been there. I was thrilled to have had him in my life at that point and so we did the "big dance."

On October 31, 1987—appropriately enough, Halloween night—I returned home from working second shift at the convenience store next to my apartment building. I had walked home and was ready for bed even though I was still wound up from the night's work and all the coffee and cigarettes I used to help keep me awake. James was in bed —already asleep—as I slipped in next to him and began to relax. My mind was going over the day's events and I was nearly ready for the final leap into sleep. Suddenly, I experienced what I call a "brain shock."

My mind was filled up with what looked like the luminous snow you see on a blank television screen. In my mind I could "see" wavy, horizontal lines and I could "hear" a very loud, discomforting hissing sound.

At first, I thought I was having a stroke. I took a mental assessment of all my extremities and when I had finally determined I hadn't had a stroke, I figured that I either had a brain tumor or that I was just plain nuts. I lay there for a few more minutes and it then happened again. Only this time I could "see" in my mind, these two very real, very strange looking eyes. It seemed real and actually in my mind, in 3D! They looked like huge cat eyes, amber in color with diamond-shaped pupils. This caused me to jump about a foot off the bed! My husband was quite alarmed by this movement and jumped with me. He asked me if I was okay, so I told him what I had seen, and how it had startled me. He was very comforting. He put his arm around me and helped me to calm down enough that I thought I'd try to get some sleep. As soon as I closed my eyes again I saw the "static," heard the noise again, and this time I heard people talking in a language that I didn't understand. I don't know how to explain what happened next, except to say that I somehow got a glimmering of understanding—just for a moment—during the course of this anomalous conversation, and I heard a man's voice say the words, "prestigious listener in November."

This made absolutely no sense to me and I jumped again, at hearing this. I told my husband what I had heard and I could tell that he was really getting worried about me. (So was I!)

James said to me, "Maybe someone is trying to tell you something. You ought to write this all down." So I went into the living room to get a pencil and a piece of paper out of the desk. I took them back to the bedroom and began to write down what I had heard. As I walked through the living room, I began to feel some kind of static electricity swirl all around me. Only it didn't feel like regular static electricity. It started at my head and swirled all around me, right down to my toes. It was the strangest thing I have ever felt and when I got back to the bedroom, I told James what I had felt in the living room and that I was feeling strange. I wrote down what I had remembered and then lay down next to my husband and tried to relax. As soon as I shut my eyes I heard the man's voice again. This time he said—directly to me—"Are you still feeling strange?" I nearly fell off the bed this time and my husband was *really* getting worried about me. I nearly screamed to James what I had just heard and I said to him, "This is not funny! Whatever is going on had better stop, now!" I lay down again, this time thinking to myself that I shouldn't close my eyes, because every time I closed my eyes I could hear him. As soon as I did finally close my eyes, sure enough, there he was again and this time he said, "Ha, ha, ha, ha, ha" very sarcastically. That did it. I was never going to go to sleep again because I would never be able to close my eyes and not hear him, whoever he was. I was so tired by this time that I finally did close my eyes and fell asleep almost immediately.

The next day, as soon as I woke up, I had the worst headache of my entire life. It felt like my head was about to explode. As a matter of fact, my whole body felt as if I had been hit by a train. This awful feeling lasted for three days, then finally wore off. I have not been the same since then. It was right after this episode that I began to have what I called "conversations with myself."

I could be driving down the street, thinking about just any old thing, when suddenly these thoughts would come into my mind from who knows where. Words that made no sense to me would bug me to the point that I couldn't concentrate on what I was doing until I wrote them down. Once I did, they would go away and I could concentrate again.

After several months—years—of doing this, off and on, I had built up quite a lot of information. All of it having to do with UFOs, other life forms, technical stuff that I didn't understand, and spiritual stuff that made no sense to me. It all sounded so crazy to me that for many years I really didn't tell anyone about what I had been doing. I was rather embarrassed by having to admit that I was hearing this stuff in my head. I was never prone to hearing voices or having hallucinations of any kind, and I thought that maybe I was just going crazy. I backed away from the whole UFO scene for a little while, feeling really burnt out on it and not wanting to have to deal with any of it. It didn't stop the messages, or "rememberings," as I call them, from coming, though.

I remembered one time I was mowing the orchard behind our house. As I sat there on that rickety mower we had, wishing that the grass would just mysteriously disappear, I began to hear this little voice in my head talking about spiritual things that were far beyond my understanding. I thought to myself, okay, I'll bite. Tell me. What is God? This is what I heard in reply:

> God is the spirit of man. Look around you. All that is beautiful, all that is ugly but with life is God. God is life. Unconditional love is the highest manifestation of life, of God. There is but one life. Man is merely another manifestation of that life, which is God.

Whoa! Okay, I thought to myself. This is getting out of hand here!

This is a photo of the mark left in my parents' backyard by the UFO. It was taken a few weeks after the mark first appeared.

This is one of the many black helicopters that have plagued my family and me over the years. This photo was taken in my parents' backyard in 1992.

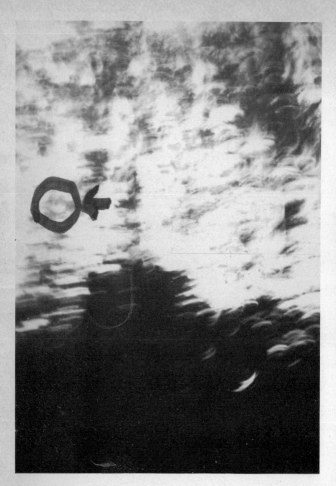

This is the first picture in the roll of film, taken of my son during our "camping trip from hell." Notice the "eye" on the left side of the frame. It's identical to an eye I saw in my mind on October 31, 1988. (The little orange fleck in the lower part of the photo is where the campfire was.) Notice the white, feathery stuff wrapping around the tree trunks and how the stuff moves in two, sometimes three directions at the same time? Photo experts have determined the image came through the lens and was not a product of bad film.

This is a photo I took in the hallway of my home. I was taking my camera to my room to put away, when I was overcome by the desire to snap a picture of the empty hallway. When I got it back from the developer, I was surprised to see all the intense red light and what looks like a "bunny" on the floor in the hall. The rest of the film came out fine and I cannot account for what I photographed.

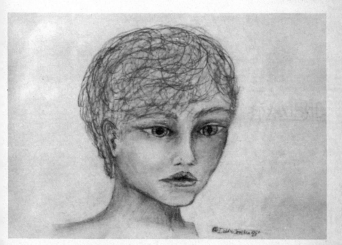

This is a drawing I did of the blond man who woke me up and asked me if I was still cold. When I finished the drawing a small, white ball of light appeared in the hotel room, moved over to this drawing, stopped, as if to look it over, and then disappeared.

These are drawings I have done. The alien male was done in 1993, the hybrid female in 1985. The female was completed in about half an hour, after having a dream about seeing her. The male is the one I have had encounters with on several occasions throughout my life.

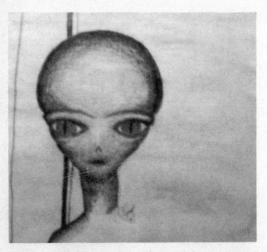

I did this drawing in 1987 after a dream in which I remembered seeing a gray head without the black eyes.

This drawing was the result of one of my first "virtual reality" dreams. I had this image of these black triangular crafts coming from the moon, heading toward Earth. 1990.

This is a drawing I did shortly after the investigation began. I felt strongly that this was mine, the symbol for me.

"Laura's" drawings of her memories. The one on the right is the full body of the larger alien and the three silhouettes of the small ones in the lighted doorway of the ship she found herself in 1966. The one on the left is of the light around the bird-feeder in our parents' backyard on June 30, 1983, as described by our mother.

This is a photo of the clay alien bust I made. It was taken from my home by an intruder in 1988.

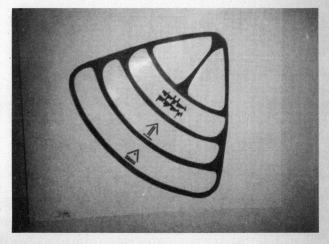

I remember seeing this design on a wall in a ship.

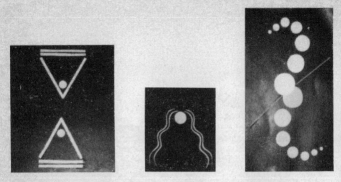

The far left and middle designs were seen by me in a ship. I don't know what they mean. The far right design came to me in a dream. During the dream someone told me this signified a merger.

Another shot of the center of the circle in Mom's yard as it grew back. Notice how dark and different the new grass came in.

I once asked about my baby—the baby I lost under mysterious circumstances in 1978. Where was she and why did she have to be taken away from me? This was the answer I got:

> The child was necessary for your development and ours. The greater good overrides all. The child is with us both. Her physical body is with us but, know this, the child's energy is uniquely yours. It is quite exciting, refreshing, hopeful. The child uses the name you chose for her. The child prefers it, to our way. The child must remain with us for now. She has much to absorb. You cannot provide what is necessary with exception of the human touch. We have not been able to simulate this yet. This will come from you. You have agreed to this. This child will then care for the needs of others. The human part of her is ever drawn to you. We do not fully understand this, nor can we prevent it. We will learn much from you and others like you. Know this, all is as it must be. All is right. These children are our hope for the future. Your future and ours. Know that we mean no harm. We only seek to grow, to become as one, as all life must!

I don't know if this means anything at all, and I couldn't begin to tell you where it came from. Perhaps my own mind is trying to justify the loss of my baby with this, perhaps it came from some outside source we don't yet recognize; I have no idea for sure. But it meant something to me and I thought I would share it with you. Perhaps it will mean something to someone else, as well.

I received/remembered a lot of technical information. None of that made any sense to me. And I had no idea as to what I was supposed to do with it. I mean, who would I tell and why would they listen to me, anyway? Thank God I met a man named John Carpenter and a man named Forest Crawford. Through them, I finally found out what I was supposed to do.

12

KATHY
The Crossover

MONTHS WENT BY AND SINCE I WAS UNABLE TO FIND ANY discrepancies in Johnny's story about his alien encounter I began to accept it as fact.

In the months since the backyard landing at my parents' house, I had tried to keep a fairly low profile on the whole subject of UFOs around my kids. I never tried to hide anything from them, I just did not overreact or play up any of the events. I have never tried to put ideas into their heads but tried to let them form their own opinions. They seemed to be evenly divided on the subject—two for and two against. The oldest and youngest children are believers and each have seen objects they feel are flying saucers or at least unexplained flying phenomenon. The middle two children tend to scoff. They listen to all the stories but aren't quite sure just what they think. Neither, to my knowledge, has seen anything out of the ordinary that we could pinpoint with certainty as being a UFO.

The oldest child, Bill, is a Capricorn, born in 1969. As a teenager he spent a lot of time in his room listening to the radio or composing tapes of his own from remixed music. He is a true night owl, and when school was not in session it wasn't unusual for him to still be awake at 5 A.M. when I got up for work. He has seen, on several occasions, flying objects that he has determined are not planes, but also not saucer-shaped, as is the classic UFO often portrayed on television and movies. He has called some of these sightings to my attention. Even though there are two small airports in a ten-mile radius from our house and numerous small planes fly overhead continuously, he and I can detect a difference in the sound of an approaching craft of unusual nature that seems to draw our eyes to the sky.

Our youngest child, "Stevie," is a Taurus, like his father. He is a high-strung little yacker who talks nonstop from morning till night. As a baby he came painfully close to death for twenty-two days, but after major surgery recovered to become a strapping young man.

Stevie is our only child to have an unexplainable encounter, so far as I know. During the early morning hours, his ninth year on this Earth, he rose from his bed and went to the living-room couch with pillow and blanket in hand. Upon waking the following morning, he proceeded to tell me about an experience he had during that night. He seemed genuinely upset. It was the first time I had ever seen him actually shake and quiver as he recalled what I determined to be a bad dream.

He claimed that he woke up about 3 A.M. and saw a round white light floating out of the kitchen. It appeared to be slightly larger than a basketball. He described this ball of light exactly the same way Mom had described the one that illuminated their bird-feeder in the 1983 backyard landing. This glowing ball of light seemed to have no source. As he watched the light, it began to travel down the hallway, stopping in front of each bedroom. It returned to the living room and landed on the table next to the couch. As he talked, I first suspected a prowler surveying the property with a flashlight. I was thinking to myself how lucky we were that he didn't go to the door or window to investigate, but stayed on the couch. He stated he began to feel extremely scared then suddenly went to sleep. He claimed he woke up immediately and where the light had been stood two small gray men dressed in gray overalls. The real clincher was these little aliens were only six to eight *inches* tall! He was extremely scared by now, but was unable to move. He claims that as he watched them, it seemed like they were talking about him—but he heard nothing. He described them as having no hair or ears and "funny big, black eyes that were pointed up in the corners." He said they had long arms for their size and they seemed to move and sway like the limbs of a willow tree in a gentle breeze.

As he continued, I had to ask him to slow down because he was talking so fast he was stammering, and his voice was shaking. He remembered that one of them called his name and then he went back to "sleep." Then Stevie woke up almost immediately. The tiny aliens were gone, but the light was still there. He then watched as the light floated out the same doorway it came in.

He claims his next memory is of waking up in the morning.

I listened halfheartedly to his adventure, dismissing it as just a dream. I listened to this story several more times that day as he would not let the subject rest. He repeated the story over and over, and he drew pictures of the tiny aliens. He honestly believed this was not a dream. The more he carried on during the day, the more I was beginning to believe maybe there was something to this. Maybe it wasn't really a dream after all.

During this time my family was now being watched, studied, and hypnotized to determine the source of the numerous encounters and the backyard landing at my parents' house. Even though I tried to keep the matter in proper perspective, I could not make up my mind whether my youngest offspring had just gotten wrapped up in the excitement, which resulted in such an unusual dream, or whether it was an actual happening.

Having an advantage over the average person, I did have some outside sources to confer with who were much more knowledgeable than I on such matters. So after my son's continued insistence that this was not a dream, I decided to call upon these sources to get their educated opinion about this occurrence.

To my surprise, I was told that encounters of this nature are relatively common to small children. Apparently these alien beings can appear in any form they choose, so that they need not be frightening to children. The only similarity in Stevie's story to any other encounter involving my family, is the floating ball of light. That light was identical to the one his grandmother saw in June of 1983. I could only assume that the idea was planted in his subconscious, coming out in the form of a very scary dream. His story was unique in that the aliens he saw were only six or eight inches tall. No other family member had been a witness to any such miniature beings, or at least remembered it.

My outside source confirmed that he had investigated numerous similar experiences involving small children having the exact encounter as Stevie had. Stevie was questioned at length by the investigator, placed under light, relaxing hypnosis, and it was determined that he was telling the story as truth and that it was more than likely a real experience, not a dream.

Well, that was all fine and good, but after careful consideration I decided to let the matter rest there. I felt that any benefit from exploring the night further by more hypnosis or regression would not outweigh any possible psychological damage that might result. I refuse to allow my child to be drilled and psychologically bombarded. If this nine-year-old child was abducted or examined in any way, it will be at his choice, as an adult. I will not accept that responsibility at this time. You can accept that choice either as a "cop-out" or as a mother's protective instinct.

Weeks passed relatively uneventfully. Summer turned to fall, fall to winter. Winter in the country takes on a completely new meaning. Where I live, a person soon learns to stock up on food and fuel because sure as the sun comes up, you'll be snowed in. You'll be immobilized in your home, which, after several days, rapidly becomes a prison. Just a few inches of snow, which hardly bothers the heavily populated areas, will blow off acres of farmland to pile up around rural homes in massive drifts, covering cars and roads, making it physically impossible to leave home.

The winter of 1984 was no exception. My family was snowbound for three days. The first day was fun in an odd sort of way. We just lay around, with no commitments, no distractions, watching soap operas and the snowfall, as it turned an ordinary yard into a showcase of white beauty. The family gathered around the television or played board games. It was very nice, the first day.

The second day we tired of the games and had eaten all the good food; cookies, brownies, and soft drinks. The living room seemed to shrink in size; people were tripping over each other.

By day number three panic began to set in. The entire family became a sickening bunch of slobs, bickering over the *TV Guide*, the last snack cake, or who's going to sit where. The living room had now shrunk to a six-foot cell. We paced from the window to the door, waiting for the snowplow to post our bail.

By nine o'clock on the third night, a rumble in the distance caught our attention. Peering down the road, head-lights of the snowplow came through the blackness of night as the blade cut into the white mountain of snow in the road. We were freed by a big, ugly, yellow machine.

Before the snowplow reached the end of our road, my family and I were in the car getting ready to make our escape down a single path to the main highway. Sweet freedom called us and we answered. We were heading for my parents' house in the city, where people know what a snowplow is for and use it. We were thankful that we had enough food and fuel to survive the blizzard and thankful that we didn't kill each other in frustration.

The fourth day we visited a friend's house for coffee and conversation. Stevie quickly walked to a neighbor's house to go shopping with them, so he did not accompany us. Luckily our road was lightly traveled, as it was still only one lane wide with mountains of snow on each side, making it impossible to pull over in the event of an oncoming car. Three or four stranded cars dotted the road and they were now covered, thanks to the snowplow.

As luck would have it, Stevie and his friends had car trouble in town and called me away from my friend's house to come and get them. Obligated to go since they had my kid with them, I made the twenty-minute trip to the local shopping center to their rescue. Trudging ahead through the mountains of snow to rescue the stranded family, I felt as if I should have had a keg of brandy tied under my chin. After completing the forty-minute round trip, I delivered Stevie and our stranded neighbors safely back to their home. I could see the back of my house from their driveway. I sat behind the steering wheel as the five people filed out of my car, noticing how pretty my house looked all covered in snow. I rarely ever saw it at that angle and it looked different from the back view. The security light in the backyard lit up one side and the back of the house and almost the entire backyard. It was a very bright evening outside. All the snow and the moon seemed to light up the whole world.

As I watched, a tall figure of a man ran from the front of my house, down the north side, around the corner, and back to the sliding glass door at my dining room. He was hunched over, apparently so as not to be seen through the windows of the bedroom. That was odd because the bedroom windows are very high up and impossible to keep clean without the aid of a chair or something to stand on. As he reached the sliding door, he stood straight up and placed both his hands on the glass, up over his head, in a "spread eagle" position, as if waiting to be searched by the police. He appeared to be as large as the doorway, even though there is a one-foot step down from the bottom of the door.

I sat there watching him, not quite sure just what to think. He appeared to be wearing some type of light-colored, tight-fitting, one-piece coverall. He did not appear to be bundled up for the weather, even though it was below zero outside. He appeared the same solid, light gray color from head to toe, and I was unable to tell where any of his clothing began or ended, or whether he was wearing a hat or gloves. He was just one solid color, everywhere.

At that time I was not aware that my neighbor had also been watching him until she asked, "What's that guy doing running around your house?" I answered that I didn't know but I supposed I had better go home and find out. In the split second it took to answer my neighbor, the man vanished around the dark side of the house. We could see that my door was still closed. Uncertain of this person's whereabouts, I left my neighbor's driveway and returned to my house to investigate. It had not crossed my mind to ask my neighbor or her husband to go with me. When I think back, that was kind of silly of me. It took less than a minute to reach my driveway. Looking about the front of my house, I noticed nothing unusual or out of place. Peeking through the window on my front door, everything inside looked satisfactory. I looked for snowy footprints on the carpet, but saw none. I felt reasonably certain that if someone had come in through the front door he would have had to track snow into my house. The dog was asleep on the couch and didn't even hear me pull into the driveway. That was the most unusual thing I noticed. The little rascal was really slipping. He was a high-strung, loud-mouthed Yorkshire terrier who would go crazy if a fleck of dust landed within three feet of him, so I was relatively certain no one had gone into my house. I still couldn't figure out why he didn't bark as there had just been a strange man running around my house right up to the sliding glass door.

I cautiously entered through the unlocked door. Now the little yapper went into his act, running around in circles, jumping up and down. I should have smacked him in the face. Some watchdog!

After being snowed in for three days with the road still extremely difficult to travel on, it seemed senseless to lock up the house. It was unlikely there would be much criminal activity on a night like this, here in the middle of nowhere. I went straight to the kitchen and got a butcher knife. How gruesome, I thought. I didn't think I could ever stab anyone, but it made me feel a little safer to be armed.

The phone started ringing. How rude, I thought. Doesn't that person know I am in the middle of a very important investigation? I answered the phone. As if on cue, it was Mom. When things get sticky you can count on her to know about it. I explained the situation, knife in hand, and kept watch down the hallway for any noise or shadows. I had not had time to search the rest of the house, and I was now beginning to lose my nerve. I was somewhat on edge. I cut our conversation short and called my friend's house to summon Johnny and my kids home. After all, he was the man of the household. He should be the one to investigate and risk life and limb. I needed to stay in one piece. Besides, someone had to be left to keep up the laundry and wash all the dishes around here.

Johnny and the kids arrived in less than ten minutes. I was waiting on the front porch, ready to make a run for it, if necessary, as they pulled into the driveway.

Feeling there was safety in numbers, we grouped together and searched each room and closet in the house, not quite sure what we would do if we stumbled onto someone. The culprit would no doubt surrender upon seeing such an on-slaught. Finding nothing, assured that no one had invaded our personal habitat, we settled in for the night.

About forty-five minutes later, we noticed a huge fire down the road, right in the middle of it, about the distance of two acres from our house. Everyone pushed to get a view from the garage window. We could make out that it was a car on fire. Flames jumped high into the night air as the entire car was engulfed.

It's surprising how much excitement you can get in the middle of nowhere. This was turning out to be a very inter-esting night.

The fire department volunteers arrived on the scene—all three of them—and the next hour was spent watching the town's finest at work putting out the blaze.

Now it all seemed to tie together. Someone was obvi-ously stuck in the snow and, needing assistance, ran to my house. Getting no answer at the front door, he must have run around the side to the back door. Seeing the light on, he must have assumed someone was home but didn't hear him. It was strange though, since the car on fire was directly in front of another neighbor's house, and they were definitely home because they were out on their front porch watching the excitement. I know these neighbors have a phone the stranded person could have used.

Still uneasy about someone snooping around my house, I decided Johnny and I should go out the front door and retrace the prowler's tracks to see if anything outside had been disturbed.

We looked around in the front, the lighted side, and the back of the house. Two feet of snow made for messy investigation. I loved untouched snow and always hated to mess it up or to have the kids walk all over it. The snow in our yard had been untouched since it had fallen. It was a perfectly smooth blanket of white, hiding all under a glistening sparkling cover.

There had been no trace of wind for two days and the eerie stillness added to the beauty.

Then it struck me that Johnny and myself were messing up the snow. It was our footprints that had trampled a flawless cover of white. It was then I realized that my neighbor and I watched a very tall, very gray man, run the width and length of my house, stop to peer in and then vanish in an instant, do all of that and never leave even a single footprint.

13

DEBBIE
Aspen: Another Turning Point

IN OCTOBER OF 1988, I WAS INVITED TO ATTEND A RETREAT and sit on an abduction panel in Aspen, Colorado. The idea was to invite a number of scientists and other experts to this beautiful place to hear what the abductees had to say about their encounters. They were going to put their heads together to try to come up with some answers. I'll bet they only came up with more questions!

It was a very interesting trip and I was glad I went, even though I didn't fare too well in the high altitude. I had an opportunity to meet some of the most important names in this field and I was impressed. I met Travis Walton, Betty Hill, and Charles Hickson, to name a few. All their stories made so much more sense when I heard them tell it themselves. I had the opportunity to "feel" their emotions as they talked—it makes a difference.

One of the most important people I was to meet in Aspen turned out to be not an experiencer but a researcher, John Carpenter. He would help me change the direction I was going in, to understand myself better and, without being fully aware of the profound influence he was having, give me back control of my life and what was going on with it. I will be forever grateful to God for bringing us together.

I'll never forget the evening I spent in John's suite with him and his wife, Denise, spilling my guts about all the strange things that I had been remembering and writing down over the years. At first I was a little embarrassed about what I was telling him, being fully aware that what I was saying sounded so crazy. But I figured, what the heck —he was a "shrink." If anyone could tell me whether I was losing my mind, he could. I think I wanted him to tell me just that. At least they have medicine to treat mental illness.

Instead, he excitedly began telling me about all these other people he had been working with recently, who were doing the same thing I had been doing for years! A part of me thought, Oh, shit! But another part of me went wild with relief and excitement. This might really mean something!

I have no idea why I zeroed in on John earlier that evening or why I felt that I had to tell him all the memories. I can't decide whether I am remembering information that someone told me long ago during my experiences, or if I am receiving some kind of communication now. A lot of the memories seem so much a part of me—who I am now— that I can't help but feel as if I were born with them already in me—in my soul. For some reason, these kinds of coincidences—"synchronicities," if you will—happen quite frequently when it comes to this type of experience. I think it must have been meant to be.

As we sat there talking, both of us got more and more excited. I became certain that what I was doing, telling John, was the right thing to do.

As I began to tell him about the things I remembered or received, he began to recite my own words back to me! I couldn't believe what I was hearing! I had not told anyone, including Budd, about all the things I was beginning to remember. Where in the hell did he hear this! How did he know? I thought to myself. This is not the kind of stuff that comes up in everyday conversation. Hell, I was still trying to figure out if I had lost my mind!

John told me about a woman he was working with named Jeanne. He thought we should meet. As soon as I heard him say those words, I jumped. I knew that was why I was there, telling him all this. I had to meet this woman. He began to tell me some of the things Jeanne had been writing down for him. I was stunned that a lot of her words were almost identical to mine!

I learned that she was as mystified about some of her writings as I was about mine. And she, too, had grave concerns about her mental health. I knew for a fact I had never met this woman, nor had we ever communicated with one another on the phone or by mail. It just blew me away that we were writing about the same things. I think John was pretty flipped out by it, too.

Before we left Aspen, we exchanged addresses and phone numbers. I thanked Denise for her patience and for allowing me to keep her and her husband up so late that night and I got Jeanne's address from John.

I couldn't wait to get home so I could write my letter to Jeanne. As my pen flowed over the pages of that first letter, I couldn't help but notice how the hand that held it was trembling. I felt breathless as I wrote page after page of memories, citing to her the correlations John had pointed out to me when we had talked that night in Aspen. Oh, how I wished Jeanne had been in Aspen! This would have been so much easier to do face to face.

My hand was having trouble keeping up with my mind and the writing on the paper began to deteriorate rapidly. I finally had to give up for the night and return to it the next morning. After all, what good would it do for me to send Jeanne this letter if she couldn't even read it?

On October 26, 1988, I received a letter from Jeanne.

John had give her my address and told her about our similarities. She apparently wrote her letter to me the same day I wrote mine to her and her first letter to me beat my first letter to her!

Her letter—more than half a dozen pages—contained almost the same things that I had written her. It was like reading my own letter back to myself. Here's a little bit of what she wrote and I quote it with her permission:

> First of all, I want to thank you for putting your experiences in book form. It was your book, *Intruders,* and the article in *Omni Magazine* that began to stir up my memories . . .
>
> I really thought I was a nut case during those two years. I used to bitch myself out for even considering the possibility of it all. Uncovering all this stuff has been a relief and a headache.
>
> I've gone through stages of terrible aloneness and feeling different from everyone I know. Here I was, remembering all these amazing, incredible things, and I had no one to talk to about it.
>
> While reading *Intruders,* I was relating to your experiences and not knowing why. There was a familiarity to it that frightened me. I knew, even back then, that I really wanted to talk to you. Now I have the chance. Everything John told me really blew me away! Damn, woman, we've obviously seen the same things! All of this really hasn't sunk in. But it's more verification, and that's what I need. I still have trouble believing it all.

I can't describe to you how it felt to hear from someone who could really understand what I was feeling. As I read these parts of the letter, I felt like crying with relief. She really understood! She knew! I won't reprint the whole letter here because it could take up a whole chapter of its own. And a lot of the things we have written are still being used as control information by several researchers. But I will tell you that the details we compared were nearly identical, along with our feelings about the whole thing.

Jeanne and I are still very close. As a matter of fact, we eventually lived together in the same house for a while in 1993—Jeanne, her daughter, my two sons, and my new husband, K.O.—one big happy family. When Jeanne and her daughter pulled up in my driveway, I felt the relief one feels when all the kids are finally home just as the big storm is about to hit. Even though she is a few years older than I, I feel very protective of her. She feels like my child.

Jeanne and I participated in a test of sorts, for John Carpenter and a man named Forest Crawford. Forest was a friend of John's and he was also a state section director for the MUFON group in Illinois. They had devised a test for abductees who were remembering-receiving information. They were looking for correlations in the information. Boy, did they find it in Jeanne and me!

With Forest's and Jeanne's blessings, I will share with you some of my information and the correlating information that Jeanne wrote:

Question: How do you use light?
Debbie—Light, in its many forms, can be used in many different ways: nutrition, healing tissue, travel, disassemble molecules/pass through (as) light/reassemble, light as a means of self-propulsion.

Jeanne—We travel by means of light fusion. We are able to travel great distances using this power. It is a transformation of light energy to light fuel. It is efficient and powerful. We have harnessed this energy and magnified it to transport us in our travels through the universe. You were brought on board our craft by means of spectral transport. Your essence was blended with the light beam. It is one method of matter transference. The light particles penetrate your atomic structure, which is recorded into the transposer memory. Matter is then reconstructed at the desired site of appearance. Light penetration of matter causes matter to become light which can be controlled and directed to the chosen area of reintegration.

Question: What is the purpose of the implants?

Debbie—Tracking, monitoring of the individual and sensory receptors, and occasionally altering the energy level of the individual to facilitate necessary communications and molecular changes for the greater good, through adjustment of energy levels.

Jeanne—The sensory implants have many uses. They are tracking devices. They record sensory input from the subjects. They register pollution levels in the subject. They measure stress levels. We are able to study migrational habits of your people. It enables us to communicate with our test subjects, even from great distances. It is a constant surveillance for our chosen ones. The implants are also warning devices capable of alerting us to certain dangers threatening the individual. It lessens the possibility of premature death of the chosen. They cannot be completely protected, but it minimizes our loss.

Question: Do you eat or drink?

Debbie—Absorption through the outer covering of the body, skin, through the soft tissue inside the mouth. Energy ray (light of some kind?), nutritional fluids. Waste excreted through the skin. We do not drink as you understand drink. Do not "swallow"; fluid is absorbed through the tissue in the mouth.

Jeanne—Our method of consumption is very different from your own. We absorb what we need from our environment and yours. It is similar to photosynthesis. We need light, mineral substances not existing on your planet, proteins, and moisture.

Question: What is God?

Debbie—There is no perfect "religion," no perfect people. There is only life. Life, in its purest form, is the beginning, the base from which all that exists originated. Yours, mine, all life, are merely tributaries of a great river. We hold all life in highest esteem, for we are all a part of that life. This is not merely blind faith. We have swum "the river," so to speak, and you, too, shall swim "the river" when you are fully prepared. These words that you restrict yourself to make it very difficult to pass on to you the information you seek. Religion is a sociological phenomenon, unique to your species. This is a creation of man. Not to be confused with the Spirit. "God" is the Spirit. Jesus was a man, created by the Spirit to help you to understand, on your own level, in your own terms and times. Obviously you were not ready. The process will continue until you have reached the level of understanding set forth for your form of life by the Spirit from which you have come. Can you possibly understand? You have made your lives of choice, and you have left no room for the Spirit within you. Now is the time to begin to remember that from which you came. Look into yourself. Look about you. All that is beautiful, all that is ugly, but with soul, all that radiates life, is the Spirit, is what you call God. You have been blinded by your lives. You have let your negativity and your fear keep the inner eye closed. Do not fear. God is life, eternal. Our greater good is that which works together to bring to the Spirit that which belongs to it. To give It strength and life. For to bring It life, we give life to ourselves, as well. Remember, there is only life if you believe, there is only love if you believe, there is only evil if you believe. If you believe that these things exist for you, then they will. If you do not believe that they exist for you, then they will not. You have been given this choice.

Jeanne—As I have told you before, God is the life essence of the Universe. We relate to this essence through respect for all life. We protect life when it is endangered. This is our goal. Our method of worship is a meditation to our inner selves. We become attuned to the universal life-force.

There is much more to the correlations that John and Forest found in their studies. I hope they will someday write a book of their own. There is no way I can put it all in here; there is simply too much. And it doesn't just involve Jeanne and me. There are many, many people, all over the country, writing the same things. Most of us have never met or heard about the other ones. I was just lucky enough to have found Jeanne, thanks to John.

I can't say whether I believe in channeling. I have had several people tell me that I am channeling this information. I really don't know. I am certainly not in any position to judge anyone else's beliefs. I just don't have enough information about channeling to make an intelligent assessment of the whole idea.

I can't help but feel that a lot of this has always been with me. Or, at least, that someone told—taught me, if you will

—all this information years ago, when I was just a little kid. And it's been locked up in my subconscious, waiting for the right time—for me to "wake up" and remember.

I would start to remember-receive information at the strangest times. I would be doing anything from washing dishes to driving my son to baseball practice, when something would come to me. I would begin to have all these thoughts invade my everyday thinking to the point where I could no longer concentrate on what I was doing until I wrote down whatever it was I was remembering-receiving. I have even had to pull my car to the side of the road and write something down because I was afraid I would have an accident if I didn't! It always seemed to hit me like a ton of bricks. I would be so exhausted afterward that I would often take a little nap.

I awakened from deep sleep more than once with whole paragraphs floating around in my head and there was no way I would be able to get back to sleep until I wrote it all down. I wrote several poems this way and it was years before I fully understood the deep meaning of the messages in these poems. (I've included two such poems in the appendix.) It just blew me away that I was writing such deep, meaningful things. Some of the technical stuff was way beyond my scope of knowledge. The anxiety I felt before something would come to me was terrific. I would sweat and tremble. I felt as if there was so much in my mind that couldn't come out, my head might burst! Then, it would finally come up to my conscious self. I'd write it down, and it would feel like some of the pressure would let up—until it built up for the next time. What an experience those few years were.

I also did several of the drawings in this book in the same manner. I was able to look at a blank piece of paper and see —on the paper—what I had to draw. It was as if something in my mind was projecting the image onto the blank paper and I just traced the images and filled in the shadows.

In 1989, someone came into my home while I was out of town and took two art pads full of sketches, two journals, and the sculpture of the alien's head I had done years before. They also read my diary. Whoever it was left our back door wide open and left other telltale signs he had been there. He neglected to touch our expensive video and game equipment or anything else in the house that was of value. I want whoever took my things to know that you can take my physical things, but you can never remove what's in my mind. Everything is burned into my mind so deeply that I will never forget any of it. I'll just make more drawings and rewrite what you took. If you have some kind of problem and need help, I pray you find it.

I had been told by "them" that sleep would bring answers. I was told that anxiety slowed the process and that sleep was optimum for remembering. So when John gave me the set of questions to answer, I took "their" advice. Every night before I went to sleep, I read one of John's questions to myself. That would be the last thing I would have in my conscious mind before drifting off. First thing in the morning, I would read the question again, and write down the first thing that came to me. This is how I finally remembered most of what I wrote. Here are a few more examples of what I remembered—or was told:

Question: Why not a face-to-face confrontation with humans?

Answer: You are physically much stronger than us. To stand face to face with many of you would be foolish and dangerous. Also, many of yours—the mind— could not accept all that we are. To physically touch us would be dangerous for your kind. The mind is not equipped. "Blow a fuse?" Understand? You, and others like you, are restructured, have the capability to absorb without danger. We radiate many things, unintentional. It is our way of "knowing" one another. Also radiate energy that is harmful to many human functions and tissue. To avoid physical contact is primarily for your [humans']safety.

Question: How do we cure schizophrenia?

Answer: Thought dysfunction; study the DNA, changes in the structure are observed with this dysfunction. Why do you continually ask for information on repairing yourselves? You have that knowledge already, why do you not use it for the benefit of all? This is wasteful. [Its tone of voice sounded as if it was pretty annoyed with me! I didn't expect that!]

Question: How do you travel in your ships? [Not the exact wording, but the general idea.]

Answer: Once here, we utilize the electromagnetic waves of your planet. [In my mind, I could see the waves of the ocean and visualized the leaf of a tree floating and drifting, riding the waves, back and forth. Don't ask me why!] We have ships built solely for use on this planet. Other, larger ships that travel much farther, utilize different means of propulsion, depending on distance traveled. Pass through glicks in the continuum by bending light and time. [your words]

This is probably the creepiest thing I ever heard them say: "Don't force memory. When we are ready, you will remember. Anxiety slows our process. Hypnosis will not reveal what is encoded into your genetic structure. Proper body chemistry will. You are currently resistive [their word]. This is understood and was expected. We have begun acceleration. Know this, all is as it must be."

I don't know what this all means. I don't even know if it means anything at all. Please remember, as you read these pages, I am only telling you things I've remembered, I'm not sure what it all means or if it even means anything at all. Somehow, I get the feeling that what we are remembering is not as important as the fact that we *are* remembering. I think *that* means something. This whole process is not quite the same as "hearing voices." It's thoughts and ideas, visual images that I, oftentimes, must use my own words to describe. That can be tough when your vocabulary is limited to begin with. It was a relief to finally meet someone who was having the same thing happen to her and to find out that we weren't alone. There are hundreds, perhaps thousands of people just like Jeanne and me. Perhaps even your neighbor or your brother are like us. It's not surprising that most people will never talk about this openly, and I realize that I took a chance when I decided to. Somebody had to do it.

John and Forest made arrangements for Jeanne and me to meet in St. Louis, Missouri. I really couldn't wait to meet her and was looking forward to the event with great anticipation.

Finally, on April 18, 1990, Jeanne and I met—face to face—for the first time. When I looked into her eyes, I knew. I could see in her what I felt in myself. I knew that there was one hell of a lot more to this whole UFO/abduction thing than anyone could have ever dreamed of. I knew that it went way beyond genetic manipulation or anything else researchers had begun to conclude. I realized that none of them was quite right in their theories. I'm not saying they are all wrong, by any means. I'd just realized that no one had it all wrapped up. What John and Forest were doing was of the utmost importance, not just for Jeanne and me, but for all human beings. I'm telling you that Jeanne, I, and people like us are living proof that something much bigger is happening and it's time for us to open our eyes and see the bigger picture. Start listening and really hear. Start talking and be truthful, not embarrassed by what you remember. Don't ridicule what you don't understand because it could, and probably will, happen to you next.

I had purchased a small crystal pyramid at a gift shop in town, several months before I started writing to Jeanne. Whenever I received a letter from her, I would use that pyramid as a paperweight to hold the pages down as I read. (I did a lot of reading on the front porch at my old house. The light was good and the breeze was relaxing.)

I had thought about sending it to Jeanne because we had several conversations about pyramid shapes and the significance they had for us. When I realized that we would be meeting in St. Louis, I held off sending it so that I could just give it to her when we met. I thought it would be a nice token of our friendship.

When I got to the hotel room, Jeanne was there. We were to be roommates. Cool! As I started to unpack my bags, I came across the pyramid I had packed for Jeanne. When I took it out and gave it to her, I thought she was going to cry. Her jaw dropped and I heard her gasp as she plopped down on the bed. After she regained her composure, she told me that she had been drawing the exact three-dimensional shape, almost obsessively, for the past week. She said that somehow she knew she needed to have one. She had been looking all over her town, trying to find one that she could buy. I told her that I thought I felt it would help her focus her thoughts. I felt that she needed to have it.

The whole time we were together, we were virtually inseparable. We realized that we could practically read each other's minds. When one thought something, the other thought it, too. It was the most incredible feeling I have ever had.

Meeting Jeanne opened up something in my mind that

had been waiting to wake up. The bond that we developed was far-and-away greater than any bond two people could ever share. It ran much deeper than the bond shared by people who have experienced the same kind of trauma. It was as if we were one entity. We are like sisters to this day.

Unfortunately I still had a long way to go, as far as getting a grip on my fear was concerned. I wasn't quite as strong as I thought I was, even after meeting Jeanne. That old saying about strength in numbers isn't always true.

On July 25, 1990, I was sitting in front of my open kitchen window, talking on the phone to John Carpenter. Earlier my oldest son had come into the kitchen to tell me his nose had started bleeding and he couldn't get it to stop. I got him taken care of and resumed my conversation. After we hung up, I decided to go back to his bedroom and check on him before I turned in for the night. It was getting pretty late. Right before I got up from my chair, I saw several flashes in the kitchen. Then there seemed to be some kind of power surge that caused the lights to get very bright. Then they grew dimmer than they should have been. I went into my bedroom and tried to wake up my husband to ask him if there could be something wrong with the air conditioner that would cause this. He was groggy as he said he had seen the way the lights were acting but not to worry about the air conditioner. Some help he was. I don't think he was ever really awake.

I decided to go to the bathroom before I hit the sack, and it was a good thing I did! As I came out of the bathroom and turned toward my son's room to check on him, I saw a small gray alien standing at the end of the hallway. I jumped about a foot off the ground and screamed louder than I thought I ever could. From the feeling I got as I looked at his face, I think I surprised him as well. I got the distinct impression that I wasn't supposed to have seen him. That didn't stop me from tearing off down the hall, sliding around the doorway into my bedroom, and slapping at the light switch with my open hand. The lights came on and then went off again as I dove from the doorway into the bed. (If you could see the layout of my bedroom, you'd know what a feat this was!) Needless to say, I woke my husband up, for sure this time! I buried my face in the pillow next to him and clung to him for dear life. He kept shaking me and screaming, ''What's wrong, Debbie? What did you see? What's out there?'' I could not talk. I guess I was in some sort of shock. I could hear him yelling at me but I could not respond. At one point, I even found myself thinking, It's just James. Talk to him. No, they just want you to think it's James. It's really them. How crazy can one get!

It took all of ten minutes before I could actually talk to him and tell him what I had seen. He was spastic. When I finally lifted up my head to look at him, I could see that the pillow I had been clutching was covered with blood. Not a huge amount, but enough to see that there was something wrong. I looked at my hands and saw two triangular gouges in the palm of my left hand. They were bleeding rather profusely. I first thought that I had cut myself on the switch plate I had slapped as I sailed around the door and into the bed. I finally got up and looked at the switch plate to see just where I could have cut myself. There was no blood on the switch plate and there was nothing I could have cut myself on. I still don't know how it happened.

Would you believe, throughout all that commotion, my son never woke up? The next day he was fine and had no recollection of anything the night before, including his crazy mother's shrieks. Lucky kid!

On August 10, 1990, we went on the camping trip from hell. Let me explain.

We all loved to camp. We had been looking for a spot to visit that was new to us. We were getting tired of the same old places. A girlfriend of mine suggested we check out Lieber State Recreational Area. Her family went there a lot and they loved it, except, she said, "for all the mosquitoes." (She warned me to take along a lot of Off.)

The morning we were to leave, I had this funny feeling that we shouldn't go, and I told my husband so. Despite my feelings, we took off for the campgrounds, about an hour's drive from our home.

Halfway there, we ran into a car accident on the highway. It was blocking our exit so we were pretty much stuck. I told James this was a bad omen.

When we got there, I hated the place right off. First they gave us a site too small for our tent so we had to switch. The only other site left was right next door to Ma and Pa Kettle, their twelve kids, two hound dogs, and a 1957 Chevy pickup with three-foot speakers in the bed blaring out the latest tunes by Boxcar Willy. If they hadn't left the next morning, I would have.

I noticed, right away, that there didn't seem to be any wildlife around this place. I mean no birds or anything. I figured the Kettles must have scared them away. I'd give it a few more days before I worried about this one. I also noticed that there were no visible bugs of any kind. I remembered my girlfriend warning me about the bugs and thought this was rather strange. Despite the fact that I and my youngest son felt something crawling on us, continuously, from the time we got there until the time we left, we never did see one bug. Nor did we ever hear a bird sing or see a wild animal of any kind (except the three cottonmouth snakes that chased us away from three different fishing holes). I thought that was rather strange, too.

I took a few pictures of the boys roasting marshmallows over the campfire late one afternoon (see photos). After we returned home and I got the pictures developed, I could see what I had only felt while I was there and I knew I was right about that place. The first photo was fine. The second one, taken a few moments later, was a mess of whirling energy and where my son should have been, there was a large, amber-colored eye with a diamond-shaped pupil, just like the one I had seen in my head on October 30, 1988. The third picture is okay except you can see the energy moving off in the background, through the trees.

After I saw these pictures, I was glad we had left two days earlier than we had planned to. Funny thing was, the kids didn't protest too much about leaving early. Normally we would have had a fight on our hands.

Halfway home, all at once, we all said out loud, together, "Boy, am I glad to be going home!"

14

KATHY
No Place to Hide

TIME MARCHED ON, TO A SLIGHTLY DIFFERENT BEAT THAN THE norm. Budd's statement that the weird encounters in our family would stop proved not to be the case, many times.

During this period I had an experience that scared me more than any other I can consciously remember. Mom and I had played bingo this particular night and I was returning home through the country about 11:30 P.M. I casually glanced east and saw three craft heading in my direction in a straight line, each probably about one mile apart. There was one large headlight directly centered on the front of each craft. From that angle I saw no other lights.

I decide to stop there in the middle of nowhere and let each pass overhead in order to get a better look. As it passed over I couldn't make out any definite shape but I saw it had a single red taillight centered directly on the rear. Again, I saw no other lights, just one white on the front and one red on the back.

I continued to sit there alone, waiting for the second craft to pass over, and I glanced back to the first craft. I was taken off guard when, instead of seeing the single red tail-light, I saw the bright white headlight and realized the first see them, but they will never know what their light did to my heart. I was almost afraid to move, half expecting the "mother ship" to be sitting there in the road beside me. I had been so excited earlier. Now I was mad, cold, disgusted, and in no mood to be blinded by such a bright light taking me so unexpectedly.

They asked me if I was having car trouble—a logical question since I was sitting in the middle of a smoke screen.

"Yes," I replied meekly. I really wanted to say, "Good guess, Barney Pfife," and get out and smack his face. I restrained myself, not wanting to top my night off in jail. Horizontal stripes don't do a thing for me anyway.

The policemen said they had to respond to an accident two blocks down the road and they would be back in a few minutes, so I should just stay in my car and keep the doors locked. I knew immediately that wouldn't make me feel too secure, this car was such a rusted piece of garbage that a six-year-old could simply rip off the entire door with little effort. I shook my head in acknowledgment and did as I was instructed.

Off they went, sirens blaring, and there I sat getting very cold.

I'm not known for my patience or doing what people tell me to do, so after about five minutes I decided to walk the block to the fire station. I knew someone would be there.

Inside the fire station, I called Mom to come rescue me. She arrived in about ten minutes and while I waited I had a nice chat with a medic, the only person I saw who was awake. He convinced me that my car had probably broken a generator belt or maybe just had a stuck choke and that I might be able to get it the four miles back to Mom's house rather than have the city tow it off or have to pay seventy-five dollars to have it towed myself. Spending seventy-five dollars for a two-hundred-dollar car certainly seemed like a waste, so I decided that when Mom arrived I would take one more shot at trying to get it back to her house.

When Mom arrived, I went outside more determined than ever to get my car back to her house. As we backed out of the parking lot, we glanced to the sky, more out of habit than actually expecting to see anything odd. We certainly felt that we had seen our limit for one night. As unbelievable as it seemed to us, we looked up to see the same large "mother ship" or whatever it was, sitting midair almost directly over the fire station. As we sat there in shock and disbelief, the huge, beautiful, unearthly craft lumbered ever so slowly off, until it was no longer visible. We started to laugh, either from fright, fatigue, or the lateness of the hour. Laughing was probably not the appropriate response to such a grand finale for such an unusual evening, but to a couple of weatherbeaten UFO watchers such as ourselves, it seemed like exactly the thing to do.

It was becoming hard to tell the players without a program now. Exactly who was watching whom? I could visualize two or three alien beings, sitting up there looking down and thinking to themselves, Why didn't that fool just leave her car alone, take her father's car home, and worry about it tomorrow? Earthlings are so stubborn. Are they looking down, reading my mind, and impressed with themselves that they have scared us out of our wits? Are they insulted when we laugh at the sight of them? Are they aware that we might sit in our car and laugh, but if that "mother ship" would have started to come closer to us, started to land or follow us, that both Mom and I would have died on the spot. I could almost see the obituary now: TWO PIG-HEADED BINGO PLAYERS WILL BE LAID TO REST FRIDAY AND THEIR REMAINS WILL BE PRESSED INTO BINGO CHIPS AND SEALED IN A FRUITCAKE CAN. A fitting tribute.

When we could no longer see the "mother ship," we returned to my car. I was now more determined than ever to try one more time to at least get the car back to her house. Surprisingly enough, the car started right up and off I went, "hell bent for election," back to her house, leaving a smoke trail behind. I looked like a skywriter zipping down the main streets. My smoke was probably spelling out CAUTION MADWOMAN ABOARD.

I made it to Mom's house and took Dad's car home. I arrived at 3:15 A.M. without any incidents along the way.

Johnny was again awake and had been since 12:30 A.M. waiting for me. I could have called home after all; his good night's sleep had been trashed anyway.

The next morning a thought crossed my mind. Maybe "someone" or "something" was trying to watch over me. Perhaps if my car had not started to smoke I would have kept driving that night and might have been in the accident the police were responding to, just two blocks away from where I had stopped. Maybe a guardian angel was trying to keep me in one piece. Maybe it was just luck; good luck camouflaged as bad luck. Maybe I was of some use to someone somewhere. Maybe the whole night was just a series of coincidences.

Whatever the case, both Mom and I know that we watched several unearthly flying craft for several minutes in several places of the city together. We knew that both of us couldn't be "seeing" things at the same time. We know what we saw, we just don't know why.

The very next evening, February 4, Mom and Dad saw a craft similar to one of the group of four she and I had seen the previous night, again over their house at approximately 7 P.M. It had one headlight, the same slow flight speed and low altitude. They could barely hear any engine noise and were positive it was no plane.

My family and I continued our daily routine, walking the fine line between reality and who-knows-what, our life occasionally broken up by the continuing series of unexpected and unexplained events. The Davis family had been discussed in various symposiums and at official gatherings of people interested in studying the UFO experience. Most of the family member's names had been changed to disguise their identity, so I felt confident that my privacy was fully protected.

My parents have not confided to any other family members, outside of us, about any of the strange occurrences they have been involved in. I often wonder how the remaining relatives will react when they find out, and no doubt sooner or later they will find out. I am not quite sure why my family chose not to include various aunts, uncles, and my only remaining grandparent. When the entire story of our family's bizarre life-style becomes public knowledge, I won't be surprised if the remaining relatives don't have stories of their own to tell. Perhaps our three-generation encounters go deeper than we even know. Luckily for "Johnny," his family all lives out of state except for one brother. They know nothing of the entire situation and are most profound nonbelievers; I am sure I will have to take the blame for corrupting their youngest son. I can almost hear them now—"I knew you shouldn't have married that crazy Hereford. Now look at what she has gone and done to you!"

There was speculation that my family was being watched not only by those not of this Earth, but also by equally mysterious people who were indeed from this Earth. We have reason to believe that our phones have been tapped, and I have occasionally caught myself picking and choosing my words so as not to appear to be a total rube. That in itself is ridiculous, since you obviously can't make a silk purse out of a sow's ear. I feel that anyone who can stand to eavesdrop on the phone in my house for any length of time, must be quite a hardy soul. After all, when there are four teenagers sharing one phone, the conversations of childish drivel would challenge even a saint's patience. Whoever has been listening must get paid quite well, otherwise he or she would have leaped off a skyscraper by now.

Mysterious black helicopters, completely devoid of any identification, are common sights around my house, Debbie's house, and my parents' house. I am positive they are also watching us. Not only are they obvious about their movements, but they appear at the strangest places. On one occasion, "Stevie" and I were driving down a deserted country road not far from our house when a loud rumbling noise drowned out even our thoughts. Since there was no other traffic, I naturally assumed my car was disintegrating, which could have been very possible at the time. I continued driving for a few blocks, but decided to stop before the car fell apart completely. The instant I stopped, a huge black helicopter continued directly above our car, so close I thought it might knock out the windshield. If I had been on the roof of my car, I could have reached out and touched someone.

When Stevie and I recovered from our shock, we braced ourselves for an explosion, because I was certain the craft would crash. After all, it would take a real lowlife dirtbag to throw such a scare into two innocent bystanders such as ourselves.

We watched for several minutes as the lowlife dirtbag continued his journey, staying dangerously low to the ground. I was beginning to wish he would not crash but maybe just clip off a propeller. The fool nearly scared me to death. Some people have absolutely no class at all.

These odd helicopters could be seen almost daily around our houses. They are so obvious about their flights it is almost comical. On occasions too numerous to even remember, they have hovered around my house, above my house, and above me for several minutes at a time, not trying to hide themselves or the fact that they are watching us. Even when I am outside and obviously watching back, it doesn't seem to bother them. They just sit there in midair, about sixty to ninety feet above the ground, whirling and watching. They are completely without identification and are always low enough so that I could easily see the pilot, if the windshield were clear glass. But the windshields are smoky black, with a finish that makes it impossible to see who's inside.

I have gone visiting friends twenty miles away and sat outside as one would fly over us. I have gone to Debbie's house many times and, upon getting out of the car, I have looked up to see a black helicopter. I have been to my parents' home and watched as one flits around behind the trees. Mom will look up and say to me, "Who are they and what do they want from us?" Then she will actually stand there and wait for me to answer like I am some kind of double agent or something. I just look at her and shake my head and reply, "Why is grass green?"

Each of us has developed the ability to distinguish the sound of these black helicopters from ordinary helicopters. They make a distinct *whomp-whomp* sound as the propeller whirls around, and they are much louder than ordinary helicopters.

When I hadn't seen them for several weeks, I made the remark to "Johnny" that they must have gotten tired of watching us work so hard. He never hesitated in his answer. He just looked up and said, "They're coming at night, I can hear them at all hours." Our oldest son agreed that he also heard them late at night.

If, as most people seem to think, they are from the government, I cannot see where I pose a threat to national security by mowing my lawn or planting flowers.

I almost feel the need to dress up before I take out the trash. I certainly hope they have taken no pictures of me. I am probably the most unphotogenic person ever to have lived. They flew over once while I was sunbathing and I instinctively tried (note the word *tried*) to suck in my stomach. Even though my basic black bathing suit was made to be slenderizing, from that angle I would surely look like a beached whale on a lawn chair.

One mid-December evening, we had friends visiting and noticed that at least two and possibly three of these unidentified helicopters circled our house. They approached from approximately five miles west and circled approximately two acres east of our house, traveling a path slightly wider than our property. At times, two of these helicopters would meet, one on each side of our house, as they continued their circular path. This went on for almost three hours. As we talked, occasionally either my friend or I would remark how odd that was and how extremely irritating.

So here we are watching and being watched. Many times we cursed the day Debbie opened the levee of our privacy to let it spill out into the cold, cruel world. Even though the rest of us opted to remain out of the limelight, so to speak, we were also being watched.

By this time Debbie was speaking at UFO gatherings and being asked to do TV and radio interviews. None of us ever thought one letter to a stranger in New York would start all this. Budd eventually wrote *Intruders,* and then the story ended up on TV as a miniseries.

Budd started the ball rolling ten years ago and it hasn't stopped rolling yet.

15

DEBBIE
Acceleration

ONE ASPECT OF THIS PHENOMENON THAT NEVER CEASES TO amaze me is the profound, undeniable changes we all seem to eventually go through, during and after our experiences. I call it "waking up." Some people seem to take longer than others, yet we all seem to be moving in the same direction. Those of us who survive relatively intact seem to be evolving into a new being. We have one foot in the linear mode of thinking—that which exists only in our minds—and one foot in the higher plane of free thought. It's almost as if during an experience we are reborn, ready to grow into a newer, better model. All priorities change and what used to be important to us, the things we used to worry about, all becomes minuscule in the broader scheme of life.

We also seem to develop the ability to sense this within others, to the point that we feel drawn to one another, like moths to a flame. The power of that attraction is so great that even geographical distance means nothing to us. We overcome tremendous obstacles just to be together. And when we are together, we quietly draw strength from one another. I believe this goes far beyond just the sharing of a traumatic event, the bonding that occurs in those situations, although I am certain that is a small part of it. When we find one another, it's as if we have found a little piece of our-selves—our heart and soul. We share an unspoken and often unconscious knowledge that no words can describe. We feel certain emotions that the confinement of human speech and written words prevent us from expressing fully. We love so deeply, so unconditionally, that it is almost overwhelming to those who have not yet discovered that part of them-selves. We all seem to share the overwhelming desire to help others feel this way, for themselves, for those around them, for this planet, and for all life.

After years of thinking about it and discussing it with family, friends, and those whom I consider to be my teach-ers in this life, I have come to the conclusion that I was born into this life with a purpose. As the years pass and I mature, the purpose has become clearer to me.

I have learned that the most important thing I can do with all the experiences I have had is to concentrate on how I fit into the bigger picture and do the best I can with what I have to benefit humanity and myself. I have realized that I cannot always control the situations I find myself in, but I can control how I choose to react to those situations, emotionally and spiritually.

I am certain that I am not the only one to finally remem-ber what we are all supposed to be doing. I believe there are thousands of us just beginning to ''wake up.''

I began talking to several researchers who were begin-ning to realize the same things and wondered what it all meant. In recent years they had begun receiving material that echoed much of what I had been telling them. One of these researchers was Linda Howe, an Emmy-winning tele-vision documentary producer and author of a UFO book, *Alien Harvest*.

We became close so quickly that I suspect she is more involved in this whole thing than she thinks she is. But I won't go into that here. I think many of the researchers in the field of UFOs are more deeply connected than they know. Even the debunkers are "driven" to debunk for a reason. (And some of them are so "driven," they are about to drive over the edge!) Love, hate, and fear are emotions of passion. In order for one to have great passion about something, there has to be some emotional investment in it. If the loudest, most obnoxious debunkers didn't have a very deep emotional investment in the subject of UFOs (personal involvement, a big paycheck, etc.), then they simply wouldn't care about what other people thought or believed. They wouldn't take it upon themselves to "set the world straight."

Whenever something unusual happened, I would call Linda. It was more like talking to a friend than talking to a researcher. She would make note of what I told her, understanding that I felt as if none of it might be important or interpreted correctly by me. But, just in case someone else came up with it, it might be good to have it written down somewhere.

In January of 1992, I called Linda. I had awakened in a frenzy, very excited and "up." I just knew that something wonderful was about to happen. I told Linda that I felt as if this was the year my life would change. That *everything* about me and my life would change and it would be wonderful!

I have awakened in good moods before, but this was ridiculous! I had never felt like this and I immediately thought to call Linda, and tell her how I felt.

In the months that followed that feeling and the phone call to Linda, lots of wild things began to happen.

In March 1992, I won a thousand dollars in a radio contest! I have never won anything like that in my entire life. I also met a really neat person that month. His name was Joe.

Joe had been having a difficult time dealing with experiences similar to mine and one of his close friends had contacted Indiana MUFON, looking for some help for him. Jerry Seivers, Indiana MUFON assistant state director, contacted me with Joe's address. We exchanged letters and soon made plans to meet.

We agreed to meet at the Denny's restaurant close to my house. I got there about fifteen minutes before Joe. My husband James and I ordered coffee and waited for Joe to arrive. Joe told me he would be wearing a sweatshirt with a wolf printed on it. Several men entered the restaurant wearing sweatshirts and I looked them over, wondering if they were Joe. They weren't. When he did come in, he was wearing a jacket. I guessed he must have forgotten he had told me to look for the sweatshirt. But for some reason I knew who he was. When he walked through the door, I just happened to be looking at it and when my eye set on him, I jumped a foot! I turned to James and said, "That's him! I know it!" James was rather shocked at my reaction but, having lived with this whole thing for some time now, he just sat back and watched.

Joe turned in my direction, made eye contact with me, and let go with the biggest grin I have ever seen. It was instant recognition and instant friendship.

The three of us, James, Joe, and I, sat in the restaurant drinking coffee for at least two hours. It was an eye-opening experience. Joe and I found that we shared a great many memories and thoughts. It was the strangest feeling, talking to Joe, as if he and I were sharing the same mind. I got the distinct impression that we had done this before, at another time, in another life, if that's possible. And I felt very protective of him, just as I had felt about Jeanne.

As we said our good-byes in the parking lot, Joe handed me a book he had read and wanted me to read. The book was called *Black Elk Speaks*. Joe knew, through our letters, that I had become interested in Native American heritage since I found I have Native American ancestry. He felt I would find the book interesting and he was right. I did. He also told me of another book he thought I should read. This book was titled *Return of the Bird Tribes* by Ken Carey. We planned for him to bring his copy of this book when we got together again at my house in the next few weeks.

Joe did return to my house two weeks later. And he did bring the other book.

I was amazed at how my animals reacted to Joe. They were all over him and seemed to sense he was a good person, a truly special person. My birds sang for him and my dog and cat wouldn't leave him alone, each wanting to sit on his lap. My animals had never reacted to a stranger like this before and I was quite surprised!

We sat up talking until late that night. Even James seemed to be mesmerized by Joe's soft voice and gentle manner.

Before Joe left that night, he handed me the book he had brought with him and I returned the one he had given me at the restaurant. I had recognized the title when he first mentioned it. Another friend of mine had asked me to read the afterword of this book several weeks before I even met Joe. I thought the coincidence of two of my best friends asking me to read the same book was interesting, so I got into the book right away. Of course, I started with the afterword. Remember, I always start a book at the ending! As I read those words I could feel the excitement rise in me. The man who wrote this book was talking about me! I know this sounds weird, but I recognized everything he was saying. I already ''knew'' what he had written and he explained things that I had wondered (about myself) for years and years. It was such a relief to read those words, to know that someone else had understood my feelings!

I called the first friend, and told him I had finally read the book he had recommended to me and I told him how I came about reading it. His comment was, "Recognize anything?" I could hear him smiling. He had known that I would really relate to the book.

All the positive messages in that book would help me get through the next few crazy months.

Shortly after Joe's visit to our house, things began to fall apart.

Twice in one week, in the month of March 1992, I woke up beet red. My body was as red as a fire truck and I felt like I was on fire. Mentally I felt wonderful! I felt as if something great was about to happen and I was excited. I was a little concerned about the redness, so I took my temperature to see if I had a fever. It was normal and after about an hour, the redness began to subside. I could watch it slowly leave my body, from head to toe, much like a thermometer goes down. One more odd thing to note in my journal, I thought to myself.

By the end of that week, James and I had noticed that the dog would no longer sleep in the bed with me. This was most unusual. I had been trying to get her out of our bed for years, and now I couldn't get her in! She would pace back and forth at the foot of our bed, whining and scratching. James would pick her up, put her in with me, and she would practically break her neck to get out and away from me. We were puzzled, to say the least.

The topper to this was, by that weekend, James came to me and asked me to sit down. He said he had something important to tell me. We poured some coffee and sat down at the kitchen table. Then James dropped a bomb.

He said that he knew why the dog would no longer sleep with me and that seeing her act strange had made him remember. He told me that one night, earlier that week, he had been awakened by the violent movement of our waterbed. He said the waves were so huge that I nearly knocked him out of bed and he could see the dog flopping helplessly around the bed, dangerously close to the edge. She was moaning and whimpering. I was nowhere to be seen and he couldn't understand how I could have gotten out of the room so quickly if I had been the one to disturb the bed. He got out of bed and proceeded to roam around the house, looking for me. Before he left the room, he saw a tremendous, bright blue flash of light come through the bedroom door. He said that it had come from the back hallway, near the garage access door. Then, for unknown reasons, he decided to go back to bed. Sounds pretty crazy, doesn't it? It gets worse.

The night he described was one of the nights before one of the mornings that I had awakened all red colored, hot, and full of excitement. All this isn't really hard for me to believe, given the person it happened to. We're all getting pretty used to this kind of stuff. What I really couldn't get over was what he said to me next.

James told me he believed he had no business being in my life—being married to me. The exact words he used were, he "was a boat anchor around my neck." He told me that I didn't belong to him or anyone else and he was afraid he'd wake up one day to find me gone, forever. (I don't think he meant I would leave him in the conventional way.) My red flags went up right away.

I really couldn't understand what he was saying. I asked him if he was trying to unload me with a bunch of UFO crap so that he could run off with some other woman and make me think it was somehow my fault. For some reason I got the impression that he had been frightened by some- thing or someone. He was adamant about there not being anyone else, and he insisted that he didn't want us to split. He was also adamant about how he felt and was certain he was right. I told him that if there was no other woman and if he really wanted to stay together then to just forget what he was worrying about, everything would be okay. He reluctantly agreed to drop the whole matter and we went on with the evening's business. Unfortunately his feelings turned out to be prophetic.

Within a week of our conversation something else happened that seemed to confirm that a change was imminent. One morning I awoke covered with cut grass. James had mowed the orchard the evening before. At first I found myself cursing him, thinking that he had dragged grass all through the house on his shoes. After I got out of the bed, I realized that there was no grass anywhere in the house and, for that matter, there wasn't even any on his side of the bed! I looked in the bedroom mirror and was alarmed to find grass stuck to the back of my gown, on the back of my head and on my bare arms and legs! I couldn't figure out what had happened. I felt fine. Actually, I felt great, like those two days when I woke up red.

I got the vacuum cleaner out and as I began to sweep the grass off the bed, I noticed my fingers start to itch. I reached down to scratch them and realized that my wedding rings were gone! Where they had been, the skin had become red and had begun to peel! I became frantic when I couldn't find my rings. I tore the house apart looking for them. I even ripped open the sweeper bag, hoping that I had sucked them up, accidentally. What in the hell was I going to tell James if he noticed they were gone? This was the *second* time that rings James had given me had wound up missing under mysterious circumstances! Was this supposed to be telling me something?

Three days passed before the missing rings turned up. That morning, I was making our bed and had shaken out the bedspread so it would lay flat on the bed. I accidentally hit one of the stones on the window ledge with a corner of the bedspread and knocked it onto the bed. When I placed the stone back on the ledge, there, in the exact place the stone had been, were my wedding rings!

I collect geodes and crystals that I keep on my window ledges so they can reflect the sunlight. They're really beautiful when the sun is bright. The window ledge was the first place I looked when the rings first came up missing. It was directly above the head of my bed and served as sort of a headboard for the bed. I thought perhaps I had taken my rings off and laid them on the ledge in the middle of the night. I looked the ledge over very carefully and the rings were not there. Now, there they were, in the most obvious place, a place I had already looked in over three days before. This seemed pretty weird. But then, so did a lot of things back then.

Our relationship deteriorated rapidly after this. I had become more and more positive that something wonderful was about to happen and, despite the poor state of my personal life, I was in fairly good spirits. James grew increasingly unnerved, to the point where every little thing got to him. He had always been rather moody, but he was getting worse by the day. On one hand, I felt sorry for him; yet, on the other hand, I couldn't let it go on the way it was going, for all of our sakes. I could never say that all the unusual experiences destroyed my marriage—I suspect it was doomed from the start. But I believe they didn't help matters any.

On June 14, 1992, I left. The boys and I moved back to my parents' home, the house where it all started. Moving was such a pain in the rear end, but I felt such a sense of relief, most of the time, that I knew I had done the right thing.

On June 18, 1992, my parents' home was hit by a tornado. Mother Nature has such a way with timing! We had just gotten unpacked, the kids in upheaval, leaving their home, their friends, and their stepfather behind in the old neighborhood. Dad had just turned in his paperwork to officially retire after thirty-five years at the same job. His retirement was to begin in less than a week.

Thank God, we all came through it safely. The house had minimal damage, a broken window, some shingles gone, broken-up guttering, damaged evergreens, broken concrete sidewalk and steps, and a leaking roof. Our vehicles, on the other hand, didn't fare so well. A sixty-five-foot beech tree, twisted off at the trunk by the tornado, bored through my van and my mother's new car. They had just sent off the last payment two days earlier, and my van was free and clear, too.

The vehicles were impaled and the tree landed within ten feet of where I was standing. I watched the tree come at me like a spinning spear and my life flashed before my eyes. I was in such shock and it all happened so fast, I couldn't move! Now, I know what an opossum feels like as he stares into oncoming headlights! The only thing that saved my life that night were the two vehicles.

As the sun rose the next morning, we began to see just how lucky we had been the night before. The whole front of the house was covered by downed trees, so Dad and I went out the back door and around front to inspect the damage. I just stood there crying, feeling as if now I had lost everything I ever had, except my children and my family (the most important things!). The van had been the final link to James.

Finding it had been a dream come true and we had made a lot of plans for that van. Every time I drove it, I thought of how the marriage had failed and how sad I felt about that. The very afternoon of the storm, I had been sitting on the front porch, looking at the van and feeling bad about the way things had turned out with James and me. Mom said someone made sure that I wouldn't have to worry about that anymore. She had a good way of thinking about losing our vehicles. She said that, perhaps, if we had been able to drive those vehicles the next day, we might have been killed or killed someone in an accident. Obviously, if it hadn't been for those vehicles, I wouldn't be here now! She believes there's a reason why everything happens, even if we don't understand right away. I think she's right.

We didn't have electricity for several days after the tornado hit. Since we are on a well and septic system, we had no water or toilet, either. But we'd learned about this in the blizzard of 'seventy-eight, so we were prepared with a generator. Unfortunately the generator had a tendency to run out of gas at the most inopportune times.

On the third night without power, I had a most unusual experience. When I had gone to bed, the generator was running to keep the refrigerator and freezer operational. Sometime during the night it ran out of gas and we lost power. I heard Dad get up to refill the tank with more fuel. As I lay there, in the dark, lonely quiet, thinking about the last few days, I began to realize that I wasn't alone in the room. A soft glow appeared around the foot and sides of my bed. It became just barely bright enough for me to see, standing all around my bed were the strangest crew of people I have ever seen. There were eight in all. Old, young, male, and female, all looking at me with various degrees of concern and curiosity. An old woman was closest to me, at the head of the bed. She leaned over to my ear and whispered, "Don't you remember us?" I lay there, as still as I could, looked over at her through the corner of my eye, and said to her, "No, I don't." Then she said, "We don't actually look like this but we know you've been through a lot recently. You've done very well through it all. We only chose to appear to you in this manner for your benefit. Look at me and you will remember." Then she got *right* in my face, nose to nose. I didn't move, but I closed my eyes as tight as I could and yelled loudly, "*No way* am I looking at you! Go away! I'm not in the mood for this right now! Buzz off!'' She kept telling me to look at her and I kept telling her to buzz off. Finally she said, "Very well. We know you are tired. We will leave you now, but we will be back. Be patient. Things will improve."

Then *boom,* I was alone. As fast as it all happened, it— they—were gone. I felt really strange. I was lying in the exact position I was in when they were there and I was sure I had been awake through the whole thing.

Suddenly the generator kicked in and the lights came back on. I lay there for a few minutes, trying to comprehend what had just happened. Exhaustion finally got the best of me and I drifted off to sleep.

The next morning I woke up, still thinking about what had happened the night before. I told my family about it and then called Budd Hopkins and Linda Howe to tell them. When I talked to Linda, I reminded her of the phone call I had made to her in January, when I had told her this was the year my life would change and it would be wonderful. Then I said to her, "Well, I see the changes, now where's the wonderful part?" I could hear her smile as she told me to be patient. It reminded me of what the old lady had said to me the night before. As it turned out, they were right.

On June 29, I had another "virtual reality" dream. This one was to give me great comfort.

I was standing in front of a small pond. The water level was very low, but rising. I could see water pouring out of a large machine on the other side of the pond. The water began to ripple out in front of me and before I knew what was going on, two men started to rise up out of the water about twenty feet in front of me. One of these men, a tall blond, well-built guy, walked across the surface of the water and right toward me. He told me they were returning water that they had taken to study and that I should come with him. I agreed, so he slipped a pair of tight-fitting rubberlike boots on my feet and walked me across the surface of the pond to the machine that was unloading water. The other man followed behind, quietly.

Inside the machine, he took me to a room with soft lighting. He sat me down and told me that I shared his heritage and that I should remember he had always loved me and always would. He also said that he had known my mother and that she had been to this place, as well. I can't remember what else we talked about, but I think it was mostly trivial stuff. When he finished talking to me, he took me back to where he had first seen me and before he left, he told me that he would be back to check on me again, someday, and to please not forget him this time. I woke up as soon as the dream was over. It left me feeling very warm, safe, and at peace with the world. What a strange way to feel after this kind of a dream!

16

KATHY
Dreamland

DEBBIE WAS BUSY SPEAKING AT CONVENTIONS AND UFO gatherings. She had been on TV and radio and had started using her own name, much to our chagrin. I remained on the sidelines by choice and watched her with a combination of shock and admiration as she exposed her soul for all interested parties. Half of me was aghast that she would actually set herself up for public approval or disapproval. The other half of me felt I should be up there with her. Some days I felt very left out and other days I was extremely glad no one knew my face.

We still feel, even after ten years, that our phones are tapped. Somewhere there could be a small skeleton wearing headphones and holding a blank sheet of paper. We don't know this to be a fact, but then we have had a lot of very bad connections, strange clicking noises, and a feeling of another presence on the line.

To my knowledge I have never been approached by any government personnel, although there were several occasions at my parents' house where strange people were seen snooping about. That's very scary to me. This might sound really off the wall, but I would rather be chased by a UFO than the CIA.

By this time in my life, Johnny had come over to the Yankee side (the lonely side), and my kids had stopped laughing at me. For the first time in many years I no longer had people tugging at me from both sides. Now I only had myself to contend with.

I even began to get encouragement from Johnny. That was a new twist. When I asked him if he wanted me to leave him out of this book, he gave me the go-ahead to write about him. Actually he said, "I don't care," and I took that for a yes. I still don't think he would agree to any hypnosis to fill in the missing eleven hours of his incredible flat-tire night, but he might surprise me someday. I guess he is prepared to deal with his friends and family. Our kids don't even know about that night yet. When this book is published they will sure be surprised. If I fill them in before this book comes out, they may want to start moving out now. They are all grown up, so I can't even use them as an excuse to hold me back any longer. They will just have to go around in wigs and sunglasses.

I am wondering now if I have what it takes to tell our encounters and if I have what it takes to accept the ridicule of the nonbelievers.

I'm just a regular person like everyone else. I hope I am capable of conveying my thoughts in an understandable manner. I really don't care what the nonbelievers think anyway. I know what I have seen and I know what I feel, and right now that is all that is important to me. I also understand the nonbelievers' views. It all seems very unbelievable and scary to someone who has never experienced anything close to it. I respect the debunkers and nonbelievers' views, as I feel everyone is entitled to his own opinion and entitled to voice that opinion.

It's not my style to get on a soapbox and preach my

views to one person or five hundred, so when the time comes, I only plan to state the facts as I know them. I don't know all the answers and I would never try to pretend I do. I only wish I did.

I can empathize with those who have never seen an unidentified flying object or its inhabitants. It would certainly be hard for them to take the whole subject seriously. To describe the alien beings to a nonbeliever as small, gray figures with large black eyes, huge hairless heads, and the ability to communicate telepathically—well, you might as well describe them as purple people eaters and expect the same response. We can only relate what we have seen and brace ourselves for the responses.

In this chapter, I would like to include some of the strange dreams we have had. I ordinarily don't have much faith in dreams and usually don't remember mine. When I do have a dream, no matter how strange it may seem to me at the time, I have tried to write it down the next day. When I have a dream that bothers me and I can't seem to get it out of my head, I can't help but feel that it must mean something, even if it's something I don't want to know or remember.

One dream I had woke me up from a sound sleep and haunted me for several days. I have not discussed this dream with any professional, the main thing that puzzles me is the fact that it doesn't make any sense to me. I will relate it to you and maybe you'll have better luck than I at figuring it out.

I was in a room that reminded me of a doctor's office, very clinical and very white. Everything around me felt as if I were in some type of sterile environment. I had on a long, flowing gown and matching robe and I remember feeling the material and thinking how expensive it must have been. The pale blue fabric felt cool and smooth like the finest satin, and as I smoothed it and felt its richness, I knew it did not belong to me. I felt as if I were in a trance of some kind, moving very slowly and mechanically. I was alone in this room, but not for long. The door opened and in walked a person of average size and height, wearing a white lab coat. I recognized this person immediately, he portrayed a doctor on a soap opera I have watched for years. How retarded, I thought to myself days later. When a person starts dreaming about soap opera characters, it's time to stop watching the soaps. As the ''doctor'' approached me, there seemed to be a conversation between us, but I cannot remember what we discussed. The ''doctor'' apparently wanted me to do something I didn't want to do, but for some reason I felt he wanted me to make the decision on my own and did not want to force me with whatever control he had over me. I don't know what he wanted, but I do remember that I refused. Upon my refusal, I was led into another room where I saw my oldest son Bill lying on a table in the center of the room apparently unconscious.

As I walked up to the table, I couldn't believe my eyes. What in the world was Bill doing here? How could they have made him go with them and why? I got very close to his face and watched him breathe. It looked exactly like Bill, but I wasn't one-hundred-percent certain it was really him. There were other people in the room, seeming like nurses, who would lift Bill up on his feet and let him drop to the ground. The nurses did this several times, much to my annoyance, and I tried to make them stop, but they paid no attention to me. At one point, they let him drop and left me there alone to try to get him back on the table myself, which I couldn't.

At that point, I was taken into another room where I found my daughter Lisa in a trancelike state, being led by two nurses. She did not acknowledge my presence as they walked her back and forth. I looked down and noticed the bottom of her feet were mutilated. The heels of both her feet had been ripped off, exposing bloody flesh to my horrified eyes. I screamed at them to stop making her walk and to lay her down somewhere to get her off her mangled feet. I picked up each foot individually to inspect the damage and now was more puzzled than ever to find that instead of bones inside each foot, there appeared to be some type of odd-looking structural support made of metal. Now this is really getting crazy, I kept thinking. If this is a robot, why didn't they make a real-looking bone sticking out to really scare me? This was probably not Lisa, but I couldn't take any chances. I had to make them stop torturing her anyway.

So now there I was with an unconscious Bill, who's probably not Bill, a mangled Lisa with bars in her feet instead of bones, and a soap opera doctor.

As the World Turns, The Guiding Light toward *The Edge of Night,* I'll be *Loving* my quest through *General Hospital* looking for *All My Children,* longing for a better life in my *Search For Tomorrow.* That does it, I have tripped over the fine line between sanity and madness, and we know what side I landed on.

By this time in my dream, I was becoming hysterical when I was led back into the first room with the phony doctor. I was totally calm immediately and walked past him, determined to pretend that he wasn't actually there.

At that point, the doctor took off his lab coat and, before my eyes, transformed into a small, revolting, very frightening being. I distinctly remember looking at his arms and thinking how awful and repulsive he was. His arms were so very thin and white, perfectly straight, like there were no muscles and just a very fragile bone holding the flesh together. They looked very pliable like a little "Gumby" arm, and I thought they could be bent and twisted into about any shape you wanted. His skin looked spongy, like a mushroom.

This part of the dream is vague. I remember this ugly

little Gumby person, very close to my face, telling me that I could never tell anyone about this.

At this point, the door opened again and "Johnny" walked in. I was screaming and crying, trying to tell him about Bill and Lisa and how these people wouldn't let me go and he had to help me get the kids out of there. As I carried on ranting and raving, I began to wake up. I somehow knew if this dream continued, I would find Johnny turning into something that wasn't Johnny.

I woke up, safe in my bed, Johnny beside me (the real Johnny) and Bill and Lisa safe in their rooms.

That dream haunted me for months and I don't know why. It was so stupid it should have been comical, but it wasn't then and still isn't now. Now I can understand why other people talk of their compelling, haunting dreams—and I can relate to them.

I only had two other dreams that were crazy like this one. One doesn't seem worth mentioning. It seems strange to me that after living such a unique life of strange unidentified encounters that I would have had many more bizarre dreams throughout my lifetime. It seems as though my subconscious should have surfaced during my sleep, recalling at least flashes of forgotten memories. Was that odd dream perhaps a memory flash of a similar incident stashed away in my mental bank? Could my mind have made the "doctor" into a soap opera character in order to exchange a frightening face for a familiar face? If it was just a strange dream with no bearing, why did it haunt me so?

My mother had a particularly strange dream that I would like to include in this chapter. You would have to know her to appreciate this dream. My mother is somewhat psychic and has had numerous dreams that come true. If she dreams about any happening more than once, you can feel guaranteed that it will happen. That sounds very strange, but we are used to it and have actually seen the end results. She has dreamed about winning money and does. She once dreamed that Johnny would be involved in a minor auto accident, related the details of the dream to me about two months before the accident happened, and it did happen exactly as she described. She recently dreamed a tree would fall through her bedroom window at night, crushing the house but injuring no one. That next summer, a giant tree was uprooted and fell to the ground, narrowly missing the house, but it crushed her car and Debbie's car.

She has had many other dreams that eventually become fact and has had two psychics tell her that she was also a psychic and apparently good enough that one psychic felt that Mom should or could give professional readings.

The strange, crazy dream she had that I am about to relate to you made no sense to either of us. She, like me, never seemed to remember her dreams, so when she told me about this one I wrote it down immediately.

Her dream started out in a huge building with three levels. It was larger than a house and unfamiliar to her. A lot of people were milling around but she wasn't sure what they were doing. She said it reminded her of Las Vegas. That was logical to me as we had been planning a trip to Las Vegas the previous month, but the plans fizzled out. She remembered that Debbie was with her in this large building and was looking at her and saying, "Somebody wants to meet you up there," as she pointed to the upper level of the building.

Mom was carrying a very lightweight, dark-haired baby (shades of *Intruders*), but she did not recognize this baby as belonging to anyone in the family or to an acquaintance.

She and Debbie went upstairs to a large room and walked down a long aisle. There they saw three or four men sitting at a large table with a microphone. She recalled looking at one and saying, "I've met you. You've been here before," but she doesn't recall what this person looked like.

He nodded and smiled at her.

She then went into another room and put this strange baby to bed, apparently having had to haul it around with her all this time. She knew this baby was not her youngest grandson because now he was there with her, standing next to her. She then went through a doorway into a huge room with a lot of machines and a lot of people. She doesn't remember what these people were doing or what these machines looked like or what their purpose might be. She wandered back into the room with the bed and watched someone come in and wake the baby. She watched as the baby and her youngest grandson left the room.

Now I was in the dream. She said she and I went searching for both kids and we found them playing in a puddle of water. The dream became more confusing as we skipped to the open highway in a car that I was driving. She was in the front seat with me and my youngest sister and her son were in the backseat. This was the same grandson who was with her earlier in the dream.

She is not sure which one of us yelled, "Oh, shit" as we all looked up and saw a huge flying saucer coming straight toward us. She remembers seeing a large red light on the bottom and it appeared to be the classical disk shape. She was aware that there were other cars on the highway and, as she glanced toward them, she commented that all the drivers and passengers were unaware of the huge disk hovering above the road.

She remembers that my youngest sister had never seen a flying saucer—at least she didn't recall seeing one—and Mom said to her, "Shari do you see that?" That's when she woke up, so we will never know if Shari saw it or not.

That was a pretty screwy dream, and I don't have the slightest idea of what it might represent. I'm not sure I want to know. I can only relate it as it was told to me. Knowing Mom's track record of her dreams becoming reality, we can only just sit back and see what happens.

As if on cue, two weeks after Mom's dream, we were invited to go on a spur-of-the-moment trip to Las Vegas and on an equally spur-of-the-moment decision, decided to go. Perhaps her dream was just a premonition about the unexpected trip and had nothing whatsoever to do with UFOs, huge rooms, strange babies, and even stranger people. Half of me was totally exhilarated about going to Las Vegas, the other half was riddled with guilt, having made my plane reservations on the easy monthly payment plan, meaning the payments are only easy until they are due.

I left for the airport in my usual state, lunacy. At thirty-three thousand feet in the air, I searched the friendly skies, but the only strange thing I saw was my own reflection in the window glass.

We will be spending three glorious days with no dishes, no laundry and no schedules, I said to myself. A well-deserved vacation, if I do say so myself. Perhaps we will hit the bigtime, perhaps we will hit the skids.

Twenty-four hours later we discovered we had hit the skids. We stayed up all night feeding the slot machines unmercifully. We fed them twenty dollars and they spit back eight dollars when they reached the point of not being able to hold any more. With a mind of their own, they seemed to know when a person mentally vows, "Three more quarters, that's all you're getting." Those three are swallowed up and the machine spits out two in a feeble attempt to keep you there a little longer. It works. You slip in those last two quarters and, bingo, twelve quarters escape into the outside world. Some of them look vaguely familiar, giving you a false sense of hope that eventually all your little coins might fall back into your bin. The slot machine has a way of making those twelve quarters sound like five hundred. Bells ring out congratulations to you like a twenty-one-gun salute and build up your confidence, making you feel like this could be the start of something big.

By midafternoon, as we sat down for lunch and the food appeared to have multicolored lights flickering in it and the ice in our glasses rang like bells as it clinked together, we felt it was time to go back to our rooms and finally get some rest. I was broke, having spent my three days' allotment in one. Walking back to the room, we noticed what a beautiful day it was. Another slap in the face. It's un-American to sleep away such a gorgeous day. I guess that served us right.

Two long days later, we were on our way back home, no money, no UFO story, no nothing. The suicide rate in Vegas must be incredibly high—as it is the most depressing place in the world when you are broke. If you're broke you might as well go home, since the casino owners don't intend to make your stay pleasant. As long as you are gambling, they bring you free drinks, one after the other. If you can't afford to gamble, you can't even find a water fountain and are forced to cup your hands together and drink out of the bathroom faucet. I am surprised they don't have pay toilets. Then the downtrodden would surely be forced to vacate even sooner or succumb to standing on street corners begging, "Hey, buddy, can you spare a dime for the toilet?"

As long as you're gambling you'll find a seat. Lose your money and you will stand throughout eternity. Even though you have donated your life savings, it doesn't entitle you to a seat of any kind. Tough luck, booby, move along. Had they made me stand up on the plane, I would have felt I deserved it. Fortunately I got to sit on the plane, and I gazed out the window humming, "Nobody knows the trouble I've seen," until we landed back in Indianapolis.

Two hours after we arrived back home, the bright lights

and ringing bells seemed to be years away. Back to the same old routine and dinner to fix.

That was eight years ago, and since that trip we have been to Vegas one more time. Mom's dream is still in limbo, and with a little luck it will stay there.

As I said earlier, I don't put a lot of stock in dreams—they probably have much more meaning than I am aware of. You are really at your own mercy while you are asleep as you cannot consciously stop yourself from thinking about a subject that you repress while you are awake. You are very vulnerable during sleep, and sometimes you can be your own worst enemy without actually knowing it.

If you are having a lot of emotional problems during your waking hours, it could be helpful if you focus your sleeping mind to a positive channel. Running away from or ignoring your problems will only slow down a recovery. You have to face the situation squarely to deal with it. You cannot move forward till you stop looking back.

It is sometimes helpful to keep a log of your dreams to check for repetition. You should go to the library and read books on the subject to get an idea of what your dreams may mean. If you're having major emotional problems, you should check out support groups or perhaps professional help.

Many support groups are free or only charge a minimal fee, and they have been a great source of strength and help for many. It is always comforting to know that you are not the only person suffering from any specific problem. Perhaps you could be a great help to another person, as we hope we have been for anyone reading this.

Had I never actually seen a UFO and remembered it, it would be easy to slough off the dreams I have mentioned here as purely dreams, with no meaning whatsoever. But after you actually see a craft or visitors, it makes you wonder if your dreams could really be unconscious memories of actual events. Could they be memories of encounters my conscious mind simply refuses to accept?

The human mind is so complicated and powerful it's hard for us to actually grasp its magnificence. Each person has the capability to not only remember and store ideas but can enhance that power with feelings and emotions, something no computer can do. I feel the visitors are lacking these emotions. They may be light years ahead of us scientifically, but perhaps all their advancement has left no room for feelings and emotions. Perhaps eons ago they were very much like us, feeling and caring beings capable of sensitivity and empathy. Perhaps they are now realizing that their civilization could possibly learn something from us.

Maybe I am way off base here. Maybe their world is very similar to ours. They might have grocery stores, shopping malls, and schools. They may have family get-togethers and mow grass on the weekend. Perhaps they have a great deal of emotion and feeling. Maybe they are just as scared and curious about us as we are about them. That doesn't seem to be out of the realm of possibility. After all, they are living creatures, and even our animals seem to have emotions and feelings, so why couldn't these beings? Maybe they dream also.

I can almost visualize a young male relating a nightmare to a friend:

> Last night I dreamed the guys and I borrowed Pop's traveler and visited the other side. I knew Momma would be very upset if she found out; she hasn't been the same since her elders never returned from their mission there. She has warned us constantly of the dangers on the blue planet but I wanted to find out for myself.
>
> For kicks, we empowered one of the giant ones to

get a closer look. Their eyes are small and wild looking and they appear to be very low on the intelligence
chain. We were terrified just thinking of the conse-
quences if not for the paralysis. Their heads were so
small they appeared deformed. But the strangest thing
of all were the millions of protuberances coming out of
the tiny holes in their coverings, especially on the top
of their cranial area. These must be antenna of some
type.

We hurried up to get out of there before we were
spotted by more of these creatures, and we amused
ourselves all the way home with the excitement of the
evening's adventures.

Momma was right, they are very scary looking, but I
already want to return again.

I felt in some way I might be able to help these
wretched creatures.

Before I awoke, I had the feeling that maybe I am
the chosen one who will be able to tame these beasts,
but I am sure glad that was only a dream.

Perhaps they will be a help to us. They obviously have
mastered space travel much more efficiently than we have.
They have perfected molecular transfer of their own bodies,
which we certainly haven't. They can levitate solid objects
anywhere they wish and they can communicate with their
minds. But the greatest advancement I see that they have
made is the monetary savings of billions of dollars a year on
cigarettes, hair supplies, and beauty products.

17

DEBBIE
Realizing New Abilities

EVEN MANY YEARS AGO, WHEN I WAS PREGNANT WITH MY thirteen-year-old, I exhibited abilities that defied explanation.

One Wednesday night in winter, my first husband, Chuck, had gone bowling with his father. They bowled every Wednesday in a league. I had gone to bed early. I wasn't feeling all that great, a normal side effect of my pregnancy.

Around midnight, I awoke out of a sound sleep with a tremendous feeling of urgency. No, I didn't have to go to the bathroom! Something was wrong. I paced back and forth for at least ten minutes. It wasn't that I was worried about my husband being late or anything like that. They would often not get home until after 1 A.M. on bowling night. I found myself drawn to the patio door several times as I paced, and I'd catch myself gazing out over the frozen lake, looking at absolutely nothing.

I slowly began to realize that there was something wrong with the lake or at the lake. I didn't know which. So I decided to go down and have a closer look. Here I was, all big and pregnant, in my housecoat and slippers, tramping through the snow outside my apartment building, looking for the reason I could not sleep. Sounds pretty crazy, doesn't it? What's new?

I got to the edge of the lake and couldn't see anything out of order. As I stood there, looking like a fool, this terrible feeling of terror and urgency hit me. I knew something was wrong and someone was afraid. And I knew that I had to help!

I still couldn't see a darn thing from where I was so I decided to walk down the shore a little farther. As I passed the next building, I could see a truck had fallen into the lake. The front end was frozen in the ice and the bed was sticking up out of the slush. I looked around the truck for footprints in the snow and even though I saw some, they were so scrambled that I couldn't tell where they were headed.

About this time, my husband and his father came walking around the building. They had come home, seen that I was gone, and come outside to look for me. Excitedly I pointed out the truck, ignoring my husband's lecture about being outside in the cold and being pregnant. He said whoever wrecked the truck was probably out somewhere trying to find a tow truck, that I should quit worrying about it and come in or he was going to drag me in. Never be bossy to a pregnant woman. I told him where to get off and that I would be in when I was ready to come in. So he and his dad went back up to the apartment and left me there to continue my search.

I stood at the bank for several minutes, looking out over the frozen lake. I thought I heard someone call for help once, but I could see nothing. Then I heard it again, and there was no mistaking it this time. I saw a small, dark object appear just above the surface of the ice. That man must have mustered up every ounce of his last strength to get himself up that high over the surface. I could barely hear his frozen voice call to me for help. I began screaming to him to hold on, that I'd get him some help as soon as I could. I yelled up to the building behind me for someone to call the rescue squad. I saw a light go on in one of the apartments, a head peek out behind a shade, and then—I couldn't believe this—that person shut off the light and closed the window! Damn, that made me mad!

I charged up the stairs to my apartment, grabbed the phone, and called 911. My husband had the stupidest look on his face. As I shouted, "I told you so!" I ran back down to the lake and looked for the man in the ice. I had told the rescue squad to meet me on the other side of the lake, as he appeared to be closer to that bank than to mine. By the time I got over to the other side of the lake, they already had him halfway out. As he was pulled up on the bank, I walked over to him and the man who had pulled him out. The rescue worker asked me if I had been the one who called. I told him I was and I asked him if the guy would be all right. He assured me that he would be okay once they got him warmed up a little but that if I hadn't found him when I did, he wouldn't have lasted much longer. I thought to myself, I've got news for you, Buddy, he found me! The "ice man" looked up at me from the arms of his rescuer and barely managed a whispered "thank you." I was just grateful that he was still alive and that I had found the source of my feelings and my inability to sleep. I walked off into the dark night, back around the lake, and back to my warm apartment, not even telling the rescuers my name. I felt as if my job was done, and I needed sleep!

So many changes have occurred in the last couple years of my life, they're beginning to seem as though they should have been decades. In particular, this last year (1992) has been a whirlwind of change for me. It's as if something important has begun, a transformation of sorts. I have learned to be very adaptable to change and I'm beginning to think that was part of the plan. Nothing surprises me any more!

I began spending more time with my friends. Thank God for them. They've helped me get through the rough parts of my personal life.

My friend Joe and I decided to make a run down to St. Louis to see Forest. Joe and Forest had never met and I wanted to introduce them. We'd made plans to hang out around the campfire, enjoy nature and each other's company. I didn't get down to see Forest a lot so this would be a real treat for me, spending time with Forest and having my buddy Joe there with me, too.

While we were at Forest's house, he had a visitor. A friend of his, a physicist named Dave, stopped in. He brought with him some experiments that Forest wanted to use to test me and a couple of other women in the St. Louis area who had also had experiences with UFOs and aliens. Dave is a very nice man. I wouldn't call him a skeptic but I know he doesn't just accept things at face value. He checks things out very thoroughly. He is a true scientist.

Joe and I had been out in Forest's backyard having a smoke and admiring the wooded lot behind his house. When I went back in, Dave had arrived. He, Forest, and the two women were seated around the dining-room table. I saw that the two women were passing a small paper bag back and forth between them, and I surmised that they were trying to figure out what was inside. Dave had brought this little experiment and was watching intently as the girls worked.

The moment I walked into the house I felt very heavy. As I sat at the table watching, I began to feel the familiar burn and tingle of my physical response to magnets.

I realized I had the ability to physically feel strong magnets a year or so earlier. I had participated in an experiment with a researcher from the neighboring state of Ohio.

During the experiment, I was blindfolded. Another person was to then move a super magnet around my head and body without actually touching me, taking note of physical and psychological reactions. I was also hooked up to a bio-feedback monitor that would record any minuscule changes in skin temperature, skin moisture, or involuntary muscle movements. The sensations I felt during that test completely blew my mind. I was extremely surprised that I had felt anything! I didn't expect any reaction at all, so when I first began to feel the heat and the tingling, I ignored it. As the test progressed, I could feel the sensations increase to the point I could barely tolerate it. I also began to feel a heightened sense of anxiety well up inside me for no apparent reason. As the physical feelings increased, so did the anxiety. Just as the feelings were about to peak, I suddenly felt as though I were being pulled out of my body through the top of my head. At that point I stopped the test. I just couldn't take any more. And I realized I had felt those feelings before. Several times.

I had those feelings right before paranormal and alien experiences. I had also felt the same sensations during an MRI test done a few years before. The technician performing the test had attributed the feelings to claustrophobia. I assured her I didn't have that problem and that I had felt funny as soon as I walked into the building. I guess she must have thought I was just nuts. I didn't realize the magnet was affecting me and I'm sure she didn't realize it, either.

Now, here I was, sitting in my friend's dining room, feeling those sensations again. There was only one thing that would cause this; therefore, I knew what was in the bag.

I leaned over the table, got Forest's attention, and mouthed the words, "I know what's in the bag." He whispered back to me, "What?" You should have seen his face when I told him it was a magnet. It was priceless! He grabbed Dave's arm and told him to listen to what I had just told him. When I told Dave that there was a magnet in his little bag and told him how I knew, he was equally blown away. That was the first real time I had any witnesses to what I had suspected I was beginning to be able to do. I'm excitedly waiting for Forest to come up with more tests we can do. I strongly believe that these are the kinds of things that researchers should be looking into if they really want to find genuine evidence for the fact that there is something very unusual going on with people like me.

I had been feeling "different," for lack of a better way to describe it. I had, in the past, exhibited some unusual abilities, such as bending metal objects with a light touch, ending people's sentences for them, and feeling, physically, certain sounds, but this was different. I noticed that recently I had begun to dream in color and in 3D.

These vivid, "virtual reality" dreams that I had begun to have were incredible experiences in themselves. They always seemed to happen just when I was about to fall asleep yet was still aware of my surroundings. The major difference between them and my regular dreams was that I was no longer watching them unfold. I was actually *in* the dreams. I had full use of all my senses and my abilities were limitless. I now understand what people mean when they talk of out-of-body experiences, and I wonder if what they are really experiencing is simply this heightened state of dream reality. I use the term *reality* because it seems to me that this state I sometimes find myself in is just another reality, an altered reality. After all, who is to say what reality is or how many realities there are.

Here's one example of a particularly vivid "V.R." dream I had recently. I had just lain down on the couch to watch some old television series on "Nick at Nite." I think it was an old "Dick Van Dyke Show" rerun. (I love those old sitcoms!)

I could still hear the TV when all of a sudden I felt myself start to slip away. With a rather loud *swoosh* sound in my head, I found myself floating in space. Just me and my Dr. Denton's. I was startled at first, but quickly began to enjoy myself. I decided to turn back and look at the Earth passing behind me. As I turned my head to look over my right shoulder, I could see this huge cylindrical object headed toward me in a flat spin. It had what appeared to be gold appendages of some kind, one on each side, that I compared to those fancy, new-fangled windshield-wiper blades. As it got closer to me I could see that it was at least as big as a motor home or school bus. As it passed me, its end spun around toward me and I could see that the end looked as if it had been blown out. Actually it looked like it had been opened with an old-fashioned can opener. And it looked very "fresh," as if it had just happened. There was a little bit of what looked like vapor spurting out of the darkened open end of this thing. This image really gave me the creeps, and I woke up instantly. The first, most insistent thing in my mind was that I had to call someone. Anyone would do, just so long as I used the telephone. I called K.O.

Bless his heart, it must have been 2 A.M. and I'm sure I woke him up. I felt like an idiot, but he seemed to understand. I was really wound up after this and it took several hours for me to finally get some sleep.

The next morning, I called Linda Howe and told her all about it. When I told my friend Liz, in Pennsylvania, about my dream, she nearly came through the phone at me! She had the very same dream on the very same night! She had written hers down, called John Carpenter, and told him about it before we even talked. So forget about thinking that we got our dream from one another's description. We have witnesses! Anyway, all this mind expanding seems to have had an effect on my I.Q.

I had to obtain a copy of my high-school transcripts when I enrolled in cosmetology school. As I was cleaning out my cedar chest one afternoon, I ran across it and had a look. I was surprised to see that my I.Q. had been scored at 111. Not too shaggy but certainly no rocket scientist. I could live with that. Later, my boyfriend talked me into taking a test for a group called Mensa. Mensa is an international organization for people who score in the top 2 percent of the country on their I.Q. tests. I had goofed around with some of their practice tests in the *Omni* magazine and had no problem with any of them. Because I already had the scores from my transcripts, I was reluctant to try. Obviously 111 isn't in the top 2 percent. K.O. reasoned to me that this would be the perfect opportunity to see if anything had, indeed, changed since I was feeling so different these days. I agreed, since the only other way to get that kind of information was to go to a psychiatrist. I didn't have any health insurance and sure couldn't afford to pay for something like that!

I was shocked when I received my test scores and found that I had scored in the top *1 percent* on the California Standard Mental Maturity Test, and the Cattell B Intelligence Test scored me at 141. Naturally, my first question was, "How could someone's I.Q. jump thirty points since the age of fifteen?" I have asked several researchers about this and they promise me they will look into it. I have tried, myself, to figure this one out. All I have been able to come up with is that I.Q. tests are worthless and we should stop using them to label people, or that I was in a really poor state of mind when I took the first tests in junior high school (which could say a lot for what learning to deal with all the experiences has really done for me), or that something is not only expanding my consciousness but also my intellect.

Three rather interesting possibilities. I would love for lots of other people like me to be able to take these tests. I bet the results would be enlightening, to say the least.

Since I was now living with my parents again, I decided to take on a few more speaking engagements. Mom would take care of my children and I wouldn't have to answer to a spouse anymore. Besides, I needed to get away from everything for a while. I had accepted a request to talk to the Gulf Breeze Research Team in Pensacola, Florida. The sun and beautiful white sand beaches sounded pretty good! I knew one of the members of the group very well and was looking forward to seeing her again. As a matter of fact, I would be staying with her at her home. I thought it would be fun, sort of like a grown-up girls' slumber party. Some uninvited guests crashed our party, though.

When I arrived in Pensacola that Friday, I was pooped! I really hate to fly! There just has to be a better way to go. My ears and sinuses weren't meant to fly and I have my suspicions about the science of aerodynamics. I really do know better than to trust my life to the precarious balance between lift and drag! I find it hard to believe there's nothing between me, in this heavy piece of metal, and the ground, except a few clouds and about thirty thousand feet of air! What's wrong with this picture?

The first night I spent in Vicki's house was wonderful. The bed was comfy, and I was ready for it! Saturday was a hectic day, sightseeing and, as my father so quaintly puts it, shoplifting. (Of course, I mean shopping for souvenirs. The prices I paid made me feel like *I* was the one being robbed!)

Saturday night was spent on my very first "sky-watch." What a neat experience that was. Except for the mosquitoes, the company was excellent, and I made a lot of new friends that night. I also ran into a few old friends, too. Dr. Bruce MacCabee was there on the beach with a couple of fellow scientists and a whole bunch of sophisticated recording instruments. I couldn't begin to tell you all that he had there that night. I'm no scientist and I had no idea what most of that stuff did. I did recognize the camcorders, the telescopes, and the 3D camera equipment. And I saw a van filled to the brim with recording devices. There were a few antennas on the roof of the van and I noticed a dish of some kind, too. I do know that one of their instruments could pick up and record each sweep of the radar that passed over us from one of the local airbases.

A few of us (the ones who couldn't take the 'skeeters anymore) ventured down to the beach, right next to the water. We set our lawn chairs in a small circle and all began to focus our minds on a similar idea. Calling "Bubba" in. ("Bubba" is the Gulf Breeze Research Team's pet name for the red lights and other objects they see in the sky down there often.) It was peaceful and cool and the mosquitoes couldn't handle the wind coming in off the waves.

After a short while, I began to feel the familiar burn and tingle of my response to strong magnets. I immediately turned to my friend Vicki and said, "Somebody's here checking us out. Closer than you think, too." Within one minute, a gal named Pat came running down the sand dune from the parking lot where everyone else was watching, to tell us that several of the people on the lot, including Dr. MacCabee, had seen a small, white ball of light whiz overhead. They said the light seemed to be moving in a sort of "dash-dash," stop-and-go way and it had come across above our heads as we sat on the beach, moving from left to right over the parking lot and us. It appeared to be about twenty feet off the ground. At the very moment they sighted the light and I had felt the magnet response and told Vicki, one of the scientists with Dr. MacCabee reported that he had picked up an unusual wave-form on one of his receivers.

Everyone thought it was interesting that not only did they see this thing with their own eyes, but that I had felt it and their instruments had picked up an anomalous reading at the very same time. I think that this kind of thing is extremely important and I don't understand why anyone hasn't heard anything more about it since that time. Even if there was a rational explanation for what the instrument picked up, I still think it noteworthy that I could feel it right before they saw it. (I did not see the light.)

We finally got back to Vicki's very early Sunday morning. I was dead tired and eaten up with bug bites. To help stop the itching and to wash off the bug spray, I took a quick shower before crashing. Once I lay down, I couldn't go to sleep. I don't know if I was overly tired or overly excited about what had happened earlier on the beach. I picked up a magazine and began to flip through it. Nothing puts me to sleep faster than reading. I have wimpy eyes.

Something caught my eye while I tried to read. I looked up and saw a small white ball of light up in the corner of the room to my right. At first I thought it might be a reflection of my reading light on the oscillating fan in the room. I watched the fan and the light and realized there was no connection. As I looked directly at the light, it shot across the room, stopped momentarily over Vicki's desk, and then shot across the room, over my head, and to my left. Then it was gone.

I really didn't feel frightened by this little incident and soon found myself fast asleep. The last thing I remembered was hearing several conversations going on in my room. I'm sure one of them was on the television. The rest, who knows.

The next morning, I told Vicki about what I had seen in the room earlier that morning. She was quite excited about it and made me promise her that if I ever saw anything like that again in her house, that I would come and get her right away. She wanted to see it, too. She said that she had heard several strange noises in the house at about the same time I was seeing this light, and she wondered if there was a connection.

Monday was another hectic day of sightseeing and frolic on the beach. Monday night there was another sky-watch. As before, we were up very late, and when I returned to Vicki's I had to take another shower to combat the itchy mosquito bites and the bug spray.

As I climbed into bed, I turned on the reading light and began to read the magazine that I hadn't finished the night before. After a couple of minutes, I began to notice a soft, bluish-white glow coming from behind my left shoulder. There was a window directly behind the head of my bed so I assumed it was just a car light of some kind, a headlight or something. When I began to feel the burning, tingling magnetic-response feeling again, I realized something was wrong with my headlight theory. Then I wondered whether the reading light was reflecting off the oscillating fan and throwing it back onto the shiny paper of the magazine and then over my shoulder. I tried several experiments with holding the paper different ways, but to no avail. I tried to rationalize the situation but nothing was working! The glow began to pulsate and grow larger with each throb.

I thought to myself, I should get Vicki. She wants to see this. With that thought, the glow stopped. I sat there for a moment, waiting for what might come next. I wasn't about to look over my shoulder to see if I could see anything. I had the distinct impression that if I did, I might see something I really didn't want to see, closer to me than I really wanted it to be.

After a minute or two, I decided that there was no point in waking Vicki up, whatever it was must have split. Precisely after I thought this, something whipped around my left shoulder. It looked like many small beams of blue and white light. Blue at the core and white around the edges in alternating fashion. *Fingers* is the word I use to describe it. It literally slapped me across the left side of my face and neck. The force was so strong that I felt stunned. I also felt a small electrical shock, and I could feel a burning, numbish sensation on the whole left side of my face. It felt as if the thing was going to wrap itself around my whole head and not let go! (There were red marks on my neck and jaw the next morning!) I immediately said, out loud, "Okay! I'll get Vicki, for Christ's sake!" With that, it let go of me and was gone.

I jumped off the bed and made my way through the dark house to Vicki's room. I didn't know where the light switch was in the kitchen, so I stood there for a moment. Then I softly said, "Vicki?"

No sooner than the words left my mouth, here came Vicki, dashing out of her room yelling, "Don't tell me, girl, I saw it, too! Blue and white lights came up from under my bedroom door, they looked like rays, and then I could see it move down the hall toward your room!" I just stood there, my mouth hanging open, not knowing whether to breathe that next breath or drop over like a fly. I felt as if I were in a daze, half there and half somewhere else.

Vicki's husband, Danny, came out of the room right after her. Both of them, eyes as big as saucers, listened as I told them what had happened in my room. Interestingly, Vicki and I had both heard a strange rattling noise in the utility room, near the dog pen, and movement throughout the house as if someone were bumping up against furniture as they passed through the house. I thought it was Vicki or Danny, and they thought it was me. It was none of us. (The following day, one of Vicki's dogs was very ill. She was quite concerned about it.)

We made our way back to my room. I showed them where all this had happened and as I retold the event, we all got more and more creeped out. Eventually, we all wound up sitting on my bed, covers half pulled up around our necks, looking for the boogie man out of the corner of our eyes. I must admit, I was the biggest weenie of all. There I was, in Florida, to talk to a large group of people about how I had finally overcome my fear and wanted to show them how they could do the same thing, and I was the most freaked out of all. I felt like a true jerk! I was never so embarrassed in my whole life! I was taken so off guard by this whole thing that I think I was more in shock than anything else. I also think that there may have been more to this whole thing than I remember because the next morning, I made a strange discovery. My trusty Timex wind-up watch was thirty minutes slow. It has kept good time for ten years and it still does today. Just for that half hour in my room that night, did it somehow lose half an hour? And I felt a strange connection to Florida after that, and I still can't shake it. I miss it very much.

After agonizing over how I would ever get any sleep that night, I decided to have Vicki drive me over to K.O.'s hotel room. I knew it was very late, but I had awakened him before, and somehow I knew he would understand. He did.

He was quite alarmed to see us knocking at his door so early in the morning, but he graciously let us in. We told him what had happened, and right away he recorded the whole thing for future reference. He's so efficient. I remembered looking in his mirror and telling him that I didn't look like me anymore. I could see something different looking back at me in the mirror. Boy, was I a wreck! He could see that I was in shock and he noticed that my eyes looked unusually bright. *Glowing* was the word he used. He thought it was so unusual that he broke out his camcorder and videotaped me. Then he fixed up the extra bed for me. I fell onto it, rolled myself up in a tight ball, reminded myself that he was there and that he would keep me safe, and then I really crashed hard. I was fried!

Monday night, K.O. decided, without telling anyone, that he would spend the night outside Vicki's house. He was very protective of me, even then. He felt that he might see something, and I guess he did.

He parked his car on a side street so that he could have a good view of her utility room. He got very sleepy despite tons of coffee and found himself nodding off a lot. At one point, however, he remembered seeing two small lights appear along the side of her house, just below the utility-room windows. They both winked out before he could get his camcorder up to catch them on tape. He said they weren't much bigger than white Christmas tree lights. Inside the house, it was pretty quiet.

I gave my talk on Tuesday. It went really well and when I told them about what had just happened the night before, everyone wanted me to spend the night with them! Now, wouldn't you have expected the exact opposite? What a group!

The entire Gulf Breeze Research Team decided to camp out all around Vicki's house that night. Each one had a post and I think they had the whole house surrounded. I felt kind of bad that they were going to miss a whole night's sleep because of me, but they wouldn't take no for an answer. I sure felt safe that night! But perhaps I shouldn't have.

I went to bed at 1:20 A.M. The window was open, the lights and TV were off. At 1:30 A.M. I was abruptly jolted out of bed by a very strong magnetic response. I lay there, a little stunned by the feelings that woke me up out of a sound sleep. Shortly I began to drift back to sleep. Again, at exactly 1:40 A.M. it happened again. This time I got out of bed, lit a cigarette, and turned on the TV. I knew the TV would impair the watchers outside, yet I did it anyway.

After I had finished my smoke, I went back to bed and

fell asleep rather easily. At 4 A.M. I woke up, quite abruptly, sitting straight up in the bed. As I looked around the room, trying to regain my composure, I slid down into the bed slowly, thinking to myself, Wow, what a trip.

The next morning, Vicki told me that at 3:55 A.M. one of the watchers, Dave, had discovered his car battery had gone dead. At that time, the whole GBRT was hovering around Dave's car, trying to get it started—nearly exactly the same time I woke up sitting straight up in bed, bewildered and confused. Dave's battery would never hold a charge after that. It was destroyed and he had to replace it.

In March of this year (1993) I was invited to participate in the making of a pilot for a possible new television series on the UFO subject. The filming was in Daytona Beach, Florida. While I was there, something interesting happened.

Budd Hopkins was also going to be on the show. I had told Budd, on the telephone, about a recent experience when I had been freezing cold and unable to get warm. I finally had to abandon my basement bedroom for the warmer upstairs couch. Sometime early in the morning, I had been awakened by a blond man who asked me if I was still cold. I told him, "No, in fact, I'm burning up." He said, "Here, let me help you." And with that, he proceeded to pull off my sweatpants and socks, fold them up neatly and put them on the coffee table next to the couch. Then he began to talk to me. I cannot remember what he said to me, but I remember at one point saying to him, "Hey, one of your eyes is weird! The pupil is diamond shaped, and it moves when you talk to me. Are you talking to me with your eye?" (What a retarded question!) He just looked at me like I was stupid and said, "Well, of course I am! Don't you remember you can do this, too?" I said, in return, "Oh, yeah, right. Whatever." Then he talked to me for a little while longer. I just remember saying, "Yeah, un huh, okay, yeah . . ." I can't remember what he said to me. The next thing I know, it's morning and there are my sweatpants and socks, neatly folded and lying on the coffee table.

I drew a picture of the man that night in my hotel room in Daytona and was going to give it to Budd the next day. After I had finished the picture, I set it up against the toaster to get a head-on view of it to see how it looked. The TV caught my eye. There was a comedienne on that looked just like Judy Garland! I love Judy Garland! I was fascinated with her and woke K.O. up to see her. He had been lying across the bed in his street clothes and had dozed off.

As we both watched TV, me standing next to the bed and him lying across it with his chin on his fists, I saw a small, white light appear between us and the TV. I couldn't believe my eyes! I watched it move slowly across the screen, past the kitchen chair, and over to my drawing. It had some kind of tail trailing behind it. It looked like a jet contrail. This thing moved like a swimming tadpole! I had never seen anything like this in my whole life! When it reached my drawing, it stopped, hesitated a moment, and then disappeared. K.O. had seen me tracking something and asked me what I was seeing. I kept rubbing my eyes, thinking that would make it go away. I jumped and yelled, "Whoa! Did you see that?" I thought K.O. was going to fall off the bed! He yelled, "What? I didn't see it! What was it?" I couldn't believe he didn't see it. It passed right in front of his face. He had let his eyes droop shut for just a minute, and he had missed the whole thing! Damn it to hell! The next time I ask him to look at something on the TV, I'll bet he doesn't close his eyes again.

On the flight home, as we sat and ate our peanuts, the whole back end of the plane filled up with a bright, white flash. I was next to the window. It was dark and I was getting sleepy. I turned my head to look out the blackened window, closed my eyes for just a second, and then it happened. The flash was so bright that it came through my closed eyelids bright enough to startle me. At first I thought it was lightning. I could see that the man in the seat in front of us had apparently seen it, too. He was looking around with this puzzled look on his face. K.O. saw it and first thought it was the peanut wrapper of the man next to us. Quickly, he realized that it was much too bright to have been merely a reflection. We waited for more flashes, thinking it might be lightning, but none ever came. That was the only one.

I looked over at K.O. and said, "Whoa, man, what if we land at Indianapolis International and find out the name's been changed to Weircook?" (That was supposed to be a joke. Weircook was the name of IIA long ago.) Oh, well.

18

KATHY
This Doesn't Look Like Kansas

As the numbers increase
of the chosen few,
We seek each out
in an attempt to renew,
our battered Earth,
our fragile minds,
for the strengthening
of all mankind.

AFTER MANY YEARS OF INDECISION, MY OWN PERSONAL CIVIL war seems to be resolving. I no longer feel myself being pulled in different directions. I have made the decision to go public and I feel I will be comfortable with that decision.

In what you have read by now, you'll have noticed that my only proof of all I've written has simply been my word. You'll have to trust me in what I've said—or at least trust that I believe it's the truth. I realize that it's possible to be sincere though deluded. So if I'm not telling the truth, it's unintentional and I hope UFO investigators will set the record straight. In other words, I want the truth to be known and told, even if it embarrasses me by showing that I was somehow deceived or fell victim to tricks of my own mind. I'd rather be hurt by the truth than to live an illusion or a lie.

The decision to go public has been difficult enough for me. If I started out on the wrong foot by lying or embellishing what I told, I am smart enough to know that sooner or later I would discredit myself in a big way. I really don't think I'm organized enough to keep track of a string of lies. I don't know what I could offer as proof anyway. Proof to one person might simply be a theory to another. As a rule, nonbelievers will accept no proof anyway. Even if I had a piece of a spacecraft control panel, there would be someone out there to debunk it. I would like to have just one picture for myself, though. It would be comforting to have something I could physically see when I begin to doubt even myself. My goal here is not to sway the nonbelievers anyway. My purpose is to convey to the thousands of others who have experienced a close encounter the method we use to deal mentally with the situations. I would like to set an example for the people who are beginning to doubt their own sanity. I would simply say that it is possible to come through these experiences and go on with your life in a relatively normal fashion.

Twenty-five years ago, when I was dealing with sleepwalking, insomnia, and the anxiety I continually felt, it would have been great to have the support groups that today's generations have. Unfortunately, at that time I was not aware of what was causing these problems anyway. Since I have always been a believer in the visitors, I would have been very interested in talking to others about the subject, but back then that subject was taboo. Saying you believe in UFOs is one thing, but saying you have seen the inside of one is another. Little gray men were for *Twilight Zone* and H.G. Wells. There was little room in the middle-class society I grew up in for the unexplainable. My generation was built upon taking care of your own problems and not airing your dirty laundry. So I took care of my inner turmoil as best I could. I just dealt with my sleepwalking one night at a time and dismissed it as a nervous problem brought on by a life too full. I did have a house full of babies and for years at least one of them seemed to have me up every night for various reasons. Alien connections were the last thing on my mind at that time of my life. Any haunting dreams I might have been experiencing then were outweighed by dreams of bottles and diapers.

Without any support other than from my parents, it has taken me many years to come to grips with it all. I am extremely fortunate that my parents are very open-minded and have never doubted my experiences. How very different things would have been if in 1965, when I first recounted my UFO sighting, they had laughed at me or accused me of lying. Of course, at the time I was not aware of the details of that evening, but what do you think your parents would say if you came home one night and claimed to have seen a giant UFO hovering over your car just a few feet from a large church and a row of houses? Bear in mind that I was just a teenager who was also late getting home. I would guess that the majority of parents would not buy that story. Fortunately mine did not laugh at me but instead were very interested. Later that night they even scanned the skies, hoping to see for themselves what I had seen earlier. That did give me some hope that I was not totally losing touch with reality.

Even though neither parent had at that time any conscious memory of ever seeing a UFO, neither one doubted me. In fact, they considered it something of an accomplishment that I had actually seen a real UFO. I guess some kids win spelling bees, some receive scholarships, and some see UFOs. Instead of a bumper sticker that reads MY CHILD IS ON THE HONOR ROLL OF HICKVILLE JR. HIGH SCHOOL theirs would read MY CHILD IS ON THE HONOR ROLL OF UFO ABDUCTEES. The bottom line was that they knew they had raised a good kid. A kid who told the truth and wasn't prone to fantasize; they believed in me and they believed me. I personally feel that they are also abductees but do not consciously remember. Perhaps that is why they were so open-minded with me. Mom has a deep oval scar on her shin with only the vague memory of being in a wooded area with a child she hardly knew. While running with this child, she remembered tripping over a log, then pulling something out of her shin. There was no blood and she can't remember how the episode ended. She also has memories and dreams of some bizarre adventures. One of her strange dreams centers around attic openings and some unknown men.

As far back as I can remember I have always been afraid of attic doors. I used to insist that Johnny nail them shut in every house we lived in. It seemed to be an unfounded, ridiculous fear. For years I had no clue as to why attic doorways bothered me so. During a hypnotic session with Mom, a strange story unfolded. Apparently, when I was just a baby she remembers trying to shove me up inside our attic to hide me because "someone" was in the house and was coming to take me. She always woke up just after she pushed me inside, so we don't know how the dream ends. Not knowing who the "someone" was or where I was to be taken, I am only assuming it is UFO related because my mom never received a ransom note. I have no memory whatsoever of that incident, but it is very strange that Debbie has a memory almost exactly the same as the one Mom related to us, except in Debbie's, Mom is being shoved into the attic and Debbie, as a toddler, is watching. Perhaps both of us had similar incidents many years apart, or perhaps she merely remembered Mom relating the story. The latter is unlikely though, as I never recalled hearing the story until Budd visited us in the early 1980s. I guess you will have to make your own decision about that. I no longer insist the attic doors be nailed shut.

Another strange incident happened when I was about twenty years old. Mom and I were alone all night because Dad was out of town on business. It was a rare occasion that he was not there. When we got up the next morning, I began to tell her of the strange dream I had the night before. I remembered being very scared as she and I were alone in the house and there were "men" all around the outside trying to get inside to us. I had the feeling that they were there to take us somewhere, but I didn't know where or why. As I began telling this dream to her, a strange look came over her face as she insisted she had experienced exactly the same dream herself that night. That was uncanny, but we just dismissed it as a coincidence and never pursued any more details.

So you can see by our background that Debbie and I have had the advantage of having some support at home. The whole world wasn't laughing anyway. I did learn very early in life that my closest childhood friends would be no support to me. When I told them I had seen a "flying saucer," they all roared. That was the last time I talked about it to them. I assumed I would get the same response from everyone else, so I just kept it to myself and my immediate family. I am keeping it to myself even now. My current employer, the people I work with, and my neighbors have no idea of my involvement in any UFO situation. Imagine their surprise when this book is published. It will be interesting to see who avoids me and who shows a true interest.

Over the years I have used humor to cope. If you laugh at yourself first, it seems to take the thrill out of it for the scoffers. I'll have to admit that now I am fairly comfortable with myself. I really don't feel any worse for the wear. I seem to be past all the anxiety I see others facing. I don't have nightmares anymore and I just take one day at a time.

But it has taken me many years to get to that point. Rolling with the flow is about all you can do as I see no way of stopping "them." It may appear to some that I am taking the entire subject too lightly, but I have merely come to grips with it. Calming my inner self has enabled me to try to find a logical explanation for our involvement. I have always felt that everything that a person experiences happens for a reason. Those reasons may be from a past life experience, karma, or a learning experience from this life. I don't know for sure what the UFO connection may be, but I feel it is for the good of the human species.

As is widely said today, we as a people are putting Mother Earth on the skids. We have not only contaminated the land, water, air, and ozone, we have contaminated our own bodies, minds, and souls. It sure doesn't take a genius to figure out that this neglect can't go on forever without some major repercussions. Earth and our species may very well be on the verge of extinction. Our scientists have worked for years helping species of the animal kingdom that are in danger of extinction. Perhaps the "visiting scientists" are working to help our civilization avoid extinction. Perhaps they are striving to help us learn more about ourselves and our own spirits.

If you compare a UFO abduction to the capture and testing of wild animals to record their migration and living habits—sedation, capture, examination, and tagging for future identification—you will find striking similarities. I like to believe these alien entities are doing this for the good of mankind. After all, it is always better to look for the good and positive side of any situation and hope for the best. Studies have shown these alien beings have been around for centuries and, like it or not, believe it or not, they will probably be around for centuries to come. Perhaps they will be around long after we are all gone. If there were harmful or destructive purposes to their visits, they would have "taken care of us" long ago.

Even though I am hoping it is for our own good, when I think of the possible involvement of my kids, it just chills me to the bone. It is one thing for "them" to do what they want with me, but I would prefer that they left my children alone. So far I don't have proof that any of my four kids have been abducted or tested. The tiny aliens my youngest son saw when he was nine is the only encounter I have heard any of them mention. That encounter was enough to let me know that my kids are involved, whether I like it or not. I have no proof that anything physical was done to Stevie, but something definitely affected him mentally. It was an experience he will keep with him forever. Perhaps one day he will decide to explore all the missing parts. My kids are all grown up now, so I have questioned them further. I will include their responses later in this book.

My oldest son is extremely interested in karma and out-of-body travel. He once told me he had been spending a lot of time experimenting with the out-of-body experience. He thought that with a lot of concentration he might be able to leave his body at will. (I would love to be able to leave mine and pick a better one—a more updated model.) He scared himself one night, though, and decided maybe he wasn't ready to float around the room after all. He claimed that just before he felt himself begin to feel "lighter," just when he thought he could really float somewhere, he began to panic and jumped out of bed. I think that was the end of that for him.

I have never heard him talk of seeing a UFO close up but he has seen many strange lights in the sky that he seemed to feel were not of this Earth. I have watched some of them with him and have to agree that many of them were traveling around in a very strange manner. Bill and Stevie did watch five red lights flying in a multitude of directions all at the same time. They first noticed them from the living room window and both went outside to watch. We lived in the country at the time and you could see for miles. They both watched as the lights would move straight up and down, from side to side, stop, then continue again. They were alone at the time so no one else got to see them, but they claimed to watch those lights for twenty minutes. Too bad we didn't have a camcorder. That would have been great to capture on film.

We had several other odd experiences during our five years in the country, including one in the middle of the night that really startled me. I always sleep on my stomach. I woke up one night by quickly "popping" my eyes open, which in itself is a little startling. I felt as if I could not move any part of my body except my eyes. I was on my side and the lighted red numbers on the clock were all I could see. I stared at the numbers and realized I could not feel the bed under me but I couldn't move any of my body to feel around for something solid. I closed my eyes for a few seconds and when I opened them again I was solidly on the bed but never actually felt myself falling or lowering, I could merely feel the bed then. I had been reading a lot on the "New Age" and during those months perhaps my mind was playing tricks on me.

One night around that same time, I had a sighting that was definitely not a trick of my mind. I had forgotten to bring in clothes off the line that evening and it was already dark outside, but since it's so tacky to leave clothes hung out all night, I scurried out to gather them up. As I stood at the line, a huge craft came from over the house traveling very low and moving very slowly. It made absolutely no noise so I didn't notice it until it was just over me. The entire bottom side was covered in lights and it was really beautiful. It appeared to be twice the size of our house, a three-bedroom ranch. It reminded me exactly of the huge craft shown in *Close Encounters of the Third Kind*. I didn't have my glasses on and the lights seemed to blur together some, but it was really magnificent. As I stood in the dark watching this craft, I felt very "chosen." This may sound weird, but I had the feeling it was a communication to me. I felt as if they were saying "It's okay now, you can tell, the time is right." I had been writing a manuscript of my own then and as I wrote, I couldn't escape the feeling that I was not supposed to be telling any of this to anyone. It was a feeling that there would be "punishment" for telling that which I had been instructed not to tell. Now I was getting the feeling that it was okay to tell, but I couldn't help wondering if it really was. As I continued to watch this giant craft, I wanted to run in and get my glasses and camera but I didn't want to leave and miss it. When it finally was past the farm property next to us, I ran inside. By that time the lights on the bottom were off and the only light on the back was just a single blinking red light. Still no sound could be heard, but I watched that red taillight for a long time before it was out of sight. None of my family would even get off the couch to come out and see it. I guess they were tiring of it all.

No one was interested in my sighting, but days later when Johnny saw a huge ball of light over the field behind our house, that was, of course, more notable. He described it as a brilliant reddish-orange circle of light as bright as the sun and as large as our house. The time was approximately 3:40 P.M. and the object was in the eastern part of the sky. He said it was approximately thirty to forty feet above treetop level, and he could hear a roaring sound. In an instant, a bright flash of light like a bolt of lightning seemed to shoot straight through it and it disappeared. The roaring sound stopped instantly.

I know power in the house had shut off and turned back

on because the digital clocks were flashing. They were the kind that flash back to 12:00 when they are disconnected and turned back on. We calculated to the time they would have been shut off and decided it would have been 3 P.M., forty minutes before he came home and saw the massive glowing ball of light. We didn't check the field or ground that was under the light. I guess we are not very good investigators.

In the midst of all these strange happenings, my dad was having his own close encounter of a more personal nature. The experience I am about to tell you seems entirely unconnected to any UFO phenomenon, or is it?

Earlier he had witnessed the same type of large craft that I had as it lumbered directly over his house one evening. After that he became extremely interested in the entire subject, which seemed totally out of character for him. He is a typical tough guy who several years earlier had announced that he was "too smart" for the aliens to interest him too much. We just told him he was too ugly for them to bother with. He declared he did in fact believe in UFOs but he wasn't about to waste too much of his valuable time on the subject.

As I write this, he is seasoning those words and about to begin eating them.

He appeared to my untrained mind to be bordering on obsession in his effort to read all he could get his hands on regarding the subject. He was not only reading about UFOs, but he also became interested in the spirit world and the power of the mind. Not having been the picture of health for the last twenty years, he was about to get a lesson on how powerful the human mind can be.

He had been plagued with angina for two decades and had apparently suffered one heart attack that he was not even aware of until it was discovered on a routine EKG. It was also discovered that his heart was somewhat smaller than normal with one side noticeably smaller than the other. Poor circulation was also a problem, leaving one side of his body feeling constantly tingly and cool. His doctor told him that if he didn't slow down, he would be dead within one year. Being the stubborn hardhead he is, he allowed that if he couldn't live his life as he wished, he might as well be dead. Undaunted, he continued his life unchanged, only seeking medical advice when the chest pains got severe enough to remind him he was no longer sixteen.

In May 1987, he ordered several truckloads of topsoil he intended to spread by hand. After spending two days shoveling dirt hour after hour, he was seized by severe chest pains and rushed to the emergency room. By the time he arrived at the hospital he was feeling noticeably better. After a couple hours of testing and waiting the doctor found nothing too serious. He released Dad and advised him to make an appointment with his heart specialist.

By the time Dad returned home from the hospital, he was feeling so good that he went right back outside and began shoveling dirt again. I'm no doctor, but something is wrong with that picture.

He told us later that his chest pain was not an actual pain but an "experience" that took him very much by surprise. He said that he felt something in his chest "break loose" and he could feel warmth on the cold side of his body for the first time in twenty years. He said he could feel the blood gushing throughout his body. He claimed it made him feel a little dizzy and that's the only reason he agreed to the trip to the emergency room.

Out of curiosity he did agree to an appointment with his heart specialist.

As the doctor compared the results of his treadmill and EKG with those done three years previously, he was puzzled—to say the least. It seems Dad had made a 60 percent improvement on the testing. The doctor was quick to say the human heart could not repair itself. Dad had suffered a definite heart problem in the past and now the condition had apparently been alleviated without treatment, a total impossibility according to the specialist.

A chest x-ray Dad had done at work also showed definite changes. The company doctor was the third to confirm a change in the heart condition. After comparing the new chest x-ray to the one done three years earlier, it appeared that not only had the smaller side of Dad's heart enlarged to equal the size of the other side, but his entire heart had slightly enlarged to normal size and appeared to be in excellent shape.

Now Dad had the opinion of three doctors that he had a greatly improved heart without undergoing surgery of any kind.

Amazingly enough, his heart had not been the only improvement. His eyesight had also improved, finding him able to see rather well without his glasses.

Last, but not least, a routine hearing test done at work showed a marked improvement over the previous test.

When I asked him what he thought of his newfound health, he replied that "they" sure had overhauled his body. That led me to believe he feels that, by some mysterious quirk, aliens have played a major part in his new and improved body.

Just a darn minute here! I am beginning to feel a little cheated. If "they" are so advanced that they can completely overhaul this old geezer, don't "they" know anything about liposuction?

As our circle of involvement grew ever larger and more complicated, we as a family were left with many unanswered questions. Why us? What makes us so interesting? Why have we remembered so much of these experiences without the aid of hypnosis while many others have not? What lies ahead for us? Will it ever stop?

After my hypnosis with Budd, I first seemed to go through a period of great fascination and interest in the subject of UFO's. Documenting all the strange events that were occurring seemed therapeutic. After about two years, though, I went through a long period of disenchantment, so to speak, something like denial. I wanted absolutely nothing more to do with the whole subject. Before this period, I scanned the skies every time I went outside. During this period I made a point *not* to look up. I decided I would never look up again. I wanted nothing more to do with any of it. Just keep it all away from me . . . period. Forever!

I stayed in that thought mode for a long time—about four or five years. I refused to even think about any of it. Every once in a great while I would peek out with one eye from behind the fortress I had built for myself and show some interest, but just a little here and there. Then I would decide, No I don't want to do this anymore, I won't ever do this anymore.

I am no psychiatrist, so I won't try to give any dimestore analysis of this period in my life. Perhaps I was finally just overloaded with it all. I seemed to have a lot of mental turmoil about the subject. I suppose I had used Johnny so long as my excuses not to become involved publicly that when he began to believe in it, I no longer had him to blame for stopping me. Therefore I just had to stop myself.

Then, ever so slowly, I began to crawl out of my hiding place. I began to see that nothing "bad" had happened to me for discussing the subject of UFOs and aliens with outsiders. I can't explain what "bad" things meant to me, but somewhere inside my head I know what that means. After all, nothing "bad" had happened to Debbie all these years. Perhaps nothing "bad" would happen to me.

So here I am in 1993. It's been ten years since we looked

at the circle in the backyard of my parents' house. Ten years of unexplained events, soul searching, confusion, and questions.

The grass has long since been replaced—like a new beginning. I have taken control of myself once again and I'm finally ready to move forward. One step at a time.

19

DEBBIE
The New Me

I WISH YOU COULD HAVE KNOWN ME TEN OR FIFTEEN YEARS ago. You would never have recognized me now.

I had been plagued by depression and anxiety for as long as I could remember. When I was sixteen, my parents took me to see a psychiatrist. I had about five visits with him in a year and a half. He wasn't much help.

Most of what I remember from these visits were conversations about how the last nerve pill he gave me worked and he always asked me if anybody had touched me in a sexual way since the last time I saw him. He gave me the creeps!

My self-image stank and I had the biggest inferiority complex in the history of the world. Between that and the depression and anxiety, you'd think I would have seen him more than five times in a year and a half.

At various times in my life, the problems I was wrestling with manifested themselves in physical symptoms. Colitis, spastic bowel syndrome, obesity, nail biting, hyperventilation, gastroenteritis, reflux esophagitis, palpitations, and the list goes on. All this just complicated my life even more. I'm sure, as I was growing up, most of the doctors I saw for various health problems thought I was one pitiful little girl.

And I believe many of them probably wondered if I had been the victim of some kind of abuse while I was growing up. I guess, in a way, I was.

I look back on these last few years and I feel that I'm not even the same person, that it was a whole other life ago. Who was that frightened, backward soul?

I can't say that my experiences with these alien beings have caused the positive changes in my life. I use the word *alien* in the literal sense—I don't know what they are or where they come from. Perhaps the changes in me were inadvertent side effects of the telepathic communication. Perhaps going through the traumatic events forced me into rising above it all, changing and growing. Perhaps these qualities were already bred into me and that was why "they" were attracted to my people in the first place. I really don't have an answer for this. All I can do is live with it and make it work for me as best I can. I do know I wouldn't change one thing about what I have been through, except maybe having them wait until I was older before they began. If I had been given the ability to choose whether to have these experiences and knew then what I know now, I would have chosen to have them with the stipulation that I could fully remember them, understand what their purpose was, and have some say as to what was going to be done to me. Not to mention the fact that a couple of Kodak moments and a few scraps of unearthly metal would have been nice, too. I don't think I would have been able to reach the level I have reached within myself, without them—the experiences, that is. But perhaps my not knowing, not remembering, was all part of the plan, the program. Perhaps if I had remembered everything from the beginning, the results would have been different.

A very close friend of mine, who is also a UFO researcher, once asked me how I could not be angry and bitter toward whatever it is that's been messing with me and my family. He felt they had used me like a lab animal, against my will, and didn't seem to care about the psychological and physical effects on me. I asked him how he could be so sure that's how it really was, that I really was used, then dumped, with no regard for my personal health and well-being. Maybe we don't understand their ways, their version of concern or compassion. I was there and I wasn't sure. I politely accused him of being slightly close-minded.

Doctors vaccinate children for protection against a rash of horrible diseases. The shot hurts and the child cries, but the older, wiser adult knows it was for his own good and yet has no way of making the child understand this. He hopes that as the child grows older, he will understand and know the doctor meant no harm, that he was only thinking of the child's best interests. How was my well-meaning friend so sure that what was done to me wasn't for my own good or the good of my species? I could have chosen to look at the whole situation from his point of view. I could have allowed myself to feel violated and used, angry and bitter, but what good would that do anyone, especially me? I believe that if we allow ourselves to stew in our own negative emotions we will create negative reactions to that response. Just as our bodies respond to positive reactions by feeling energetic and strong, I believe we can make ourselves feel weak and tired, lowering our immunity to disease and attracting more negativity. We lose control of ourselves, our health, our state of mind, and our lives. Did I really want to live my whole life feeling bad over something I may have misunderstood? Was it really worth making myself sick over? Or should I try to look for an alternative response? One that might benefit me and could possibly help others feel better, too. Did I want to choose the constructive path or the destructive path? Being a fairly intelligent, reasonable person, I choose to feel the alien's treatment has been beneficial to me. I don't allow my feelings to eat me alive. After all, as

I've said before, I can't always choose the situations I find myself in, but I can choose the response I make to them. As a result, I will always be in control of myself, my health, and my life. I have begun to look at the human mind as a giant computer. And I am the programmer. I can program my mind to take me anywhere I want to be in life; it can lead me to be anything I want to be, for me. When I came to this realization, the experiences began to change. They moved from the physical (the scars, the mark in the yard, the physical exams, etc. . . .) to the psychological, the spiritual. This new way of thinking has only come along for me in the last couple of years and has been the single most important change in me since all I've told you began. I was never really as bitter as one might expect I would be, but I was terribly frightened. With my newfound sense of self-control, I have found new strength and an easing of the fear. It's amazing how much more clearly you can think when you're not afraid of what you must think about.

I realize how strong the human mind can be—so much so that I have learned never to trust in my memories of the experiences 100 percent. I realize that the mind can do many things in order to protect itself. I can be as skeptical of my own memories as any Phil Klass, a notorious UFO debunker and skeptic. But I have learned to trust in me. I have faith in myself and my instincts and, of course, in God. The more I trust in these, the stronger I get. When realizing your own encounters, keep in mind, all is not always as it appears to be. And remember this: Most people I've met who worry about whether they have gone crazy, usually haven't. The ones who think they are "normal" and that everyone else is crazy are the ones I watch out for!

It helps to keep notes of everything strange that happens. It also helps to remember that every bump and bruise, every weird little thing you notice, does not necessarily mean they have been messing with you again. It's important to keep your perspective in all this. You can't imagine how much clearer things can become once they are written down. Re-reading your journal is like watching a movie three or four times. Each time you watch it, you pick up something new that you missed the time before—at least, I do. Something new about the experience, something new about me. And sometimes a more prosaic explanation will make itself clear to you after the initial shock has passed and you calm down a little. Keeping journals can actually help explain a strange experience after a little time has passed.

I have experienced, on more than one occasion, what I call abductee burnout. It happens because you can only talk about this stuff and think about it so much. Pretty soon you'll feel like your head will burst if you say or hear the words *abductee, alien,* or *terrified* one more time. It's very stressful to relive, in your mind, the frightened, helpless feelings and the physical pain of the experiences, not to mention imagining the ridicule you might have to face. When I found myself in this state of mind, I withdrew. I just backed off it all for a while. I refused to talk about it, read about it, and if I saw something on TV about it, I turned it off. Eventually something would shove me back into the whole thing again, but the reprieve was nice. I wouldn't be surprised to find that a little distance, every once in a while, could actually be good for you, if you can manage it. Most people don't seem to realize that we didn't ask for this to happen to us. We're just trying to understand it, to understand "Why us?" Sometimes I'd get angry and find myself yelling out into the dark night sky, "Why don't you just leave me alone? I don't want this life, I don't want this change. Please! I just want to be like normal people!" I didn't want the changes at first. Even though the changes were for the better, they were uncomfortable because they were new to me. Sometimes even good changes are scary, if they are unfamiliar.

The best medicine is to talk about it. There are people who will listen without ridicule and judgment. Just being able to talk about it releases a lot of pressure. I believe that if you have found the inner strength to reach out to someone else and talk about something that bothers you, half the battle has been won. I can't give you any advice about how to stop the experiences. I don't know how to do that and I don't need to, now. I have learned to cope with them, integrate them into my life, and find some inner peace. That I can share with you.

I can also tell you about how it feels to be under hypnosis, for those of you who are considering it as a tool for investigating your cases. I was scared to be hypnotized in the beginning. Between what I had seen on television and what my sister went through when she tried it for weight loss, I wanted no part of it. Hypnosis was nothing like I imagined. As a matter of fact, you have felt the feeling before if you have ever fallen asleep. Have you ever been on the verge of sleep and the phone rings? You jump up to answer it and it takes a minute for you to realize who you are talking to and where you are. That's the superrelaxed state I found myself in when I was under hypnosis. The first time or two I wasn't able to relax quite that much, but after that, I felt more comfortable with it and when I realized I was in control, I could let go a little more. Heck, the first time I ever had hypnosis, I didn't even think I was under until I woke up and realized that almost two hours had passed! It seemed like fifteen minutes! If your therapist died during a session, the worst thing that would happen would be that you'd fall asleep, wake up a few hours later feeling refreshed and good, until you found out your therapist croaked! If you decide to undergo hypnotherapy, please try to find someone who is experienced and knowledgeable in hypnosis. And be sure you really want to do it. I come from the old school of thought, "If it ain't broke, don't fix it." If you are not having problems sleeping, health problems, or other problems that are seriously affecting your life, think hard before you decide to possibly open a can of worms. Even though I have not remembered all of the night in June of 1983, I will not be having any more hypnosis for it. I feel okay and I figure that when I am ready to remember it, it will come back to me.

I've been very fortunate in that I have always had the support of my family and all my friends. I realize that there is no support for many of you. I know that must be very hard for you. That is one of the reasons I wanted to write this book—perhaps the most important reason. I want to pass along to you some of what I have been blessed with. I feel that part of what I am here to do is help people and teach people how to cope with being witness to and frightened by something most people don't even believe exists. It has only just begun. We have come a long way and yet we still have a long way to go. I want you to realize that if I can come through this intact and stronger than ever, so can you. What I have to say has nothing to do with "New Age" philosophies or religious beliefs. I'm not trying to start some kind of cult or get people to "follow" me. That's the last thing I want. It's just an alternative way of thinking and feeling about things that might help some other people who are like me and have experienced the sort of things I have. It works for me. I want them to know they are not alone. Someone understands and wants to help.

My feelings on just about everything from life to death, have changed since our family was investigated and all the things we have experienced have become public. Through all the questions, interviews with neighbors, family, and friends, all the medical testing, psychological testing, voice stress testing, employer interviews, and everything else I allowed myself to be subjected to in the name of research, I have slowly changed, learned, and grown.

I had a near-death experience when I gave birth to my first son. I feel it was somehow connected to my other unusual experiences. I'm not sure why yet, though. It was not a conventional NDE, if there is a "conventional" one. I did not see any bright, white light at the end of a tunnel. Nor did I see angels or devils or God. (*No.* I didn't see aliens, either!)

I had to have my son by emergency C-section when my kidneys failed as a result of a disease called eclampsia. I was semicomatose by the time I was anesthetized for the delivery. Suddenly I could hear my doctor's voice yelling at me to fight. His voice, and those of the other fifteen people in the delivery room, began to fade, then get louder, then fade again. With a loud swooshing sound, I found myself trapped in what appeared to be a black box of some kind. I could not see my body but I could feel my fists as I pounded violently on the cold, black walls before and around me. I kept screaming that I wasn't dead yet and for someone to please let me out. With another swishing sound, I found myself being lifted off the table and onto the stretcher. I couldn't breathe but I couldn't get anyone's attention. I had apparently been given some kind of drug that paralyzed me. Frantically I tried to shake any part of my body to get someone's attention. I finally got my legs to move a bit and as soon as the doctor looked at me, he realized that I was in serious distress. I was heaved back onto the table, where oxygen was forced into my lungs. As I felt the oxygen flow in, I practically gulped it down in relief.

I had been awake for nearly the whole operation. I assume they tried to give me as little anesthesia as possible, for the baby's sake, but this was a little bit much! I told the doctor later that I could feel him cut me and that it was like a burning pinch and pull rather than what I would have assumed as being just a cut. He seemed a little surprised that I knew that. (Believe me, I would rather not have known!) Then I told him that he and someone else had been talking about sailboats before all the rushing and screaming began. Again he looked surprised. But when I told him about hearing them screaming at me, being trapped in a black box, begging to be set free, screaming that *I* wasn't dead yet, he looked at me like I was nuts and ordered me an antidepressant tablet! No wonder most people never tell their doctors about these kinds of experiences!

No one ever told me why, when I received my bill for the hospital stay, I had been billed for two emergency resuscitations during the delivery.

I have come to believe, after that close call with death, I must be here for a good reason—or else I would have left that day. I wasn't allowed to get even close to leaving. I guess God knew if I ever got a look at that light, I'd never go back!

My baby and I had less than a fifty-fifty chance going into the delivery room. I remember, at one point, praying to God. I told God that if he would let me and my baby live, I promised to teach my baby the kind and loving God that I knew. I must have said something right because seven days later my son and I went home. God kept his end of the bargain, and I've kept mine, too.

Between this experience and the other weird experiences I've had, I have come to believe, wholeheartedly, that death is only a change, not the end of a life. As a matter of fact, many of the things I used to worry about are no longer at the top of my list. All my priorities have changed. I see the bigger picture now. You've probably heard the expression, "He can't see the forest for the trees." Well, I don't just see the forest anymore. I see the whole planet!

On September 1, 1990, I had the most incredible dream of my life. This dream had such an impact on me that I will never forget it as long as I live. I told everyone I knew, and even a few strangers, about it! I told an Episcopal priest about it and she told me that God had spoken to me and I was blessed. I told some of my Native American friends about it and they called it my medicine dream. They told me that the hummingbird was my totem and that was a pretty cool totem to have. Here is my medicine dream:

I was sitting in a lawn chair in my parents' backyard. I was sitting right where the mark in the yard was, right in the middle of the circle. My children were playing in the yard as I watched. I enjoyed hearing their laughing voices and feeling the sunshine on my face. All of a sudden, I heard this loud buzzing noise whizzing around my head. I instinctively picked up the little Whiffleball bat that was lying on the ground next to my chair and began swatting at the small, dark thing flying around my face. I assumed it was a bumblebee and that it was going to sting me. I hit the thing and it fell to my feet. I leaned down to get a better look at this thing and was horrified to see that what I had struck down wasn't a bumblebee. It was a tiny, precious hummingbird. As it lay there, trembling, I scooped it up into my hands and began to cry. At that very moment, I wished that I had been the one that bat had hit. I cried out to the sky, "God, please don't let this poor creature pay for my lesson with his life. Take mine instead." At that instant, the world changed. The familiar sunlight took on an unusual quality. Shadows changed and sound stopped. I could no longer hear the voices of my children, nor could I even see them. It was as if the whole world, time itself, came to a screeching halt. Then, from all around me, I could hear this gentle, male voice softly speak. He said, "Do you understand this?" I shouted to the sky, "YES! I struck out at this poor creature before I even knew what he was. I judged much too quickly. I could have just gotten up and walked away, yet I chose to strike out at something I didn't understand. Please forgive me and please don't let this innocent life pay for my lesson learned. I will never forget this!'' Then, I heard the voice say, ''Very good.'' The next thing I knew, the world and time were back to normal and the tiny hummingbird I had cupped in my hands was coming around nicely. I took him inside the house, nursed him back to health, and he stayed in our house for the whole winter. He stuck to me like glue and followed me everywhere. The following summer, I set him free and we never saw him again. (This was a long dream!)

This was to be the first of many ''virtual reality'' dreams. I hope they will all be this educational and enlightening.

Maybe I did speak to God that night in my dream. He taught me a powerful lesson that applies to many things in life, unusual experiences included. Maybe it's not such a bad lesson for us all to learn.

20

KATHY
Rebirth

We are viewed upon
and analyzed,
with dark and endless
liquid eyes,
seeking our souls,
ignoring our cries,
and leaving few
to sympathize.

I ONCE HAD A PSYCHIC TELL ME SHE SAW ME AS A TEACHER somewhere in my future. At the time she told me that, I thought she was crazy, and I was thinking of asking for a refund. Perhaps sharing my views through this book and my public appearances will be my way of teaching. That sure seems like a great deal of responsibility, and I hope I can do well. My mind will probably go blank the first time I have to speak in front of a group of people. I'll wear red so the tomato stains won't show in case they decide to pelt me with vegetables.

The same psychic also said that Johnny and I were soulmates who have shared many previous lives together.

She claimed we were so closely tied together she kept pick-ing up messages from both of us and couldn't tell them apart. To see us, a person would find that extremely hard to believe. We appear to be as opposite as oil and water. He is a small-town country cowboy through and through, with a deep southern drawl. He loves bluegrass music and is the greatest fan George Jones ever had. I, on the other hand, could be considered a borderline workaholic, always doing my work and his too. I get tired of waiting on him to do it. I love Motown music, stamp collecting, and working in my flower garden.

He is always the "half-empty" while I am the "half-full." He looks for the negative side to every situation while I search for the positive. I am the "nest builder" while he is the "nest sitter." Yet, in spite of it all, I feel he is truly my other half. Over the years we have seemed to balance each other in some unexplainable way. In our last life I feel like I was his parent and he my child. I feel the same past-life karma with my kids and family. We have all evolved over the years in numerous lives and will continue for numerous lives in the future. I probably will live again even though I vowed this would be the last unless I could come back as a rich, thin man. Or maybe just rich—I'll buy thin.

I have to wonder if Johnny's involvement with the visi-tors is because of his involvement with my family, or is it simply his time to know and grow? Have we been chosen for a special purpose somewhere down the line to perhaps carry on the remains of a weakened civilization? Have we been chosen to replenish an endangered population? Have we been chosen to spread the word and educate the majority of nonbelievers? Any one of those possibilities is pretty radical coming from a suburbanite like myself.

I haven't felt "chosen" lately, especially at night after working all day with little to show for it. Actually I feel a little silly, lying on the floor in my nightgown, writing my brains out with a vision that I might actually make a difference somewhere. I'm not sure what force is behind me, guiding me through this, but I will just let that force show me the way. If It is meant to be, it will be. There must be a special purpose ahead for Debbie and me because we have felt compelled to finish this book. After its publication, I am considering further hypnosis to uncover the rest of the missing parts of my life. At this point, I feel like I have just uncovered the tip of the iceberg. Each incident I have told is actually a story in itself. I'm not ready to put myself through all that just yet. It is very time consuming trying to work, write, and keep the house together, but when this book sells, I will have an obligation to find out all I can. I might even talk Johnny into taking the plunge with me. Perhaps after the initial shock of going public wears off, he will become more interested in learning all the missing details of his own encounters.

I am not only finely tuned into Johnny, I also feel I am tuned into anyone I meet. I have always been a very good judge of a person's character from the minute I meet him, but I try never to make a judgment about someone from my first impression. I have always had a talent for empathizing with others and almost always know what a person is trying to say before he finishes the sentence. With my family and close friends, I sometimes know exactly what they're feeling or thinking. Many times it's not what I would want to hear or know. Everyone is different and they are entitled to different opinions, so when I feel we have very conflicting ideas on a subject, I usually just keep my opinions to myself. I have found in life it's usually better not to push people into thinking as I do. Pushing people only tends to put them on the defensive anyway. I have learned that my family and kids are each their own individual personalities and that individuality is what makes life interesting. There is something to be learned from everyone.

Actually I am not the only family member "tuned in." All of us are spirtually connected to each other. I'm not saying our family is more advanced than everyone else; we are simply more aware of our surroundings. I have in- creased my own awareness by concentrating on the inside forces I have and not letting the outside forces overwhelm me or sway my feelings. Debbie and I seem to share this increased awareness in a great number of ways, yet when we disagree it's like a mental star wars. I told her once that the reason she and I had so many inner conflicts was that each of us had such strong spiritual forces that we could be like opposite ends of a magnet, putting out such strong vibrations it was impossible to get each end near the other. I suggested that if we combined these forces and directed them toward a similar goal, there would be no telling what we could accomplish.

I witnessed the strength of her mind on one occasion and if I hadn't seen it for myself I would never believe this story. A few years ago, I had taken on the task of refinish- ing the kitchen cabinets at my parents' house. Debbie and her kids were living there at the time. The second day of stripping and sanding was beginning to wear my patience thin. I was working like a borrowed mule and as I watched Debbie read magazines and do her nails, I decided she could kick in some physical labor herself. I gathered up all the hinges and handles in a bowl for her with a bottle of cleaner and a rag and told her to make good use of herself. After about an hour of rubbing and polishing the handles, she began to slow down to a snail's pace. As I sanded my guts out, I looked over and saw that she was methodically rubbing one of the handles while staring into space. I told her to wake up and use a little "elbow grease" or she would never get done. She didn't care because she never sped up, but shortly after that she said, "Look at this handle, it's all bent up." Oh sure, right, I thought to myself, just a trick so she could stop working. I went over and snatched the handle away from her to see for myself. Sure enough, it was bent like a half moon. We tried to bend it back by hand but neither one of us could straighten it out. I had to take it outside, lay it on the concrete, and hit it with a hammer before it would go back to its original shape. I told her if she was that good she should be the one sanding and I would clean the rest of the handles.

I have never tried to bend any handles with my mind, but I can stop a migraine headache without any medication. I have had migraines for a number of years, since my session with the hypnotist to lose weight. I have found that with just a few minutes of uninterrupted relaxation and concentration, I can stop these headaches myself. This method also works for other aches and pains. I simply clear my mind totally and with each breath I take, I visualize the bad or negative forces leaving my body as I exhale and the healing or positive forces entering. I can completely relax myself and feel 100 percent better in just a matter of a few minutes. It's sort of a mini-meditation—and everyone should try that every day. It's very refreshing.

The human mind is very powerful and can sometimes play tricks on you. That is one explanation by the UFO debunkers. I can speak for myself only when I say that all of the situations I have described here previously were not mind games but actual events related to the best of my knowledge. I rarely jump to conclusions and always look for a logical explanation for every event that concerns me. I have only included the occurrences that I am certain have actually happened, and I will let you be the judge of my character.

You are probably wondering why I have gone from ufology to past lives and karma and are probably thinking that these subjects are totally unrelated. Perhaps so, but to my family, especially Debbie and me, they seem to be very relevant to each other. In 1985, as I wrote my own manuscript about events of my family, I spent almost a year putting it together. I never contacted any agent and only sent three copies out to different publishing companies. Two of the publishing companies never even acknowledged my existence and the other forwarded a pleasant rejection letter without reading my manuscript. That manuscript was put away and untouched until Debbie and I started writing this book. I'm sure I would not have attempted this writing had I not had that old writing to use as a reference. At the time I was struggling to write it I had no idea that it would be so valuable to me years later.

Debbie's boyfriend K.O. has also played a major part in this book. He came into her life through his involvement in ufology and she has known him as an acquaintance for many years. After her divorce from James, she again moved back to Mom and Dad's house. Their house is a lot like a highway rest area. Other family members move in and out so fast the mailman can't keep up with the names. K.O. set up Debbie with a computer and printer and taught her how to use it. I didn't even know she could type when she first mentioned writing a book. The more she talked of her plans the more I wrestled in my mind trying to decide whether to approach her about writing with her. It seemed like the perfect opportunity to combine our spiritual forces in a single project.

She did have a major advantage over me as she had been involved in UFO studies, had spoken before large groups, and had done interviews for the last ten years. I, on the other hand, have only gone to work, done laundry, and washed dishes. She knew many people from all over the country and they knew her. No one knows me. Her face, her story, and her artworks are recognized by many, while my face was buried in the sand. That is why I originally chose to write this book under the name Laura Davis. Since I am

Laura Davis in the book *Intruders,* I figured no one would have a clue as to who I am if I used my real name. Second, if I used my real name people would really be confused, since my name is Kathy. As you remember, Kathie was the main character in *Intruders.* But I've decided not to hide under the name Laura Davis. I am only trying to simplify matters in an already complicated story. I won't be able to hide any more unless I put a sack over my head.

Even though Debbie seems to have all the right connections, I feel I can offer an equal share of interest in our story. I stand not only as a character witness but also as an eyewitness to our family's ongoing involvement with the paranormal for three generations.

In a strange way, I feel I laid the groundwork for this book in 1965 in that empty church parking lot.

For eighteen years, I was the only family member to actually remember seeing a UFO, close enough that there was no question whatsoever in my mind about what I had seen. I think that because of that incident, and because we talked about it freely among ourselves, Debbie's courage was bolstered to find the missing pieces to the 1983 backyard incident. It would have been very easy to simply dismiss the entire event as a nightmare. It would have been easier to just assume the large circle and long path burned in the yard was due to sewer problems or lawn chemical overdose. After all, that would seem the logical explanation to the average person. That may be the answer for someone not as aware of their surroundings as our family seems to be. That would be the answer a person could simply state, then file away to be forgotten. But the easy way out is not always the right way out. The only way to face a complicated problem is head on and don't look back.

That is what Debbie did. At the time none of us were too thrilled about the idea. There were too many unanswered questions, and each question uncovered another eerie, unexplainable event. Each event was a complicated story in itself that seemed to form mind-boggling experiences for all of us. Was it going to be worth it? It would have been very tempting to hide it away or sweep it under the rug so none of us would have to deal with our inner selves, our unconscious minds that continually tried to remain silent.

As Debbie worked to uncover all she could, we trudged along behind like baby ducks following their momma. I was surprised at the great number of people out in the real world who had experienced incidents much like our own. These were average-appearing, intelligent people who were all very pleasant and open about their lives. I guess I thought I would meet a roomful of people who were wearing tinfoil triangles on their heads or something, but that was not the case. In fact, many of them appeared to be much more intelligent than I am. These were everyday people, struggling with bills, kids, and life, just like me. That was kind of reassuring. I met many highly educated, professional people who showed great interest in the entire subject and never even cracked a smile. That caught me off guard. I had been used to people laughing at the first mention of UFOs and aliens. Now I was meeting a completely new culture.

Even in this relaxed, more open atmosphere I was reluctant to say too much about myself or my family. It's hard to break old habits. I had visions of revealing my inner thoughts to someone and midway through a crucial part of the story, she would say, "Yeah, right," and begin to giggle hysterically. Besides, it never seemed to be a subject I could describe quickly or simply. I could never just say, "Oh yes, I've seen UFOs and aliens," and leave it at that. It's much more complicated. Then after you include a few of the details, you feel the need to add some defensive tactics for self-preservation.

It seems a real shame that an innocent person has to continually be on the defensive because of a situation that is totally out of his control—a situation he did not ask to be included in and usually ends up wishing he had not been in. I think a great majority of the ridicule that nonbelievers dish out is due to fright. They are afraid of what they can't understand. By refusing to acknowledge its existence, they simply "will" it away. Maybe they feel that if they pretend such things don't exist, they will be left alone.

I don't think that will work.

I had no idea what determines the aliens' way of selecting people to become involved with. I could be snooty and say they would most likely pick a clean, pleasant-appearing, extremely bright, and hysterically funny person.

I don't think that will work either.

The chosen ones I have met appear to be a mixture of people from many walks of life. Perhaps what makes them similar is that which we can't see. Perhaps it is that which we can only feel. There appears to be a kind of unspoken bond that links us spiritually. Perhaps that bond was formed between people who have shared a similar, frightening experience, holding on to the opinion that there really is safety in numbers. Perhaps they share this unspoken bond for a reason they are neither consciously aware of nor consciously remember. Perhaps we are being prepared for a great purpose somewhere in the future.

I feel in my heart this purpose will be good. I have never felt alien intervention was for a negative cause. If I had felt that way, I would never have begun writing this book. Being the bearer of bad tidings is not my bag. I have never felt the visitors were evil . . . only scary. That which we don't fully understand can be very scary.

I truly believe that I am now at a point in my life where I am no longer afraid. If a craft landed in my yard I would welcome the occupants into my home. If only they gave us the choice to meet with them instead of taking people against their will. The resentment I feel is because of my obvious lack of control over the encounters. Being snatched up and examined without any choice whatsoever is just too tacky for words. I suspect "they" would have many willing volunteers if "they" were only open and honest about their intent. There would be many people who would welcome a little gab fest, so to speak. An open exchange of ideas. A real learning experience. I believe two civilizations, one of extreme intelligence and one of extreme sensitivity, could successfully merge to help each other. If they would just quit snatching people against their will and learn a little from our sensitivity.

It would be so much nicer to get a pleasant little invitation, requesting our company. Something like:

> Dear Kathy,
>   Long time no see. Hope this finds you and your family well.
>   This is just a note to let you know that we will be in your area on the 22nd of this month at 1:15 A.M. Look for us in the northeast corner of the Joneses' wheat field.
>   We look forward to seeing you again. Feel free to bring a friend.
>
>   Pleasant dreams,
>   Q

Now that would be a much more sensitive and personal way to communicate. At least we would have a choice in the matter.

That's not scary at all.

I may be way off track here. I certainly don't have all the answers. I'm not sure I have any answers at all, only questions. Whether I am right or wrong, I feel I must come forward now and see what happens. Because of my past involvements, I must share my opinions now and hope I can help a few people come to grips with themselves.

I must abandon the "Do not air your dirty laundry" syndrome. I must learn to trust in myself and others enough to become more open. I need to keep reminding myself that this is no longer the 1960s and I am no longer a kid.

I haven't had all the interaction with people Debbie has had. I have had no groups of people applauding me for encouragement, but I will catch up fast. As I begin to crack my shell, I feel all the pieces are falling into place. The time must be right.

21

DEBBIE
The Future

PLEASE: KEEP AN OPEN MIND AND AN OPEN HEART AS YOU READ this chapter. It contains my feelings about what the future may hold for the human race—and for me. At this point in the game, none of us can really have much more than feelings, intuitions, and educated guesses.

I hate predictions. I try not to make them. If I do make public my feelings about the future, I try to reinforce the thought that these are only my feelings and may mean absolutely nothing. On a personal level, I believe there are several paths we can follow and our fate is determined by our choices. But I also believe that divine guidance is there for us—within us—should we ever decide to ask for it—and listen to it when it is offered. As for the bigger picture, I was raised to believe that there is a reason that ''big'' things must happen, even though we might not understand it at the time. And little things happen so that something bigger can happen later.

Most of the predictions I've heard other people make simply did not happen. On the rare occasion when someone hit it right on the mark, I thought to myself, Either he just got lucky or he must be a very special, gifted person. I doubt I am gifted in that way.

It doesn't take a rocket scientist to see where we are headed if we don't start taking care of this planet and of each other. Most predictions are really logical observation. But that doesn't explain all predictions.

Animals are often aware of impending earthquakes due to changes in the electromagnetic fields that surround the planet. And you may have seen your family dog hide under the couch before a big storm hits. Animals can sense change coming before we do. This might be what's happening to me. My awareness of my surroundings has been so amplified that sometimes I sense things before most people catch on. Perhaps this is what happens to us as a result of our experiences, and that's why so many experiencers tend to make a lot of predictions. An overabundance of inner awareness spills over into the physical realm we live in and we become supersensitive to that, too. It makes me wonder if something isn't being awakened in us—something in all of us that was long lost and is now being found again. I see it as an awareness of the planet we live on and the connection we have to it, to each other, and to all that is life—God (or whatever name you choose to call it).

I feel as though I'm beginning to remember another world, another existence. My sister and I have both, at various times in our lives and independent of one another, made the statement that if one of us were to ever fall ill with some catastrophic disease, we would know exactly what to do. We both felt that we had been told to go alone and find an open field, lie down, go to sleep, and the next morning, when we wake up, we would be healed. Neither one of us had ever mentioned this to the other and it only came out after the investigation started with Budd.

I had also had a recurring dream that began when I was very young. In the dream, I was lying in a ditch, covered by fallen trees, hiding from the violence all around me. The sky was a funny color, a very dark, ominous purple/blue mix. There were blue and red streaks of light flashing back and forth across this frightening sky. The wind was ferocious and rain was falling so hard that it blew horizontally across the open field in front of me and stung my face as it hit me. There was a large hill about seventy-five feet in front of where I was lying. I was trying desperately to get to this hill. I crawled on my belly toward the hill, digging my fingers in the dirt as I crawled so as not to be blown away by the terrible wind. The noise all around me was deafening. I felt pure panic. My only hope seemed to be making it to that hill. As I finally got to the base of this hill and was able to look up, I could see a man standing at the very top. He was dressed all in white; he was dry and the wind seemed to have no effect on him. He was very beautiful, with golden hair draped over his shoulders. His eyes were bright blue, radiating pure love and calmness. When he spoke to me, it was as if he spoke directly to my heart and my mind. He said, "It's time to go. You are safe, now." Suddenly the most incredible feeling of relief and calm swept over me and then the dream would end. Last year, when I went to visit Cahokia Mounds in Illinois, built by Indians hundreds of years ago, I found the hill and the trees and the ditch that I had dreamed about before so many times in my life. I can't describe to you the feeling I had when I stood atop that hill (a mound) and looked back at the ditch and trees. It was a combination of peace, relief, and an uncomfortable twinge of anxiety. I don't know what it all means, but if I ever find myself in a situation similar to the one in my dream, I'll know where to go!

My sister and I have both said, also at different times and independently, that the world would be a very different place by the turn of the century. But it would only be for the young and the strong. Whether that means physically, emotionally, or spiritually, I don't know. I did know that I would be a part of it. And she knows she will be, too. I do know that no one need be lost in the changes. If people do become lost, it will be by their own choice.

I feel that some of the changes will be real, physical ones. Things will happen to change the whole look of the planet. Major governmental and social changes will occur. For some reason, I feel like these are a few of the things I'm supposed to watch for because they will be my triggers. They will help me to remember what I am supposed to do next.

I feel as though the whole world, all of humanity, is about to embark on the greatest journey of all. As time passes, I think it will become more and more obvious.

As a species, we are beginning to go through some profound changes. I feel that part of why I am here is to help open as many hearts and minds as I can so these changes will come as easily as possible for those who are still bound by fear. The only way I know how to describe the changes that I feel are coming is to say that the human race is about to take the final step on the evolutionary ladder. This change will not be a physical one; we won't lose our pinkies or our appendix. We will lose our fear, our sense of separation and individuality. We will learn how to escape the confinement of our linear-time thinking and realize our potential as "one." The veils of our minds will finally part, and we will remember what we really are and why we are here.

I can't really explain to you why I think aliens have something to do with this. I only know they do. Perhaps they are simply another manifestation of the life that we are all a part of and are helping us to remember, to evolve, so that they can, too. After all, I believe that all life is somehow connected. That includes them, too. Maybe in helping us, they are helping themselves. Maybe we are holding more than just ourselves back with our fear, desire for control, and lack of responsibility, and they're getting tired of waiting for us. Perhaps our encounters are gentle or not-so-gentle reminders. Anything is possible.

Most of the time, I believe that all the answers we spend a lifetime seeking have always been within us. We waste so much time looking for it everywhere else, not wanting to take responsibility for our lives and our feelings, that we miss the whole point—learning, growing, loving, and becoming one.

As of late, I've learned to run on instinct. I'm letting the universe guide me. I have found that the more I trust in it, the better it gets. When I stopped fighting my instinct and started listening to it, my life really took off. I found my direction and purpose. Instinct is what led me to my fiancé, K.O., and I include our coming together in this chapter because this is one instance where I believe it was orchestrated. All my rationalization and reasoning just can't explain why we are together. And without him, this book would have never happened.

It was 1987: Budd Hopkins had come to DePauw University to give a talk on UFOs. He had just finished his book, *Intruders,* the book about my family. My sister, Kathy ("Laura"), my new husband, James, and I had gone to the university to hear him talk. This was our first experience in seeing how the public reacted to the subject. And it was a chance to see Budd again. We didn't get to see him as much as we would have liked.

K.O.'s daughter was attending the university at the time. She knew of her father's great interest in the subject of UFOs and had informed him that Budd would be giving a talk there. He and his wife attended that night, as well. Budd asked my sister and me to stand up and say a few words about what our family had experienced, and K.O. videotaped the whole thing. (I look at the tape today and laugh. I was so nervous you could hear my voice shake as I spoke.) K.O. was fascinated with our story and with me. The investigator in him wanted to learn more.

As the years passed, I would see him at various functions, MUFON meetings, and conferences. As it turned out, we shared mutual friends in Rose and Charlie Rich, and we would see each other from time to time at their home. I never thought of K.O. as anything more than a nice, kind of nerdy, really intelligent friend. Besides the fact that we were both married, he was fourteen years older than I and definitely not the type to whom I was normally attracted.

Here's the story:

It all starts one week after I had become engaged to my second husband, James. While I was a junior instructor at the local beauty college, my students got me to do something I never would have done on my own. On their lunch hour, they had called a psychic who would give one free reading over the phone. After much begging on their part, I agreed to talk to the guy, but not without quite a nasty little attitude about the whole thing. The ancient voice on the other end of the phone line asked me, "What's your name, honey?" I said, in a hateful tone of voice, "Debbie," and I thought to myself, You're psychic, you tell me the rest. Immediately, he said, "You're going to be married three times." I said, "I don't think so." He repeated himself in the same hateful tone of voice that I was using with him. I then informed him that I had just gotten engaged to number two and there would be no number three if I had anything to say about it. He then said, "Go ahead and marry him. It won't last more than five years." (James and I did split on our fifth anniversary.) Then he proceeded to tell me that number three would be an older man, someone several years older than I, who would satisfy me and protect me the way I needed to be protected. He would give me all I needed so I could do what I had come here to do. I told the old psychic that he was out of his mind, he needed to get a real job, and then I hung up on him. I told my mother about the phone call when I got home from work that afternoon and we had a good chuckle. But she never forgot it.

In June of 1992, my husband and I split. This was a hectic time in my life (see chapter 15) and I was experiencing a multitude of feelings. I was leaning on my friends heavily and had spent a lot of time on the phone to one of my best friends, Forest Crawford. We had talked about everything imaginable. I had read some books on the subject of angels and found it fascinating. Once, Forest made the comment to me that if I ever had a question as to the direction of my life, I should just ask the universe. And if I listened really closely, I might hear an answer. I thought that was a neat idea.

One night, while driving home from my soon-to-be exhusband's house where I had collected some more of my belongings, I began to think about my conversation with Forest. I had mentioned to him that I was feeling a sense of urgency that I had never felt before. I felt as if I needed to be with someone—someone I already knew—before something wonderful could happen. I had run a mental list of all the eligible men I knew who might be what I was looking for. (K.O. was not even on that list!) As I drove down the dark back roads of the shortcut to Mom's, I remembered what Forest had told me earlier. If I asked, someone would answer.

Thank God it was dark and the road was deserted, because I began to talk out loud to myself. I'd have died if anyone had seen me! "Okay," I said, "Forest says you guys will answer my questions, so I've got one for you. Who is it I'm supposed to be with?"

I swear on a stack of Bibles, I heard—as plain as day—a woman's voice in my car say the name "Carl." It was as if she were sitting right next to me, yelling in my ear. It startled me so much that I nearly drove off the road!

Although it's a nice thought, I never really expected to hear an answer! I don't know what possessed me then, but next, I began to question that answer!

"Carl?" I said. "I don't know anyone named Carl. What is this, some kind of joke? I know it's someone I already know, so why are you telling me this name?"

Then I said, "Well, I have an uncle named Carl, but he's dead, and I don't think he would count anyway. We're related, you know."

Twice more I heard the name Carl, each time more insistent than the last. The final time almost sounded as if the woman were getting upset with me for questioning her. I really felt like some kind of nut! When I got home, I told my mother about this and we both laughed, but I still felt kind of weird that I actually heard this voice. Maybe I'm cracking up, I thought to myself. I called my friends, Rose and Forest, and told them about it too. I'm glad I did.

A few weeks passed. I was slated to give a talk on my experiences to a group in Pensacola, Florida, that August. K.O. had heard that I was going to go do my talk alone. Knowing the circumstances under which I would be leaving (see chapter 15), he thought it would be nice for me to have a familiar face from home there, lending me moral support —rather presumptuous and not at all like him, but a nice thought. He had separated from his wife the year before and had taken up traveling as a hobby. Also, being an investigator, he was interested in hearing my talk.

He was somehow able to purchase a ticket on the same flight and for the seat right next to mine, even though my flight had been booked months in advance. He even booked himself a hotel room five minutes away from where I would be staying. I was surprised to find out he had made all these plans before consulting me, but I was truly flattered that he thought that much of me. We were at Rose and Charlie's house the night he told me that he had made arrangements to go on my trip with me.

At one point, I looked at him and said, "Hell, K.O., here I am going to travel with you and I don't even know your real name. What does K.O. stand for, anyway?" He looked over at me and smiled really big as he said his full name to me for the first time: "Karl Osburn Learner II." Immediately I remembered the voice in the car and the name it had spoken. I looked at my friend Rose, who had apparently also remembered what I had told her. She had this great big grin on her face! I was thinking to myself, Oh, my God! No! This can't be! What is this, some kind of joke? Fortunately my thoughts were only known to Rose.

I know this sounds terrible, but he was one of the last men I would have chosen for myself. Not that he's not a good guy. It just didn't fit. As it turned out, he couldn't have been a better choice for me! It's a good thing I decided to let someone else do the choosing this time! It didn't take me long to realize that I had made some pretty crummy choices in my life previously. If I wanted things to change, I knew I had better change my choices.

The day after K.O. and I returned home from our trip to Florida, I began to feel guilty. I had treated him so poorly during the whole trip that I was ashamed of myself. All the time we were down there he was as attentive and protective as he could be. I fought back in my own mind. How dare someone or something force me to be with this man! I didn't like the thought that I had no choice in the whole affair.

All my friends commented on how much he appeared to care for me. Vicki, a really good friend, even said to me, "Girlfriend, that boy's in love with you! If my husband can see it, anyone can!" I told her to shut up and not let anyone hear her say that! I was, briefly and to the point, a bitch from day one of the trip. The second day after we returned, it was as if a light came on in my head and I could hear that woman's voice again, this time in my head. She said, "Do you really want to push away the best thing that's ever happened to you? This is it, girl. This is what we've been waiting for." I called K.O. up and apologized for my horrible behavior. The first thing he said in response was, "You know, something told me to give you a little space, that you'd come around." Two days later, I started writing this book.

After K.O. and I had dated for a while, we began talking about getting married someday. My mother then reminded me about what the old psychic had told me on the phone that day, several years before. That pretty much cinched it for me.

K.O. has been instrumental in the writing of this book. He got me my first dinosaur computer and taught me how to use it. Before him, I couldn't even turn one on! He has supported me emotionally, spiritually, and financially. He helped me find the confidence in myself to do what I feel I have to do. He taught me to believe that I could write, in book form, all the things that were in my heart—and that it might help others in the process. I love him very much and I thank God every day for my blessings.

There's so much in my mind and heart that I want to share with you, but I have yet to find the words to express it fully. I think you have to feel it rather than hear it. I wish I could climb inside each and every one of you and make you "know," but I can't. You'll have to come to the realizations I have come to on your own for them to have any real meaning for you. All I can do is plant the seed and hope it grows.

The things that I find myself feeling and thinking, amaze me. To remember where I came from, to know where I am, and to see where I'm going really seems incredible to me. I feel I'm living proof of a larger plan. In a way, sharing it with others feels kind of weird and embarrassing. I feel naked right now. I realize that I still have much to learn. This growing and changing process I have found myself in has only just begun. Through reading this book, I hope you have been able to see where I came from and where I am heading. If I can get this far, so can anyone else. No one was ever more terrified than I was.

There's really no good way to end this book. The experiences, the changes, and the growing never seem to end. The only thing I can do is keep looking up and in, keep having faith, and keep writing. And remember that no matter how weird it gets, it never stops feeling right.

22

KATHY
The Future

As I near the conclusion of this book, I realize we're nowhere near the end of our story. It is merely a stopping place. I feel like I am just beginning to get on a roll with this writing stuff, and I think I like it. I was once told that writing would be good therapy for me. I took that comment as a hint that perhaps the person thought I was one brick shy of a full load. I see now that it has been good therapy. It's very cheap too. I would recommend it for anyone who has experienced any kind of trauma in his or her life. It's very therapeutic to document your thoughts on paper, even if later you just pile up the sheets and set them on fire.

I began polling my kids a couple of weeks ago for their opinions on the subject of UFOs and visitors. None of them seemed to be really cooperative, but I did manage to get a sense of their feelings. When I asked my daughter Lisa her opinion, she made a snarly face. She is now twenty-three, married, and has a daughter of her own who is four months old. That makes me a grandma now, really antique. Her answers were exactly what I was expecting to hear. I had always felt she had never seen any unidentified craft or alien beings. She did state that she felt there was life on other planets and people on this planet have more than likely seen the visitors and their crafts, but she had not.

I asked her if it was going to embarrass her now that I am committed to go public with our story. She claimed that it would not and she seemed to think her friends and co-workers would not put her through the wringer too much. Her close friends already know the story anyway. Lisa, like me, picks her friends and keeps them for life, so they were around when *Intruders* was published.

When I asked Mike, who is now twenty-one, what his beliefs are, he said, "Catch me later on that, Mom." So far that is all I have managed to get out of him.

Mike was the kid with Johnny on the night he had the flat-tire incident. He wasn't with him during the incident itself, but he was the one left waiting all night at the cabin for his dad to return. Mike had not read *Intruders* and, as I suspected, had no idea of his father's involvement. We never discussed Johnny's experiences in front of any of the kids. When I told Mike the details of that night recently, he was surprised to say the least, but he was not what I would call flabbergasted. Mike was also with Johnny the morning he stopped on his way to work and watched an unusual craft in the early morning hours. At that time, he claimed that he had no memory of seeing anything in the sky but did remember his dad stopping the truck. Now, as I reminded him of that incident, he denies any memory of that morning at all. It certainly didn't make much of an impression on him. I don't think I have to worry about embarrassing him; he's oblivious to the world. He's only interested in subjects that involve horsepower, RPMs, and bikinis.

I did get a little more cooperation from Stevie. He remembered seeing the tiny aliens in the living room when he was younger. He also admitted he hadn't shared this story with any of his current friends—just with a couple of friends at the time it happened. That's pretty understandable because it was a very bizarre situation. When I asked him if he would be embarrassed for his friends to see his mother openly talking about our lives, he said, "That's cool, as long as you don't drag me around with you."

I questioned his views on why he thought aliens were visiting and what he thought they wanted to accomplish. He stated he thought they were here to help us progress. To him, progress meant showing us how to make more electronic gadgets to make our lives easier, perhaps a floating car for better transportation.

He thought the government knows a lot more than they tell us, but he didn't expand on that idea.

When I asked him why they don't just make themselves known to all, he said that he thought they didn't think we were capable of handling the reality of them. He went on to say that they would make themselves known "when the time is right."

It was very eerie for me to hear that phrase come out of the mouth of one of my kids. Those exact words "when the time is right" have been popping up in my head as long as I can remember. Since this kid doesn't read about UFOs, never read *Intruders,* and I don't talk much about the subject in front of him, it seemed like a great coincidence that he would use those exact words. It was more than a little chilling for me just thinking of all the possibilities that phrase might represent involving my youngest child.

Last of all, I asked him what changes he thought we would be seeing by the year 2000. He didn't seem to think we would see that many changes so soon, but perhaps later in the next century.

He is eighteen now and just graduated from high school last night, by the skin of his teeth, I might add. He has come a long way from the scared little kid watching miniature aliens on the coffee table. He seems to be a typical teenager and doesn't show any signs of being traumatized by the long chain of incredible events we have experienced as a family.

My heart tells me I made the right decision all those years ago not to make a major issue of the UFO phenomenon—at least as far as my kids are concerned. They were all at such impressionable ages then and life itself is frightening enough without adding to the burden.

My oldest son Bill has apparently been contemplating his ideas now for weeks. He is contemplative by nature anyway and never answers a question outright; even the simplest question seems to him to deserve great thought.

I have quizzed him several times and he simply evades giving me a direct answer. I am sure he is a believer, but for some reason he refuses to state his opinion. It surprises me that he refuses to cooperate with me. I somehow felt he would have the most to offer since he is not only the oldest but there was a time when he was extremely interested in the subject. He is by far the most talented artist in the family but I couldn't even get him to draw a contribution. By the time this comes out in print, he will no doubt have a hundred ideas to offer.

Now comes Johnny. His complete turnabout from staunch nonbeliever has been extremely hard for me to grasp. He is beginning to talk very openly about the entire subject. He told his mother about this book last week. He didn't go into much detail, but it was a great step for someone who had not breathed a word of this to her for at least the last twenty-five years that I know of. His parents, to my knowledge, were not even aware of our mention in *Intruders*. As I sit here writing, Johnny is talking to one of his sisters on the telephone and comparing ideas about ufology. As it turns out, she has been a believer for years but also, to my knowledge, had no idea of our family's involvement.

I never thought I would live to see this day. I wonder how different things might have turned out if he had showed this encouragement ten years ago. I don't blame him for my decision to be excluded from the UFO scene. I realize I was excluded by my own choice, but perhaps his approval would have been enough to sway my decision.

In a way, I feel I have been on the back burner, so to speak, all these years. I believe everything happens for a reason though, when the time is right. I feel that the last ten years have enabled me to grow spiritually and put things into the proper perspective. Ten years ago I did not want my kids involved in any way. It seemed to be the only way I had any control over their involvement. If they have been tampered with by any alien forces, I certainly had no physical way to stop it. I simply wanted to protect them, not only physically but also mentally. That's why we limited our UFO discussions to the bare minimum. They were at a very impressionable age back then and it is a very scary subject to many.

Now they are on their own. I think they are all mature enough to separate fact from fiction and make their own decisions. I would never try to contaminate their beliefs for any reason. They are free to make their own choices.

As a family, we have some physical and psychological similarities that may or may not have anything to do with the visitors. Johnny, Debbie, Mom, and Mike have the deep oval scars on their shins that are sometimes connected to UFO abductions. Mom, Debbie, our other sister Shari, and I all had carpal tunnel syndrome that involves nerve conduction to our hands. Debbie, Shari, and I all had an infected pilonidal cyst. That is a cyst that forms at the base of the tailbone and is extremely painful. My brother and I were the sleepwalkers. Many of us suffer from a variety of allergies, to penicillin, various other antibiotics, mold, dust, and weeds. I had the rarest allergy of all. For an entire year beginning at the age of ten, I was allergic to cold. If anything cool or cold touched any part of my body, I would instantly break out in huge hives accompanied by extreme itching and swelling. As the area was warmed up, the symptoms would subside. The hives would appear not only if I was exposed to cold air or a cold surface, but appeared if I ate or drank anything cold. That was really a bummer. No cold drinks, cold food, ice, or ice cream—or my mouth, lips, and throat would begin to swell and itch and my throat would begin to close up. If I went outside in the fall or winter I had to be totally covered head to toe. I had to carry medication with me everywhere I went. I felt like a sideshow freak because everyone I encountered wanted to see for themselves. I was constantly laying an arm on a cool surface to offer proof and receive "oohs" and "aahs." This lasted for one year and seemed to stop rather abruptly, but it was a great source of embarrassment and discomfort to me during that long year.

It did leave me with a feeling of great empathy for those people suffering from physical disfigurements, as I will never forget the crushing embarrassment I felt then.

I'm not sure whether these similarities have any meaning or not. Probably many families share traits that way.

Debbie and I shared the desire to save and collect seeds. It was a short-term event for her, but I have saved and replanted flower seeds for many years. At one time I had the notion to save seeds from every conceivable plant. I also had a mental vision that I should be stocking some type of shelter with tools, food, water, medical supplies, seeds, and books in some underground house of sorts. I haven't done that—I just felt I should, sometime, for a reason I don't know and don't care to speculate about.

I feel that by the end of this century we will see many great changes in this world. There may be some difficult times ahead, but then again, change of any kind can be difficult. I feel that there is always something to be learned from all the events that happen to us, good or bad. It's not what life deals you that makes a difference, it's how you deal with your experiences. How you deal with positive and negative changes determines how you grow mentally and physically. Life is like going to school to enrich your inner self. All our life experiences also serve as teaching experiences. No one can experience every conceivable event possible in a single life, so we as a people share and compare our experiences in hopes of helping others understand how we have dealt with all the events that affect us.

As people listen and learn about these different experiences, they begin to enrich their own understanding. Even if people don't believe or agree with all they see or hear, they should keep an open mind, because no one has all the answers. What is right or relevant to one person may not concern another, but there is still something to be learned.

All the experiences I have conveyed to you in this book were my learning experiences. In my effort to share them with you, please keep an open mind and don't judge me too harshly. Remember that many, many years ago, the people here on Earth thought the world was flat. No one had a clue as to what gravity was, and travel in space was a great stretch of the imagination. As I said, no one has all the answers. With the growing number of believers in the UFO phenomenon and the growing number of eyewitnesses coming forward, a person would have to have a very closed mind to think it's all just a figment of the imagination.

A closed mind is a very small mind.

Far too many people have seen UFOs and aliens to dismiss these phenomena as purely imaginary. Far too many alien craft have been captured on film to label the subject a hoax.

Granted that over the years there have been many elaborate hoaxes. Some people have gone to great lengths to duplicate the UFO phenomenon. For reasons only they can explain, these people spend a great deal of energy trying to fool the public. I suppose they don't have anything better to do with their time. Sometimes it appears that the public enjoys these hoaxes. They seem to offer an easy way out of a subject that makes people uneasy. Since it's simpler to prove a hoax than prove the real experience, it's simpler to say all UFOs are just a hoax and sweep the subject under the rug.

As I wrap up this final chapter, I would love to be able to include a photo as some solid proof, but so far I have nothing to offer. About seven years ago I had a picture to submit, but unfortunately it disappeared under mysterious circumstances. I was coming home from an errand one evening around 9 P.M. and noticed two very large, extremely bright headlights from two separate craft traveling slowly toward my house from the southwest. They appeared to be side by side, but I knew they were two separate craft because the span between them did not stay the same as they would move slightly up or sideways. I can't explain why I was sure these were not planes, but I just "knew" they were not of this Earth.

I ran inside to get my camera and dashed back outside, hoping they would travel directly overhead so I could get a good shot of them. Of course that did not happen. I would estimate the craft to be about one mile away from me as I took the first two pictures. Then they began to turn away from me as I snapped the third picture. I realized then I was at the end of the roll of film, so I just watched as the craft stayed together and began traveling away from me in the direction from which they came. On the back of each craft was a single red light. I saw no other lights on them and could not make out any distinct shape or hear any sound.

I sent the roll of film to a photo finishing service by way of mail, ordering double prints of all the pictures. When I received the pictures back, I was disappointed to find I only had a double print of only one picture; the other two were missing. As I looked at the picture I was dismayed to see only what appeared to be one blob of light, not the two lights I had seen. Where the second light should have been was just a light spot in the picture, appearing to have no shape to it at all. I disgustedly put the two identical pictures and negative in my china cabinet and forgot about them.

Three years later, I stumbled upon the film envelope in the china cabinet. I removed the first picture from the envelope and held it at a sideways angle. As I looked at the blob of light, I noticed it had a definite shape. It struck me by surprise to see this picture resemble a UFO, because when the picture was held straight the shape was not noticeable at all. The light was perfectly domed on the top, at the bottom edge on each side it angled in at the same length and the bottom was perfectly flat. Circling the light was a thin red line at what would be the edge, making the shape of this light quite distinctive. I could not believe I had not seen that three years earlier.

I immediately sat down, wrote a note to a friend of mine involved in a large UFO organization, and included the negative and one of the duplicate pictures. The other picture I placed in a mail order film envelope with instructions to have it enlarged to an eight-by-ten-inch size.

As weeks went by I began to wonder why I hadn't heard from either my friend or the photo company. After contacting the photo company, I learned they had lost my order. Debbie was going to visit our friend and I asked her to check on my letter to him for his opinion. When she came back I was really surprised to hear that he had not received my letter at all.

So that was the end of my picture. I sat outside many nights after that fighting heat, humidity, and bugs in hopes of getting something else on film, but it never happened.

As I sit here now writing, I am on the deck of our friend's cabin where Johnny had his first UFO and alien sighting many years ago. I have my camera ready next to me, my glasses on, and four willing eyewitnesses inside. I have been sitting out here for an hour picking gnats out of my drink and slapping mosquitoes off my face. It's a very overcast night and I can only see a handful of stars, but I know the visitors are out there and the least they could do is cooperate after all the anguish they have put us through.

I sit here like a dope thinking perhaps I can "will" them to fly over to somehow back me up as character witnesses. That's really rich. It's certainly very assuming of me to think I am so special they would love to accommodate my every whim. Just sitting out here surrounded by nature is enough to make a person realize just how dwarfed one soul is in the grand scheme of life. When you think past the vastness of Earth into space and the universe, it's hard to imagine one human could feel any more special than any other living creature. You're born and you die. Whatever you accomplish somewhere in between is totally up to you.

So now, after an hour and a half, I am giving up and going inside. Again with no pictures. I guess I'm not so special after all.

My friends waiting inside, bug free and cozy, would have loved to have gotten a glimpse of a UFO. One of my friends, who I'll call Lou, had a UFO experience many years ago, when an unidentified craft flew next to her car for several miles through the country. She claimed it was flying at the same speed as her car and very low to the ground, raising to pass over houses, barns, and poles. She doesn't know if there was any unaccounted time and has no memories of any occurrences.

Lou also saw a large craft hovering over a small patch of trees down at the end of the road leading to my house. Her mother was with her and they pulled to the side of the road and watched this craft for a few minutes before it sped off. Each remembered the craft differently, which was a little surprising. After the craft left, they came down to my house, but there was nothing left to see.

Lou and her husband lived about four miles from my house, possibly three as the crow flies. They were awakened one night by a large light shining through the sliding glass door in their bedroom. As they watched the light, they thought it was very close to being above my house. They watched for several minutes and tried to call us but, since school was out for the summer, our phone lines were tied up nearly twenty-four hours a day.

Johnny and I slept through this, totally unaware of anything.

Lou said she read about one of these sightings in the local paper the next day, but I didn't see it.

In conclusion, I would like to think that somewhere, someone who is reading this will understand why we have opened ourselves up to the public. I hope I have conveyed my thoughts and ideas in an understandable manner. As I finish the last of my contribution to this book it still hasn't sunk in to my mind that Debbie and I have actually accomplished this feat. It has all happened so fast I still find it hard to believe. This book has gone from an idea to almost three hundred pages in just a few months. Considering the fact that neither of us were aspiring authors or even experienced writers, but that we are just everyday people, makes this book even more of a small miracle. Our guardian angels must be worn out guiding us through each page. Even though we have worked very hard, the task seemed to fall in place effortlessly, as if it was meant to be. I won't try to have you believe that our royalties won't be welcome, but in all honesty, the money will be quite secondary.

We have a literary agent. That sounds so "Hollywood" I can't believe it's really us. Obviously I'm still hiding behind my security blanket because after we signed with him, Debbie asked me if I had told all my friends at work we now have an agent. I looked at her and said, "Are you crazy?" I knew then I had a long way to go.

I don't know why we have been chosen as intergalactic guinea pigs. I don't know the itinerary for the future. I don't know what the visitors hope to learn from us. I can only imagine what they must think of us. We must appear to be overgrown, dumb, hairy mammoths. A culture of people who fight among themselves, litter their world, and base their existence around material possessions.

Physically we humans may be a good specimen to breed with their species. Our large bodies and their small ones might produce a medium-size frame such as our race was many centuries ago, and we certainly have plenty of hair to go around. Their super intelligence might balance out our much lower level of intelligence, and our sensitivity just may soften their coldness. It may be a match made in heaven, so to speak.

Perhaps one day in the future, earthlings and non-earthlings will coexist in harmony.

Perhaps we will bond with a wholly new culture of friends, each helping the other in different ways.

Perhaps one day alien spacecraft will fill the skies in view of everyone, the way our aircraft clutter the skies now.

If the day ever comes that a UFO is looked upon by us humans with no more interest than we give to a passenger plane, it will be a little sad to lose one of the greatest mysteries of all.

23

DEBBIE

"Emily"

Excerpts from original medical records:

> 2-23-78: Problem with catching and clicking with R T-M joint. X-ray ordered. Preg. test done which tends to be pos. *[The x-ray was canceled.]*

> 3-13-78: Preg. test—neg. *[Two entries that day.]*

> 3-13-78: In for preg. test which was neg. Two wks. ago it was positive. Will order another test at the hosp., most likely she is. *[Never had hospital test.]*

This part of my story—the possibility that I have a missing daughter, is the most difficult to talk about—for a variety of reasons. The most obvious reason is that it's the strangest part of the whole abduction phenomena and the hardest for people to believe. It's also embarrassingly painful for me to recall. In addition to the high strangeness of it, I also have to deal with all the normal emotions a woman has when she loses a baby—the feelings of inadequacy, the loss, the longing. In my case, they are still there and still strong.

Fifteen years have passed since then, yet even now I feel a knot in my stomach when I think about it. It's something I'll never forget—and I'll never stop feeling.

I have a really hard time believing this first pregnancy was a hysterical pregnancy. I am under the assumption that women who have hysterical pregnancies desperately want a baby. I definitely didn't want to become pregnant at the time. Born in 1959, I was barely eighteen years old! I wanted to have children someday, but not then. My boyfriend and I had gotten engaged in December 1977, decided to marry the following June, and were looking forward to having some time alone together before we started a family. When I actually heard the words, "You're pregnant" come from my doctor's mouth, my first reaction was "Oh man! No, not yet!"

I must backtrack a little here to tell of a strange experience I had with a couple of girl friends in November of 1977—because it will become an intricate part of this story and must not be omitted.

About 2 A.M., Dorothy, Roberta, and I were driving around on the country roads of rural Indiana. I was supposed to be spending the night with Dorothy and she was supposed to be spending the night with me. I'm sure that's not the first time teenagers have used this excuse to gain some freedom. It's a classic. We really didn't have anything to do, but the thought that we were "free," that we were actually doing something we weren't supposed to be doing because we were still classified as children by our parents, gave us a "charge." I guess it made us feel more like adults even though, in retrospect, it was kind of stupid. When you're eighteen, you think you know it all.

There was nothing else three teenage girls could legally do at two in the morning. We were basically "good kids."

Besides, we were on a "mission." We were going to spy on Dorothy's boyfriend. He lived in an old farmhouse, and we were going to see if he was where he said he was going to be. We figured he might also be using the "I'm spending the night with her/him" excuse.

While driving north on a dark, deserted country road, I noticed a bright, white flashing light begin to move toward us from the east. At first it seemed pretty steady, and I assumed it was an airplane. Teasing my friends, I said, "Hey! Look you guys. It's a UFO!" (Don't ask me why I said that because I have no idea!) Dorothy and I started to giggle as Roberta jumped up from behind me to get a better look at it. The startled look on her face was priceless.

We had been watching the light for a minute or two when suddenly it started to flash really bright and dance all over the sky. It was quite a magnificent sight even though we were all startled when it began to "dance."

Dorothy and I were fascinated—almost mesmerized—by it, although I also felt myself becoming a little anxious. Roberta, on the other hand, became *very* upset. She dove behind my seat, curled up on the floorboard in the fetal position, and began to whine, "Come on, you guys, let's get out of here! I'm getting scared!" I looked over at Dorothy with an ornery grin on my face and then turned around in my seat to look at Roberta. I was quite amused to see her lying there with her coat over her head.

When Dorothy slowed the car to get a better look at the light, it suddenly shot almost directly overhead. Dorothy and I shouted, almost simultaneously, "Wow! Check this out!" I could feel the blood rush to my face as my heart began to pound with a mix of anxiety and excitement. Roberta went ballistic and began screaming at us to "get the hell outta here, right now!" Dorothy and I looked at each other and started to giggle hysterically. The odd light was creeping us out, but it didn't bother us as much as

Roberta's reaction did. We were nervous about the whole situation and when teenage girls get nervous, they giggle.

That was the last conscious memory I had of that night for a long time. The next thing I remember, we were driving back into town, feeling kind of dazed and disoriented, when Dorothy looked at her watch. She seemed surprised at the fact that it was now four-thirty in the morning. She said something like, "Time sure flies when you're having fun!" There was a hint of sarcasm in her voice.

I had nightmares about that night for years afterward. None of them made much sense and I quickly tried to forget the details as soon as I woke up. I had vague dreams of feeling chased and hunted, like a wild animal. And I always seemed to wake up just before I could get a good look at my attacker's face. I remembered dreaming about pain, lots of pain.

When Budd began investigating my family's experiences, I underwent hypnosis to recall details of this particular night. I remembered seeing the light in the sky and snickering at Roberta for being such a chicken. I remembered the car stopping and seeing a bright flash of light in the car, as if someone inside had taken a flash picture. Then I saw a big, black craft racing toward the car from directly in front of us. The whole car was enveloped in a black cloud. I remembered being pulled from the car—legs first—by some unseen force and suddenly being in a white room with strange-looking balconies and railings. I remembered feeling naked and cold, helplessly lying on a very hard, narrow, elevated surface. I couldn't see it but I figured it was a table of some kind.

I remembered feeling a tremendous pressure on my abdomen, right above my pubic bone, and feeling as if I would explode. Then I felt the same kind of pressure under my right breast and heard an extremely loud sucking sound, like when you're drinking a milkshake with a straw and get to the bottom of the glass. Then I heard someone tell me—in my head, "It's over." My legs were then propped up and I just laid there. As the entity leaned over me from above my head, I could see the gray face that I have seen so many times since. The huge, black eyes looked into mine very intently and told me to rest.

The next thing I remembered, I was back in the car. I could see stars and sky out the window, but the inside of the car was black. I could feel my hand on the door handle but I couldn't see it. I could feel the seat under me. I wanted to get out and run, but I couldn't. I couldn't move, I couldn't see anything inside the car and I couldn't hear anything, not even my own breathing. But somehow I knew Dorothy was no longer in the car with me. I panicked and wondered if they were doing to her the same thing they had done to me. I wanted to help her but I couldn't and I somehow felt responsible for what I thought was happening to her then. I felt guilty for teasing Roberta about being chicken. I wanted to cry, but I couldn't even do that.

Suddenly the blackness was gone and I could see Dorothy standing outside in front of the car, looking up at something unseen.

I could move again. I could hear Roberta whimpering from the backseat. Quickly forgetting everything that had just happened, I jumped out of the car and walked over to Dorothy. We both stood there for a short time just looking up at the clear, starry night. I asked her if she could still see the light. She told me, "No, they're gone now." I remember looking at her kind of funny, thinking, What's this "they" stuff? Then our eyes met. I didn't have to verbalize my question. It was as if—for one brief moment—we both realized what had just happened and then just as quickly forgot it. We walked slowly and silently back to the car. We got in, told Roberta it was gone, and drove off.

Budd interviewed Dorothy when he came to our house

during the investigation. When we arrived at her apartment that night, we told her about June 30, 1983, and the investigation. Then Budd asked her about that night in November and the light we had seen. She piped up with, "Which light are you talking about? The light in the sky or the light on the ground?" Her comments took me by surprise because I hadn't remembered any light being on the ground.

She said she remembered getting out of the car to look at the light on the ground. She didn't remember much after that except for remarking at how the time had flown by. She did not want to undergo hypnosis. The thought of it made her very nervous. She really didn't want to remember anything about that night. Thinking about it made her stomach hurt. I can't say that I blame her!

Funny thing about this whole affair—after Budd interviewed her, Dorothy and I kind of drifted apart. I got the distinct impression that being with me was triggering a memory in her that made her very uncomfortable. Whenever our eyes met, I could see the pain in her. And I recognized it all too well.

We did run into each other several years later. She told me that, after I had brought Budd to meet her, she could not stop thinking about that night in November and the light on the ground. That's why I think my explanation of why we drifted apart is fairly accurate.

I have often wondered if this incident in November 1977 was actually the night I got pregnant and not the night in December, when my boyfriend "Eddie" asked me to marry him and we had sex for the first time in our relationship. I guess no one will really ever know.

For sanity's sake I have always assumed that my first pregnancy was my boyfriend's baby, and I suppose I always will. I really detest seeing headlines in the tabloids that read, I HAD AN ALIEN'S BABY! and certainly never want my experience to be put in the same category with these ridiculous stories.

I had a light period in January 1978. Despite this, I felt I was pregnant. (As it turned out, I had periods for the first couple of months with my two son's pregnancies, and was later told this is not at all uncommon in some women.) I had all the symptoms of pregnancy. Nausea in the morning (and sometimes evening, too), tender breasts, fatigue, more frequent urination, and a curious one—gagging whenever I brushed my teeth. (I also had this one with my other two pregnancies.) My friends kept telling me, "Girl, you're pregnant!" And I kept saying, "No way!"

When you're pregnant, live in the Midwest, have a daddy like mine, are eighteen and not married, you'd better make damn sure you're pregnant before you go telling your father about it. No one would want to incur the wrath of Daddy without good cause!

By mid-February, my period was late. I talked to my mother about it and she took me to our family doctor. He gave me the standard pregnancy tests and pelvic exam and told me I was, indeed, pregnant. If I recall correctly, there was even some debate as to how far along I was. He felt I was farther along than I did. I was counting back from the night in December when my boyfriend proposed to me. Except for remembering the light in the sky, all conscious memory of the experience in November had slipped into the shadows of my mind.

Everything seemed normal and, as the days passed, I began to accept the fact that I was going to have a baby and began to look forward to having a child to share with my soon-to-be husband.

We decided to move the wedding date from June to April so I wouldn't look so pregnant.

One weekend in mid-March, I had gone to my sister "Laura's" house to babysit for her and her husband's kids so they could have some time off. I figured it would be good practice for me since I would soon have a child of my own. Besides, I had always been the free babysitter in the family.

After I had put the kids to bed for the night, I went into my sister's bedroom to watch TV and talk on the phone with my fiancé. While I was talking to Eddie, I started to get the feeling that someone was looking at me through the bedroom window. I couldn't see anything, but I sure could feel it! I cut off Eddie quickly without telling him how I had begun to feel and moved into the living room after we hung up.

As soon as I left the bedroom, the feeling went away. I dismissed my anxiety as "pregnancy nerves" and eventually shook it off. I lay down on the couch to watch the "Bob Newhart Show," one of my favorites. I grew sleepy after a while and decided to roll over and get more comfy. I figured I could "listen" to my show just as well as look at it. (That's one of Mom's favorite excuses for falling asleep on the couch in front of the TV.)

As I lay with my back to the TV and my face stuffed into the pillow, I began to feel someone gently stroking my back, shoulders, and the side of my face. I was startled at first but, almost instantaneously, the thought *It's just one of the kids* popped into my mind. A lovely feeling of peace and warmth washed over me. I quickly relaxed and let the soothing strokes lull me to sleep.

Years later, partly under hypnosis and partly on my own, I remembered the rest of the story:

> I was on a strange table. It seemed to be in sections and the bottom dropped out of it while the legs began to elevate. I was somehow stuck to this table and it pulled my legs so far apart I felt as if I were going to be ripped in half. Then I could feel something large and cold going into my vagina and I felt as if I were

being opened up inside like a pupil dilates. I could feel my pelvis bones. They felt as if they were being pulled apart, strained to the limit. I felt like a wishbone! Suddenly, I felt as if my abdomen was being sucked flat from the inside out. I could feel the pain and wanted to scream out but I couldn't. Then I saw her.

She was being held by the gray, black-eyed entity. His hands were cupped and I could see something moving around in them. At first I didn't realize what it was. She was so tiny! As soon as I realized what had happened, I screamed—in my mind I think, not with my mouth—but he heard it anyway. I screamed, "It's not fair! It's mine! I hate you! I hate you! It's not fair! You son-of-a-bitch! You bastard!" I felt he was actually taken aback by my reaction to the whole thing and took measures to quiet me down immediately.

That's all I could remember after that. I think I may have actually passed out after that because to this day, I can't remember anything else.

The next morning, I woke up in my little niece's bed. I had no memory as to how I got there. The very first thing on my mind was, How in the hell did I get in here? The second thing I thought was, Oh my God! I'm not pregnant anymore! My little girl is gone! I looked all over the bed for signs of a miscarriage. Then I got up, went to the bathroom, and checked myself. Nothing, not a sign of a miscarriage anywhere.

I couldn't figure out why I felt like I was no longer pregnant. At that point, I had no conscious memory of the night before. I was panic-stricken and I felt really stupid. How could I explain this panic? What in the hell was wrong with me?

I called Mom from Kathy's house and told her that I thought I was having a period and needed to see the doctor right away. I was actually spotting lightly but I didn't know how to explain it or justify why I wanted to go to the doctor. I needed confirmation that I was still pregnant for my own peace of mind.

Mom called the doctor, who told her to tell me to not be alarmed, just put my feet up for awhile and if it got worse or I experienced pain, to call him back.

Well, that didn't satisfy me. I called my friend Dorothy and told her how I was feeling.

She told me that she was going to Planned Parenthood the following Monday to get some birth control and she suggested that I go in with her. She suggested I tell them that I wanted a pregnancy test and not tell them I had already seen my doctor and had been confirmed pregnant. That way I would get a positive result and I'd feel better. Plus it wouldn't cost me anything, I wouldn't have to tell anyone how I felt, and I wouldn't have to explain why I wanted another test.

I thought it was a great idea, so Monday morning Dorothy picked me up. We then picked up Roberta, and off we went to the Planned Parenthood clinic.

I proceeded as planned. When the nurse called me back to the exam room to tell me my test was negative and if I didn't start my period within the week I should return to them or talk to my family doctor, I went into shock.

In the car on the way home, huge tears streamed down my face. I sobbed, over and over, "They took my baby! That was *my* baby!" I'm sure my friends didn't have the slightest idea about what to do with me, but they didn't question what I was saying, either.

Dorothy dropped me off at my sister's house, and from there I called Mom again. I told her she had to take me to the doctor because something was terribly wrong. I couldn't tell her what because I didn't understand it myself, but she heard me crying and must have thought I was in pain. She picked me up right away and on March 13, 1978, we went to the doctor's office.

When we got there, I told them I had what appeared to be a period and that I had had another test that turned out to be negative. They looked at me as if I were nuts, but they nevertheless gave me yet another test. When we got the results and it was negative, too, they took me to a room and set me up for another pelvic exam.

During the exam the doctor was very quiet. When he was done, he motioned for me to get dressed and told me to meet him in the office and bring my mother with me.

I remember the look on his face as Mom and I sat there. It was obvious that he was as confused and concerned as I was. Then he said to me, "I'm not quite sure what went on here, but you are not pregnant. I see nothing out of the ordinary. You look healthy, completely normal. Sometimes these things happen and we can't explain them. You're young and healthy. You'll have more children someday."

As I sat there, quietly crying, he told me, "I think the best thing for all of us to do is to just forget this ever happened." I remember saying to him, "Oh, I'll never forget this, as long as I live!"

My mother asked him if I would need a D & C since I had been pregnant and now wasn't. He said that he didn't think there was anything to clean out, that I felt normal size and looked just fine but if I should start having problems, I should come back. He mentioned something about sending me to the hospital for another pregnancy test before he did the pelvic exam, but afterward decided not to.

After the incident of June 30, 1983, I began to think of that first pregnancy again. I cannot explain why looking at the mark in my parent's backyard triggered memories of this lost pregnancy, but I think that fact is significant in itself. Even though I didn't consciously think about that part of my life much, I had never forgotten it. I had been able to control my feelings and keep how I felt about it to myself for many years. I never talked about it with anyone except Dorothy. After Dorothy and I drifted apart, I was alone with my memories of that time in my life. And that was okay with me until that night in June.

During one of Budd's trips to Indianapolis to interview some of our family and friends, I told Budd about the missing baby. I really don't know what possessed me to tell him about her.

We had been at a nice little restaurant having lunch. On the way back to Mom and Dad's house I began to think about the baby again. We pulled up in the driveway and as Budd started to get out of the car, I just sat there. Budd sensed there was something on my mind and began to question me about it. That's when I blurted out the fact that I had lost a baby when I was eighteen. As soon as I realized what I had said, I felt like such an idiot! I felt so sorry for him at that moment. The look on his face was like he might have been thinking, Well, I'm really sorry to hear about that but, what the hell does that have to do with anything? Then, I thought to myself, Jesus H. Christ! What have I done? I told him I had no idea why I felt I had to tell him about the baby except, for some reason, I believed there was a connection between whatever happened in my parents' backyard that night in June of 1983 and my lost baby.

I'm not really sure exactly what Budd thought that day. I do know that after he had time to think about it and began to hear of more cases very similar to mine, things started to fall into place for him in his mind. Eventually I told Budd about seeing my baby again, a few years after losing her.

I've had a few "dreams" about seeing my daughter over the years. The "presentation" in Budd Hopkins' book, *Intruders* was the most dramatic. That "presentation" was also depicted in the miniseries of the same name that aired on CBS in May of 1992.

On October 3, 1983, "they" showed my daughter to me and "they" let me remember. Because I couldn't take her with me and I felt such strong emotions about her, I believe someone—the entity I always seemed to recognize—felt sorry for me. Remembering this presentation was a way I could take some of her with me. But that is only speculation. I felt as if a lot more had happened earlier that night, but the only part of it I remembered without hypnosis was this part. To this day, I never have remembered the beginning of this incident:

I had been sitting on a table in a really big white room. The gray entity I always seemed to recognize helped me off the table and stood next to me as more gray entities came into the room. I knew something was up, but didn't know what. This had never happened before and I felt some kind of electricity—excitement—in the air. They all seemed quite pleased with me and I even remember one of them reaching out to touch my shoulder, as if in support. Of course, that was my *interpretation* of the touch. It could have been for some very different reason. Whatever the case, until then I had never remembered feeling that much emotion from them.

As I looked up, a small girl was escorted into the room, flanked by two of the grays. For some reason, I felt these two grays were female. Outwardly they didn't look any different from the rest but something about their eyes and the way they "felt" made me think they were female.

The little girl was about the height of a four-year-old child, but she was very tiny otherwise. She had tiny ears, set low on her head, a tiny mouth, and large blue eyes. Her forehead was very large and her body seemed very thin and frail. She had snow white hair that was patchy on her large head and her complexion was very pale.

I remembered thinking how strange she looked when she blinked. Her eyeballs rolled back and her eyelids met in the middle of her eyes. Nevertheless, I thought she was absolutely beautiful! I was in love, and my maternal instincts overwhelmed me very quickly.

She looked like an angel, and my first instinct was to run up to her, grab her, and hold her. It was almost as if she read my mind because as soon as I had that thought, she jumped and tried to hide behind one of the entities holding her hands. My heart sank when she did that.

It was then that I realized she was just as afraid of me as I had been of the grays. The mere sight of me frightened her.

Looking back, I could see how I must have looked huge and scary to a little kid if all she had ever known were the little gray guys. But at the time, all I could feel was crushed. I decided not to go to her, so I wouldn't frighten her even more. I remembered how I had felt when I was younger and I thought the grays were going to touch me. But holding myself back was really hard to do!

As soon as I had the thought that I would not grab her, I could have sworn I saw her crack a tiny, timid half smile as she peeked at me from behind the entity. It was the sweetest thing I had ever seen and my heart felt as if it would burst!

The gray standing next to me looked at me and I felt he somehow told me that this was a good thing and I should be proud that I had done well. He didn't quite seem to understand my mixed emotions.

He told me many things, most of which I still have not remembered. I do remember him saying something about a father taking care of his children. That is when I asked him if I could please take her home with me. He told me no, that I could not feed her. He promised me I would see her again and then told me that I had to leave soon or I would get sick.

He walked me over to this round platform. As I stepped up on the platform, I turned toward him. He stepped in front of me and took my hands in his. He felt squishy and cool. He looked up into my eyes. Suddenly I began to feel all kinds of emotions shoot through me like bullets. I thought to myself, *What the hell's wrong with me? Why am I feeling all these feelings?* Everything a human being could possibly feel, I was feeling—all at the same time! That was probably the most intense moment of my life.

Suddenly I realized that I wasn't the one having all those feelings. I believe they were coming from him. Like some lame attempt at "feeling" for me, of relating to me in my own human terms.

He let go of my hands and then the whole room— and he—began to look as if I were seeing them through the heat of a fire, real shimmery and wavy.

The next thing I remember, I was lying on the grass behind my parents' home. I looked up and could see a craft above me, starting to move away. It looked like a headband with white lights on it.

I got up and went to the house, but all the doors were locked. I stood at the back door and called for my mother to let me in.

Mom heard me and quickly came to answer my call. She never said one word to me. She just let me in and went back to bed.

* * *

Mom says she remembers hearing me call her name that night, but she doesn't remember letting me in.

I know the entities are famous for lying to their "subjects," but I choose to believe them when they tell me I will see her again someday. I have to believe it.

I keep telling myself that people who find out they are adopted almost always, eventually, seek out their biological parents. I figure if the little girl really is a part of me, like I feel someone told me that night, then someday she'll feel "the pull." The human part of her will drive her to find me. I can only hope.

Many people ask me how I came about naming her "Emily." That's a pseudonym Budd chose to use in his book. The real name I gave her was Elizabeth.

The entity I have always been able to recognize during all my encounters told me that if it made me feel better about leaving her with them, I could give her a name and they would use it for her while she was with them.

Elizabeth was a name I had always liked. As a little girl growing up, I had always said if I ever had a little girl, I would name her this. I believe this is pretty common with little girls who want to become mothers someday. I called various dolls by this name throughout my childhood. It was a name I held close to my heart. It was a name intended for that first child, had she ever been born to me. It was an appropriate name in light of how I felt about the little girl I saw in my "dream" that night. That's how real she is to me.

This aspect of the abduction phenomena is the most emotional and the most ridiculed part of the entire experience. Can you blame people for not wanting to tell others about something like this? Would you want to open your heart up to what you knew would be ridicule and pain?

I didn't want Budd to put anything about the baby in the

book. It took considerable convincing on Budd's part for me to finally give in and let that part of my story be included. I just didn't know if I could handle having to talk about something so bizarre, so unbelievable, and yet so personal and emotional. And I felt it would lower the credibility of the rest of the case. Certainly I could never expect anyone to believe a word of this! I never would have, had it not happened to me. And I still can't be sure of exactly what happened. I still prefer to call "the presentation" a dream. It's the only rational way I can live with this.

What convinced me to finally reveal the "baby" part of my abduction experiences was the fact that I was not alone. Budd began to hear from literally thousands of men and women like me all over the world who have lived with something like this. And if ever anyone knew their secret heartache—their confusion and isolation—it was me.

I thank God I have the support of my family and friends since this has come out. Many of you won't be so fortunate. My prayers are with you, always.

If I had been able to tell someone about this earlier without being dismissed as a total nut, perhaps my life would have taken a different course sooner. If I can spare one person from going through what I went through emotionally, then it will be okay that I have told my story.

No one will ever know exactly what is happening to me and my family or why I've remembered the things I've remembered and seen the things I've seen. I find it intriguing that hundreds of thousands of men and women have remembered and seen exactly the same things I have. That tells me that *something* is going on. What that is, we can only speculate. When I hear someone say they have all the answers, my red flags really go up fast. Hell, I've been there and I still don't know much of anything for sure! I know my feelings and the hard, physical evidence are certainly real, but as for the rest . . . ?

I am assimilating all this with a human brain, a human mind. And we still haven't quite figured out how these work yet. Perhaps some of the answers lie there, as well as in the world and the universe(s) around us. If you find any of the answers, I'd love to know them, too.

24

KATHY
Family Ties

SINCE *INTRUDERS* WAS PUBLISHED, THE ISSUE OF GENETIC experimentation and the possibility of alien offspring has been widely discussed. What about my own case? If there has been any, I am not aware of it. I'm not sure I want to know! Is it just coincidence that our youngest sister *passes out* every time she sees a newborn baby?

I believe that the visitors have for years used humans for a purpose only known to them. An alien hybrid program seems logical, if only from a human point of view. Producing a half-human—half-alien baby would appear to be a sensible step for such a scrawny-looking species as the grays. Comparing our species and theirs, we appear to be far superior, physically speaking. They are no doubt eons ahead of us mentally. If we could combine the best attributes of both breeds, just imagine the possibilities of such a civilization. The large, physically strong and healthy bodies of humans with a superior mentality, sprinkled with psychic abilities, and topped off with a nice head of hair, sounds quite appealing to me. Why wouldn't it sound good to them, too?

I feel they must be at least curious and possibly envious

of our sensitivity and ability to empathize with each other. I feel that even though the visitors are apparently able to control us physically, they may be having a hard time figuring out how we feel emotions. Emotions are useless when you are dealing with technology and machines. The visitors' extreme intelligence has left little room for emotions. Perhaps feelings and emotions have nurtured our race to the size we are now. Adrenaline—a hormone that can be produced by emotion—responsible for the survival of a species by creating the fight-or-flight response, also produced growth. Interestingly enough, Debbie suffers from hyperadrenalism with no known organic cause. Is this a coincidence?

I have heard people claim if you talk to and nurture a plant it will exceed normal growth. Maybe the visitors are like the untended plants that are smaller and frail, only given in life what is needed physically to survive. Maybe in a small corner of my subconscious, I know why, and perhaps someday I'll remember.

But what about Debbie's claim to have had a missing daughter and that her pregnancy may have had something to do with her experiences? I can't say for sure, but I can describe how we lived during the time this was supposed to have taken place and tell what I remember of how these events were accepted by our family.

At a very early age, I came to the conclusion that in this lifetime I was destined to raising kids and being surrounded by them. I haven't really decided if it is a blessing or a curse.

I was an only child until I was eleven. Then Debbie arrived. She was my first sister and was followed by two more babies in rapid succession. Mom was told she could probably not have any more children several years after I was born. Within six months of moving to our house on the East Side, Mom realized she was pregnant. Imagine her surprise when she found she was going to have another baby after all those years!

Naturally we all doted on Debbie as if she were a new toy. I was at the "mother's little helper" age and spent a great deal of time playing mom and fussing over her. I spent many hours teaching her to walk and talk. I took her all around, showing her off.

Our brother was born a year later, and the thrill of another baby soon began to give way to the work they both required. Being the only boy of the children did give our brother a little advantage and he seemed to get his share of the attention.

Unfortunately for our youngest sister, who was born shortly after him, she would have had to have been two-headed to get much quality time. Three babies in practically as many years was the mother lode of chaos in our household.

The house seemed to get smaller every year. Privacy was merely an interesting idea that someone else must have had. Almost every day when I came home from school, I would find my personal belongings had been tampered with or something of mine had been totally destroyed.

By the time I had reached my midteens I made a personal vow to never have children of my own.

I still had fun with the kids occasionally as I watched them grow up and develop their own personalities. By the time Debbie started school, she was a painfully shy child. You would think that with all the attention she received she would have been more outgoing, but that was not the case at all. She didn't mix in well at school. She seemed too shy and backward to make many friends. She was chubby, which was very detrimental to her self-esteem. Getting her to attend school was a huge problem. For the twelve years she went to school, every day was a war. Kids are so cruel;

a chubby, shy kid is like a gift from the devil for the class bullies.

As the years passed, life with Debbie was rough. Mom ended up taking her to a psychiatrist looking for a solution to her problems. The constant battle to get her to school every day was taking its toll on both of them. The psychiatrist put Debbie on antianxiety/antidepressant medication, which seemed kind of drastic since she was then just in her early teens. The medication didn't seem to help much and was soon discontinued. The doctors also discovered she had high blood pressure when she was only about fourteen or so. My poor baby sister was practically a wreck! No one could figure out why. Now—in retrospect—it all seems to make a little more sense.

In the midst of all the uproar, I got married and made a run for the border. The vow I had made to myself to never have children didn't hold up so well. By the mid-1970s I had four! I also had my own chaos to deal with and I became less aware of what was happening with my brother and sisters.

Saturdays were my night to escape and have a few hours away from home responsibilities. Johnny and I usually got a babysitter and found somewhere to go. Since Debbie was now a teenager we often used her to babysit. Many times she would spend the whole weekend with us, occasionally bringing a girlfriend to keep her company. I always suspected she was afraid to be alone after the kids were in bed. It would not be unusual for us to come home to find her afraid for one reason or another. Debbie's friend Dorothy had also babysat for us a few times when the kids were younger. Her brothers were close friends of my husband.

I remember once when Dorothy babysat for us, she reported that someone had been snooping around the house. Upon inspecting the grounds the next morning, we found small muddy footprints *going up the side of the house* under one of our children's bedroom windows!

During that time, I myself was having some problems with sleepwalking and was unwilling to be alone. I understood where Debbie was coming from when she showed signs of being nervous when alone in the house.

By the late Seventies Debbie was tired of babysitting and had found a steady boyfriend. It must have been serious because she announced her pregnancy about 1978. I was sympathetic although I sure didn't want another kid to raise. I was glad it was her instead of me! What really amazed me was how well our parents seemed to take the news. I didn't live in their house though, so I am sure I missed some of the fireworks. I knew there had to have been at least a minor explosion. Our dad was a clone of Archie Bunker—need I say more?

I really don't remember very much between the time Debbie announced her pregnancy and then announced she wasn't pregnant. Although Debbie would talk to our mother, she tended to keep her feelings to herself back then. It didn't seem to be too long between those events. They only seemed like two acts of God to me, and they were soon put to rest somewhere in a far corner of my mind. And in Debbie's, too.

I don't recall thinking about the situation again until *Intruders* had been published. During the many months Budd worked on that book, amazingly enough, no one in the family was aware of any possible connection between Debbie's pregnancy and any alien intervention. Through all of Debbie's trips to various places for hypnosis, medical tests, interviews, and a lie detector test, never once did she fill us in on the whole story. She only divulged her inner feelings to Budd near the end of his investigation. I guess it took her a while to trust him before she would tell him what she had kept to herself for so many years. Can you blame her?

Imagine our surprise! None of us wanted too much coverage in the book to begin with—even using fake names—and our memories were tame in comparison with her bombshell.

After I became aware of the whole story, I probably had as many questions and theories as a total stranger would have had, maybe more. The first question naturally was whether she was telling the truth. Despite her problems earlier in life—and perhaps *because* of them—I couldn't believe that she would make up such a wild story. She knew during the entire time Budd was writing the book that she would be expected to make public appearances in order to promote it. It would have been hard enough for a person of her timid nature to go before the public with just the mildest parts of our memories. To relate the alien-baby memory would be a total impossibility for someone who already felt threatened by life in general. Knowing in advance that she must expose her soul to the world, I think she would have made it as easy on herself as she could. So to answer the question of whether she deliberately lied: No, she didn't. I believe she told the truth.

Of course my next question when *Intruders* was published was whether such an event could be a clue to why there is alien interest in our people. I believe that it is. I don't know why or how, but I'm sure the aliens are advanced enough to figure it out. We have our test-tube babies after all. One hundred years ago, who on Earth would have believed that?

My third question was: How many others have had the same thing happen to them and are they aware of it?

I had many other questions too, such as:

Has it ever happened to me?

Once or many times?

Where are all these babies now?

Are they alive and well?

Do they breathe air like us?
Do they eat our food?
Who or what is taking care of them?
Do they have hair?
Do they look like us or do they look like them?
When did it all start?
When will it stop?
Do they know who we are?
Do they care?

Sorry to say, I only have questions—no answers. As far as my opinion of Debbie's memories, I can only say I have tried to weigh the possibility against the impossibility and I must vote for the possibility. I hope that as I begin to explore my own hidden memories, a similar event does not surface. I'm still trying to deal with meeting the little gray men and people who look like insects.

I wish I had all the answers, but I'm not sure I have the nerve to share them anyway—at least not yet. Someday, maybe, everyone will know. Perhaps in years to come we will look back at our questions and be amused at the innocence of the last century. Our generation must advance or be left behind in our own ignorance. The time is upon us to look for *all* the answers. We must open our minds to all aspects of life—not only in our small existence but in the universe. A closed mind is a small mind. We must look ahead to the future and learn to accept changes and leave behind negative attitudes. You can't move forward if you're always looking back.

If you were able to compare Debbie's personality now to her personality ten years ago, you would have a hard time believing she is the same person. She has gone from a shy, backward kid with a self-esteem level of zip, to an outspoken, self-assured person who appears to know where she's going in life. The change has been so extreme that a person would have to wonder if the alien intervention played a part in this transformation. Of course everyone changes over the course of his or her life. Life's situations bring many changes upon us, and I believe the aliens are just a part of life. But the change in Debbie seems much too dramatic to have been the result of normal life and gradual maturity. It would appear that Debbie and the rest of our family could possibly be pawns in the alien grand scheme of things. A person might wonder if perhaps we have been nurtured or "programmed" from a very early age to spread the word in an attempt to prepare our peers for a future of civilization integration. (Like, our shopping malls aren't crowded enough now!)

Perhaps they merely want to show us a better way of life. Perhaps they want to protect us from ourselves. A lot of humans have a somewhat self-destructive manner. There is too much stress involved in just surviving in today's society. The need people feel to acquire material possessions seems to overpower the need to feel inner peace and happiness. People equate happiness with possessions and then find that when they acquire the possessions they are still not at peace with themselves, only think they need more possessions. Our society tends to connect the word *rich* with possessions, when in fact the really rich people are those who know the meaning of inner peace. I wonder if the alien interest in us involves their quest for inner peace. Or do they already have that gift and want to educate us?

Perhaps we are just a game to them. Maybe we are just a hobby, like a big ant farm. I like to think that their interest in us has only good intentions. There is already too much negativity in the world. If the visitors had devious motives, we probably would have been aware of it many decades ago. One fell swoop would have done us in, yet they continue discreetly mingling with us, quietly performing a task we don't consciously understand. Quietly entering our personal worlds totally without warning. Quietly toying with our minds. Quietly etching their presence permanently into our deepest memories. Quietly awakening memories. Quietly wreaking havoc.

As I prepare myself to enter the harsh light of public scrutiny, I must continually remind myself that in order for people to really understand these galactic interlopers, all available knowledge must be shared, whether we like it or not. It is time for every person who has been affected by these beings to come forth and be counted. It is time for the nonbelievers to open their minds and look beyond their fear. It is time to make contact. It is time to understand . . . *finally!*

Postscript

OCTOBER 13, 1993: I HAVE RECOVERED FROM SURGERY enough to be able to sit at the computer and tell you about it. On September 29, two weeks ago, I had a complete hysterectomy. Everything happened so fast that I still find it all hard to believe.

I hadn't felt well for quite some time. When I realized the problems I had been experiencing during my monthly periods were now responsible for making me feel so crummy all the time, I began to get a little worried. Ever since the night of June 30, 1983, I had, in the back of my mind, worried that what had happened to my dog as a result of her being outside with me that night, would eventually cause me some major problem. But how could I ever explain my fears to my new family doctor? I had never told him anything about my experiences or about that night. I was afraid he'd think I was nuts. He may still, if he ever reads this.

Basically, I lived with my pain for many years, complaining occasionally, but always chickening out when it was suggested that I do something about it. I was afraid I had cancer, like my dog, and I didn't want to know.

Eventually the pain finally drove me to the doctor. I just

couldn't take it anymore. As soon as he looked me over, he told me it was time—I couldn't ignore this anymore. He believed I had a large tumor and I needed a hysterectomy right away. I had suffered enough.

As soon as I realized it was going to happen, I called Budd Hopkins. Budd didn't seem to be too surprised with what I told him. He said I was probably one of the last remaining female abductees to still have all her female parts, that this happening to me was probably just a matter of time. He definitely felt that there was some connection between my current physical problems and the experiences I have had.

I don't know how much of a comfort that was to me in light of the fact that I was so terribly worried about what had happened to me and my dog in 1983. Nevertheless, I did appreciate his support and his encouraging words about how good I would feel after it was all over.

Six days before my surgery, on September 23, 1993, we had a terrific UFO sighting right out in front of our house.

Four of us—my fiancé K.O., my friend Jeanne Robinson, who then lived with us, her daughter, and I—saw and videotaped a tremendous bright light as it hovered and skipped across the night sky just west of the farmhouse where I live now, having moved upstate from Indianapolis.

I had been sitting on the couch in the living room, watching television. A bright, flashing light outside the front of the house caught my eye. I watched it for a moment, thinking to myself, It must be some kind of airplane. After about thirty seconds, I realized it was moving too erratically and was much too bright to be just an airplane. I jumped up from the couch shouting, "Hey, you guys, look at this!" K.O., Jeanne, and her daughter all came running for the front door. After a few moments of "What the hell is that?" we all ran onto the front porch, tripping over each other to get a better look at it.

I immediately told K.O. to get the camcorder. The rest of us ran to the driveway. Seconds later, K.O. returned with the camcorder and we videotaped several minutes of the light as it got brighter and then grew dim again. Soon it appeared to drop just above tree level and move off into the distance.

We watched for several more minutes, until it was out of sight. Suddenly I realized something was walking down the road toward me and the other two girls. I tried to reason in my mind that this must be some kind of wild animal. "A deer, that's what it is," I said to myself. When it reached the end of the fence, it stopped, cocked its head at me, and began to walk backward! Wait a minute! A deer couldn't walk backward. Besides, its legs and shoulders were moving in a funny way; it was kind of gangly-looking. This was the strangest thing I had ever seen. It was too tall to be any kind of dog. I estimated its height to be about four feet. It was very thin and very pale in color. It was very dark out that night and I figured the only way we were able to see it was because it was reflecting the moonlight. As a matter of fact, it almost looked as if it wasn't quite all there, as if it weren't fully materialized. Its head was light-bulb shaped and its neck and shoulders were very thin. Its legs and arms were quite long and thin, too. On the videotape you can hear Jeanne's daughter saying, "Momma, what's that in the road coming toward us?" Then you can hear me scream. Suddenly the mood changes and you can hear us talking excitedly about the light we had just seen. Nothing more was said about the thing in the road. K.O. had his little handheld two-meter radio outside with us by this time and you can hear a British fellow talking about how he could see colored fingers of light in the northern sky. He believed he was seeing the northern lights. The only thing we could see when we looked north were clouds. Then you can hear K.O. talking about how he is recording some strange beeping sound that appears to be coming from our cattle barn, north of the house.

Later in the tape, you can actually hear the beeping sound as K.O. takes the recorder closer to the barn. Then we saw another light shoot behind us from the west, heading southeast. This light turned a deep, blood red before it shot out of sight.

After we finally went back in the house and began to review what had just happened, we realized there was some time missing—and several minutes of video, as well.

After we had seen the "animal" coming down the road toward us, but before K.O. began to record the beeping sound, I had recorded some of the sound myself.

After we lost sight of the light for the last time, K.O. had gone in for a few minutes to call a friend of his who was on the other side of town. He wanted to have him look outside and see if he could see anything. Jeanne and I were outside alone at this point. This is when we first noticed the sounds.

Jeanne remembers the red light being on when I was taping and she also remembers how I marked each beep with a verbal confirmation. I even remember telling K.O. to turn the camcorder back on because I had shut it off before he came back outside. And he remembered turning it back on before he went to the barn to record some more of the sound and check on the cows. But my whole part of our tape is missing.

Later, as he went back over the times and the tape we had, we realized we could only account for about eighteen and a half minutes of a forty-five-minute episode. To this day we still aren't sure what happened to the rest of the time —or to us.

When I went back to my surgeon for my six-week checkup after the surgery, I asked him exactly what he had found. I reminded him that the doctor in Springfield who read my ultrasound scan told me I had a tumor in my uterus. I also reminded him that my own family doctor had felt what he thought was a rather large tumor in the same place.

I was very surprised to hear him say that he found no tumor at all but that I did have something called adenomatosis, cysts on both ovaries, scar tissue, adhesions, and endometriosis. I definitely needed the hysterectomy but had no tumor. As I write this in December 1993, it's been twelve weeks since my surgery and I still have no need for any estrogen supplements, even though I had a total hysterectomy. No symptoms of menopause, whatsoever.

I wonder what happened to whatever the doctor saw on my ultrasound film. No one will ever know, yet I can't help but think it might have had something to do with the sighting we had just before I went in for the surgery. Under the circumstances, wouldn't you?

Several people have made the comment that perhaps now that I don't have the equipment for making babies, "they" will leave me alone. I have a feeling that it will only change my "job description." I guess time will tell. Something seems to be taking very good care of me for some reason.

On December 3, 1993, K.O. and I were married in Las Vegas, Nevada. If anyone had told me as a young girl that this was how my life would go, I would never have believed it in a million years. No one will ever be able to convince me that this phenomena isn't "real." How can something change your life so drastically, if it isn't "real"? I am very fortunate that my changes have been for the better!

Even though it's been several years since the book *Intruders* was published, I still receive letters about it.

A few days ago, I received a letter from a lady who lives in Indianapolis. In it she told of events—alarmingly similar to mine—that happened to her on the same side of town. Our dates and times weren't too far apart, either. The confirmation never seems to end.

APPENDIX
Debbie

THE EVENT ON THE NIGHT OF JUNE 30, 1983, AWOKE something in me that had lain dormant in the deep recesses of my mind. My spirit was somehow set free.

From the latter part of 1983 until well into 1987, I did things that I had never been able to do before. Even more astounding was the drive with which I did them.

I was not previously inclined to be artistic or poetic. I believe what I was able to do was a direct result of my experiences.

The desire to share with others what I had created was like nothing I've ever experienced before or since. I felt as if a part of why I was able to find this within me was to help others find it within themselves. I felt that what I had done would be their trigger.

In September of 1983, I began to get incredible images in my head and I felt the need to put them down on paper for others to see. I began to make collages. I spent every penny I had on materials to make these things, and, once I started working on one, I couldn't stop until it was finished. I knew when I would be making a new design because I would feel very anxious and fidgety for a day or two before the actual work began. That was my cue to go to the dimestore for construction paper and glue.

Then, early in the morning—usually around 2 or 3 A.M.—I'd wake up and feel shaky and sweaty. That meant it was time to start. (I realize how weird this sounds and I'm a little embarrassed by it.)

I started to "remember" words, phrases, and ideas at some of the most inopportune moments.

I remember driving down the street and beginning to "hear" things about God, life, and the connection between the two—that God and life were actually one and the same. It got so intense I had to pull my car over to the side of the road and write down what I was getting before I could go on. Once I wrote it down, the "remembrance" went away and I could continue with what I was doing.

A lot of what I wrote during this period was stolen from my home when my husband and I were out of town. Fortunately, the thieves can't erase my memory. All the stuff that I "heard," "remembered," or whatever you want to call it, was burned into my mind forever. It has become a part of me. Perhaps it always was.

It was during an episode like the one mentioned above that I wrote the following two poems. I was feeling very agitated and anxious a few days before they surfaced. They were like the steam of a teapot gradually building up. When I wrote them down, some of the pressure was released.

I woke up out of a sound sleep to write these, and afterward I collapsed onto the bed and fell away, relieved, at last.

The next morning, I awoke to find all these chicken scratches on my notepad. I had to rearrange a few words and sentences for them to make any logical sense. This is the first one I got. I call it *Song for Per:*

When I look into your eyes, I become you.
I pass through to the inner core, which is the true
   self.

Reaching in, I bathe in the warmth of your highest
  essence.
I comfort and ease the coolness of your human emotion.
I open your heart and your mind in the name of
  love.

All memory, we now and forever share.
Fused by the power of our soul.
We are all but one soul.
Massive and eternal.
One memory, one love.

In the beginning, split with fear,
We now struggle to learn, to return to the place,
When we will come, once again,
Together, forever.

When I wrote these poems, I was much too frightened
and weak to have ever thought of touching someone else's
soul, or reaching so deeply into my own. There was no way
I could have come to the realization that I was truly connected to all living things and that these words had come
from my connected spirit. That they were meant for me, for
healing.

Several years passed before I fully understood the meaning of what I had written. When I showed it to a few of my
close friends, they couldn't believe I had written it. As I
read the words, *I* couldn't believe I had written it!

Keep in mind, during this period of my life, I was sleeping in the daylight and staying awake, on guard, almost all
night. I was gripped with debilitating fear and anxiety. Days
would go by when I wouldn't even get dressed. I spent a lot
of time in my ratty old housecoat.

I was not a religious person and had only attended

churches with childhood friends whenever I spent the night with them. In my anxiety-ridden state of mind, I was nowhere near up to hearing all this. Or at least I didn't think I was.

During this period of time, James and I were dating. We broke up for a short time before we eventually married. While we were apart, I remember feeling very sorry for myself and very angry at God. One night in my room, I blurted out to myself, God, or whomever would listen, "Why did you give me so much inside and no one to give it to? No one here understands love or understands me. I scare people off with my intense feelings. Why did you do this to me? I don't want to be here anymore! I don't belong here. I'm too sensitive."

Suddenly it was as if a huge set of warm, loving arms surrounded me. I heard in my mind and felt in my heart these words: "Don't you realize that all you've been trying to give has always been meant for you? Once you learn this, it will come."

That night was a turning point for me. It was as if the lights came on and I could finally see. For the first time, I understood.

Shortly after that, I wrote the last poem I was to write in this manner and, with it, the tumultuous period in my life quietly passed on. This is what I wrote. I call it *Prophet's Prayer:*

Why, oh why, must I be the one
To feel the light, yet share with none?

Understanding this human soul
Will, I fear, take its toll

Grant me strength to carry on,
To be again, with you, as one.

Send to me what I've searched for so long,
My fate fulfilled, my duty done.

How long must I wait? My patience wears thin.
A lesson to learn before I begin?

You are my heart, my life you command.
Yet all that must be, I cannot comprehend.

The message is vague and yet just within reach.
Am I not the pupil or is it I who must teach?

Afterword

WHAT HAS JUST BEEN PRESENTED TO THE READER IS AN incredible and sincere gift from two healthy and marvelous human beings. Debbie and Kathy have stepped forth as sisters to bravely reveal family secrets and perplexing mysteries that have intruded into their lives. Despite the bizarre nature of their experiences, they have learned over time to cope. With the patience and understanding of researchers, friends, family, therapists, and other participants in this puzzling phenomenon, they have grown in many ways. They wanted to share their experiences with candor, sensitivity, humor, and a sincere hope that what they may share may actually help someone else to not feel so alone or crazy. They *know* what that feels like!

They are not trying to become professional writers nor profit in any way. They wanted to share themselves as simply a gift of thanks to all those who helped them and to all of those puzzled individuals who could still receive help and have not. This book is a gift of love not a scientific document. It is written in the earthy, good-natured, and sensible style that truly characterizes these two lovely sisters. This is a sharing experience—and they hope that the readers benefit from their openness. As more participants in this phenomenon come forth as Debbie and Kathy have, we may learn how similar these personal tales truly are. Then we all may have the chance to grow and learn what we may *need* to know for our future.

John S. Carpenter, MSW/LCSW
Licensed Clinical Social Worker
Psychiatric Hypnotherapist

Debbie's first public talk, described above, is available on audiotape and videotape as part of the proceedings of the conference at which she spoke. For information, write to Omega Communications, P.O. Box 2051, Cheshire, Ct, 06410-5051, USA.